National Wildlife Federation

COOKBOOK

On the cover: "Dayton Farm – home covey" painting by Jonathan Wilde

© National Wildlife Federation MCMLXXXIV
1412 16th Street, N.W.
Washington, D.C. 20036

Library of Congress Cataloging in Publication Data
Main entry under title:
The National Wildlife Federation cookbook.
    1. Cookery.   I. National Wildlife Federation.
II. Favorite Recipes Press.
TX715.N338 1984   641.5   84-81650
ISBN 0-87197-184-4

Page 1 recipes on pages 122, 125, 136 and 170.
Page 2 recipes on page 169

A Dedication...

to the millions of members and supporters of the National Wildlife Federation.

Through your concern and generosity, our magnificent wildlife and natural treasures remain a reality to be enjoyed by all.

About
The National Wildlife Federation

The National Wildlife Federation represents conservation at its best. It is made up of private citizens who want to help NWF promote the wise use of our national resources.

In addition to our individual members and contributors, NWF — a nongovernment and nonprofit organization — has affiliated organizations in forty-nine states, Puerto Rico and the Virgin Islands.

NWF believes:

- That the welfare of wildlife is linked to that of all living things.

- That wildlife is an indicator of environmental quality — and when properly managed, is a source of inspiration and recreation.

- That awareness, understanding and action by concerned citizens are necessary to protect our life-supporting environment.

- That life and beauty, prosperity and progress depend on how wisely we use the gifts of clean air, rich soil, pure water, mineral wealth, and our abundant plant and animal life.

For more information on the National Wildlife Federation's membership, education and conservation programs, write to:

National Wildlife Federation
1412 16th Street, N.W., Washington, D.C. 20036

BRANDIED PEACHES FLAMBE

1/2 c. sugar
1/2 c. Brandy
4 lg. fresh peaches, peeled,
sliced
2 tsp. cornstarch

Combine sugar, 3/4 cup water and 1/4 cup Brandy in chafing dish. Bring to a boil, stirring constantly. Add peaches. Simmer for 10 minutes or until tender. Blend cornstarch with 1/4 cup water. Stir into peaches. Cook until mixture thickens, stirring constantly. Warm 1/4 cup Brandy; ignite. Pour over peaches. Spoon into dessert dishes or over ice cream. Yield: 4 servings.

Contents

Recipes compiled and edited by editors of Favorite Recipes Press.

Feeding the Birds

Do you feed birds? If so, here are a few choice recipes to help you give your feathered guests a sumptuous feast. In addition, we've included a table of preferred foods of some of the most common birds. Since different birds prefer different foods — and populations change from time to time and place to place — you should find just the right ingredients for your favorite species on the list.

Remember, too, that summer feeding is not harmful, and can be very rewarding by bringing young birds and parents, and birds in bright breeding plumage, to your feeder.

Some helpful hints: (1) Put food out in the evening; most birds eat between 7 a.m. and 9 a.m. and again just before dusk. (2) Keep your feeder clean and check every day to refill. Birds get used to your food supply — and you want to keep them coming to your feeder. (3) Keep a birdbath filled with clean water all year.

There are four feeding levels:

I. GROUND FEEDERS

Kinds of Birds:	blue jays, sparrows, juncos, quail, doves, pheasants, towhees, red-winged blackbirds, house finches.
Foods They Like:	millet, wild birdseed mix, cracked corn, peanut kernels.
Kinds of Feeders:	Scatter seeds on the ground or in a shallow tray.

II. TREE TRUNK FEEDERS

Kinds of Birds:	chickadees, titmice, nuthatches, creepers, woodpeckers, many seed-eating birds.
Foods They Like:	suet or suet cakes and peanut butter mixtures.
Kinds of Feeders:	wire mesh holders, plastic mesh vegetable bags, log holder.

III. TABLETOP OR WINDOW FEEDERS

Kinds of Birds:	cardinals, chickadees, purple finches, grosbeaks, goldfinches, mockingbirds, catbirds, jays, house finches, titmice.
Foods They Like:	sunflower seed, wild birdseed mix, peanut kernels, raisins or currants.
Kinds of Feeders:	Place trays on picnic tables, benches, or posts, or attach them to windowsills.

IV. HANGING OR HIGH POST FEEDERS

Kinds of Birds: chickadees, cardinals, goldfinches, purple finches, pine siskins, redpolls, titmice, nuthatches.

Foods They Like: niger seed, sunflower seed, wild birdseed mix, peanut kernels, nuts.

Kinds of Feeders: plastic tube feeders, round or square post feeders (some shaped like little houses), recycled milk cartons, detergent or bleach bottles.

PLANT A NATURAL FOOD SUPPLY

Here is an idea to feed the birds and add to your fruit bin, too. Plant small crab apple, hawthorne or mulberry trees. Once the trees are established, suspend birdhouses from the branches. Birds will find caterpillars and other insects as well as the fruit — a regular storehouse of food — for themselves and their young. And, the tree will benefit from its tenants.

HUMMINGBIRD FEAST

1/4 c. sugar
Red ribbon (opt.)
Hummingbird feeders

Stir sugar into 1 cup boiling water. Cool. Tie ribbons around the feeders to attract hummingbirds. Fill feeders with sugar mixture. Do not substitute honey for sugar.

PEANUT BUTTER SURPRISE

Soft drink bottle caps
1 small log
1 c. cornmeal
1/2 c. peanut butter
Wild birdseed or sunflower seed

Nail bottle caps to log. Combine cornmeal and peanut butter in bowl; mix well. Add seed; mix well. Fill bottle caps with seed mixture. Suspend "feeder" from tree branch.

BIRD CAKE

1/2 lb. suet, chopped
1 12-oz. juice concentrate can
1 c. wild birdseed
or sunflower seed

Melt suet in double boiler pan. Cool until hardened, then remelt. Line juice can with mesh, allowing the mesh to extend over edge of juice can. Stir birdseed into melted suet. Pour into lined juice can. Cool until mixture hardens. Place juice can in bowl of warm water. Let stand until suet is loosened. Gather mesh at top; remove from can. Close top with string. Hang the "suet-in-a-sack" high in a tree outside your window and wait for the birds.

PREFERRED FOODS OF SOME COMMON BIRDS

Mourning dove	oil (black) sunflower; white and red proso, and German (golden) millet
Blue jay	peanut kernels and sunflower seed of all types
Scrub jay	peanut kernels and black-striped sunflower
Chickadees	oil (black) and black-striped sunflower; peanut kernels
Tufted titmouse	peanut kernels; black-striped and oil (black) sunflower
White-breasted nuthatch	black-striped sunflower
Red-breasted nuthatch	black-striped and oil (black) sunflower
Brown thrasher	hulled and black-striped sunflower
Starling	peanut hearts, hulled oats and cracked corn
House (English) sparrow	white and red proso, and German (golden) millet; canary seed
Red-winged blackbird	white and red proso, and German (golden) millet
Common grackle	black-striped and hulled sunflower; cracked corn
Brown-headed cowbird	white and red proso, and German (golden) millet; canary seed
Cardinal	sunflower seed of all types
Evening grosbeak	sunflower seed of all types
Purple finch	sunflower seed of all types
House finch	oil (black), black-striped, and hulled sunflower; niger
Pine siskin	sunflower seed of all types
American goldfinch	hulled sunflower, niger and oil (black) sunflower
Rufous-sided towhee	white proso millet
Dark-eyed junco	white and red proso millet; canary seed; fine-cracked corn
Chipping sparrow	white and red proso millet
Tree sparrow	red and white proso millet
Field sparrow	white and red proso millet
White-crowned sparrow	oil (black) and hulled sunflower; white and red proso millet; peanut kernels and hearts; niger
White-throated sparrow	oil (black), black-striped, and hulled sunflower; white and red proso millet; peanut kernels
Song sparrow	white and red proso millet

From the National Wildlife Federation booklet, WILD BIRD FEEDING PREFERENCES
by Aelred D. Geis and Donald B. Hyde Jr.

Trail Recipes

SALMON-ZUCCHINI BUNDLES

4 6-oz. salmon steaks
1 can tomato soup
2 tsp. capers, drained
1/4 tsp. garlic powder
1 med. zucchini, thinly sliced
1/4 c. Parmesan cheese

Cut four 14-inch squares heavy-duty foil. Place 1 salmon steak in center of each foil square. Combine soup, capers, garlic powder, zucchini and cheese. Spoon over salmon. Seal foil around salmon to make tight packages. Place on grill 4 inches from hot coals. Grill for 25 minutes. Yield: 4 servings.

11

Trail Recipes

Snacks

BASIC GORP

1 c. peanuts
1 c. raisins
1 c. M and M's

Mix together equal amounts of peanuts, raisins and M and M's. Package mixture in individual plastic bags to be carried by each camper.

Note: You can substitute or add cashews, walnuts, shelled sunflower seeds, chopped dates, chopped apricots or shredded coconut to the Basic Gorp recipe. In winter you might add miniature marshmallows.

BEEF JERKY

3 lb. lean steak, 1 to 1 1/2
in. thick, partially frozen
1/4 c. soy sauce
2 tsp. garlic salt
1/2 tsp. pepper

Trim steak; slice in thin strips. Put soy sauce, 3/4 cup water, garlic salt and pepper together in bowl. Marinate steak in this mixture for 2 to 3 hours. Drain steak on paper towels; blot dry. Lay individual strips on the oven rack so that they are not overlapping. Dry in slow oven with door ajar for 6 to 8 hours until steak is brittle.

GRANOLA BARS

7 c. granola
1 c. dry milk powder
1 c. whole wheat flour
1 c. honey
1 c. peanut butter
1/2 c. fruit juice concentrate

Combine all ingredients and mix well. If too dry, add liquid fruit juice by spoonfuls until it sticks together. Spread mixture on cookie sheets and pat firm. Dry in slow oven with door ajar for 8 hours. Turn over. Dry for 4 hours. Slice into bars. Dry for 3 to 6 hours longer.

Vegetables

WILD GREENS

Edible wild greens
1/4 c. vinegar
1/4 c. bacon drippings
Salt and pepper to taste

The young, tender leaves of dandelions, lamb's quarter, pigweed, purslane, sheep-sorrel, nettles, Russian thistle, miner's lettuce, shepherd's purse and violets can be cooked like spinach or used raw as a salad. Either way, combine vinegar, bacon drippings, salt and pepper to make dressing that complements tart flavors of greens. Flavor will also be improved if you change the water several times while cooking the greens.

Note: For creamed greens, cook and drain greens and add 1 cup white sauce.

Main Dishes

POCKET STEW

2 lb. hamburger 2 potatoes, sliced 2 onions, sliced 2 carrots, sliced (opt.) 1 c. peas (opt.) 4 slices bacon Salt and pepper to taste	Place hamburger patty in center of 12 x 18-inch square of heavy-duty foil or double layer of regular foil. Cover with thinly sliced potatoes, sliced onions, carrots and peas and top with 1/2 slice bacon. Season with salt and pepper. Wrap in foil, forming thick handles for turning on both ends of the package. Place directly on coals for 15 to 20 minutes. Slit open and serve. Yield: 8 servings.

Note: Easy to serve to large backyard crowd, or can be made at home, frozen after wrapping, and taken on the trail for cooking the first night out.

Breads & Desserts

BASIC BANNOCK OR SKILLET BREAD

2 c. flour 1/4 c. dry milk powder 1 tbsp. sugar 1/2 tsp. salt 2 tsp. baking powder 2 tbsp. shortening	Combine dry ingredients in plastic bag before you leave home. At camp, add 1 scant cup cold water gradually and mix into a stiff dough. You can do your mixing right in the plastic bag or in a pan so the dough can be scraped out more easily. Melt shortening in skillet until hot. Turn dough into skillet, patting into oversized biscuit. Brown over fire. Turn when crusty and firm and brown other side. Stand skillet on edge before coals, using it as a reflector. Turn bread frequently and adjust distance from heat to keep it from getting too brown. Bake until bannock sounds hollow when tapped. Break into pieces and serve with margarine and jam.

FRIED PIES

1 pastry stick 1/2 c. jam 2 tbsp. shortening	Mix pastry stick using package directions. Roll out egg-sized chunks into 8 circles. Place 1 tablespoon of jam in center of each patty. Fold pastry over; press edges together. Fry in lightly greased skillet on both sides.

FUDGE

1 c. sugar 3 tbsp. cocoa 3 tbsp. dry milk powder 1 tbsp. butter Nuts (opt.)	Combine dry ingredients in plastic bag before leaving home. At camp, stir 1/3 cup of water into mixture. Cook over low heat until syrup boils and forms soft ball. Remove from heat. Add butter. Stir when cool. Pour into greased bowl or skillet. Add nuts. Cut into pieces.

Appetizers

Get company in the company mood! Dainty, tempting appetizers are charming introductions to any meal and, with a little ingenuity, can be thrifty ways to use up leftovers too!

Appetizers are served all over the world, but Americans prefer three main types — hors d'oeuvres, canapes and cocktails.

There's no limit to the kinds of meat, poultry, fish, cheese, fruits and vegetables that can be selected for appetizers. And there's only one rule to follow: don't serve any food as an appetizers that will be repeated in the main meal. Remember, appetizers are a part of the whole menu and should whet the appetite, not satisfy it.

Choose complementary flavors which contrast in texture and taste. For example, a simple appetizer of crisp apple slices pleasantly contrasts with slices of hard cheese. Appetizers don't have to be exotic to be good. And after the party? Your family will love the leftovers. Especially when they taste recipes like "Parmesan Twists," "Crisp Won Tons," and the "Sweet and Sour Mini-Spareribs." All delicious!

Serve your appetizers with flair and confidence, for the recipes that follow are guaranteed to please.

← PARTY CHEESE DIP, Recipe on page 23.

Appetizers

ARTICHOKE NIBBLES

2 6-oz. jars marinated
artichokes
1 onion, finely chopped
1 clove of garlic, crushed
1/4 c. dry bread crumbs
1/4 tsp. salt
1/8 tsp. each pepper, oregano
and hot pepper sauce
4 eggs, beaten
8 oz. sharp Cheddar cheese,
grated
2 tbsp. minced parsley

Drain and chop artichokes, reserving half the marinade. Place reserved marinade in saucepan; add onion and garlic. Saute until onion is tender. Discard garlic clove; drain. Add bread crumbs and seasonings to marinade; stir in eggs, cheese, parsley, artichokes and onion. Spread in greased 7 x 11-inch baking dish. Bake at 325 degrees for 30 minutes or until set. Cut into 1-inch squares. Yield: 6 dozen.

PETITS CHOUX

1/2 c. oil
1 c. flour
4 eggs
1/2 c. finely chopped Swiss cheese
2/3 c. sour cream
3/8 c. mayonnaise
2 tbsp. chopped onion
2 tbsp. chopped chives
2 tbsp. chopped pimento
Salt and garlic powder to taste

Combine oil and 1 cup water in small saucepan. Bring to a boil. Stir in flour. Cook until mixture forms ball, stirring constantly. Remove from heat. Beat in eggs and cheese. Drop by heaping teaspoonfuls onto baking sheet. Sprinkle with additional cheese. Bake at 400 degrees for 20 to 25 minutes or until golden brown. Combine remaining ingredients in mixer bowl. Beat until blended. Serve with warm puffs.

FOUR-CHEESE BALL

2 3-oz. packages cream
cheese, softened
1 5-oz. jar sharp Cheddar
cheese, softened
1 5-oz. jar Roquefort cheese
spread, softened
1 5-oz. jar smoky cheese
spread, softened
1/2 onion, grated
1/2 tsp. Worcestershire sauce
1/4 c. evaporated milk
1 c. chopped walnuts

Combine all ingredients except walnuts in large bowl; mix well. Chill for 2 hours or longer. Shape into large ball. Roll in walnuts. Chill until serving time. Yield: 10 servings.

Appetizers

CAVIAR PIE

2 tbsp. butter, softened
9 hard-boiled eggs, finely
chopped
1/4 c. mayonnaise
1/4 tsp. each salt and white
pepper
2 c. chopped green onions
1 8-oz. package cream cheese,
softened
2/3 c. sour cream
1 4-oz. jar lump fish caviar

Grease bottom and side of 8-inch springform pan with butter. Combine eggs, mayonnaise, salt and pepper in bowl; mix well. Spread over bottom of prepared pan. Sprinkle green onions over egg mixture. Blend cream cheese and sour cream in bowl. Spread over onion layer. Chill, covered, for 3 hours to overnight. Spread caviar over cream cheese layer. Remove side of pan. Garnish with lemon slices and parsley. Serve with wheat thins or rye rounds. Yield: 16-20 servings.

CRAB MEAT APPETIZERS

1/2 c. tomato juice
2 eggs
1 c. dry bread crumbs
1/2 tsp. salt
Dash of pepper
1 tsp. finely chopped parsley
1 tsp. finely chopped celery
leaves
1 tsp. finely chopped chives
1 6-oz. can crab meat, flaked
1 tsp. lemon juice
Fine dry bread crumbs
Oil for deep frying

Combine tomato juice and 1 beaten egg in bowl. Add 1 cup bread crumbs, seasonings, crab meat and lemon juice; mix well. Shape into 3/4-inch balls. Dip in remaining egg; coat with fine bread crumbs. Deep-fry in 365-degree oil for 2 to 3 minutes or until golden. Yield: 2 dozen.

SWEET AND SOUR MINI SPARERIBS

3 lb. spareribs, cut into
finger-sized pieces
Salt and pepper to taste
2/3 c. packed dark brown sugar
2 tbsp. cornstarch
2 tsp. dry mustard
2/3 c. vinegar
1 c. crushed pineapple
1/2 c. catsup
1/4 c. finely chopped onion
2 tbsp. soy sauce

Arrange ribs, meat side up, in single layer in shallow baking dish. Bake at 425 degrees for 20 to 30 minutes or until brown. Pour off excess drippings. Sprinkle with salt and pepper. Combine remaining ingredients and 1/2 cup water in saucepan; mix well. Cook over medium heat until thick. Spoon half the sauce over ribs. Bake at 350 degrees for 45 minutes; turn. Cover with remaining sauce. Bake for 30 minutes longer.

Appetizers

BEEF WELLINGTON BITES

1/2 lb. beef filet
1/2 c. teriyaki marinade
1 2-crust pkg. pie crust mix
2 1 7/8-oz. jars chicken
liver pate
1 egg, beaten

Cut beef into thirty six 1/2 x 1-inch pieces. Marinate in teriyaki marinade in shallow dish for 1 hour. Prepare pie crust using package directions. Roll into two 9 x 12-inch rectangles on floured surface. Cut into 2 x 3-inch strips. Spread a small amount of pate on each piece of beef; place on pie crust strip. Fold to enclose beef; seal ends. Brush with egg; place on greased baking sheet. Bake at 425 degrees for 20 minutes. Yield: 3 dozen.

SEAFOOD-DEVILED EGGS

18 hard-boiled eggs
1 6-oz. package frozen shrimp
and crab meat, thawed, drained
2/3 c. mayonnaise
1 tbsp. chili sauce
1 tbsp. grated onion
1 tsp. minced green pepper
1 tsp. chopped pimento

Cut eggs in half and remove yolks; reserve whites. Mash egg yolks in small bowl. Add remaining ingredients; mix well. Spoon into egg whites; arrange on serving plate. Garnish with parsley and ripe olives.

CHILLED MUSHROOM HORS D'OEUVRES

1 lb. mushrooms
1/4 c. vinegar
1 tbsp. parsley
1 clove of garlic, halved
2 tbsp. olive oil
1/2 tsp. salt
Dash of pepper
1/4 tsp. oregano

Cook mushrooms in boiling water in saucepan for 3 minutes; drain. Combine remaining ingredients in bowl; mix well. Add mushrooms. Chill for several hours. Remove garlic before serving.

PARMESAN TWISTS

1/4 c. butter, softened
1 c. Parmesan cheese
1/2 c. sour cream
1 c. flour
1/2 tsp. Italian seasoning
1 egg yolk, beaten
1 tbsp. poppy seed

Cream butter and cheese in bowl until light and fluffy. Beat in sour cream gradually. Blend in flour and seasoning. Roll dough on floured surface into two 7 x 12-inch rectangles. Cut into 1/2 x 6-inch strips. Brush with mixture of egg yolk and 1 tablespoon water; sprinkle with poppy seed. Twist each strip 2 or 3 times and place on buttered baking sheet. Bake at 350 degrees until brown.

EMPANADAS

1 lb. ground beef
3 med. onions, chopped
1 ripe tomato, chopped
2 sm. green peppers, chopped
Salt, garlic salt and chili
powder to taste
1 tsp. sugar
Flour
Hot peppers to taste
1/3 c. chopped Spanish olives
4 capers (opt.)
1/2 tsp. salt
1/2 c. margarine
Beaten egg yolks

Brown ground beef in skillet, stirring until crumbly; drain. Add onions, tomato and green peppers. Simmer until vegetables are tender. Add seasonings, sugar, 1 tablespoon flour, hot peppers, olives and capers; mix well. Cook for 5 minutes. Set aside to cool. Mix 1 1/2 cups sifted flour and salt in bowl. Cut in margarine until crumbly. Mix in 1/4 cup cold water. Shape into ball. Chill for several minutes. Roll on floured surface. Cut into 4 1/2-inch circles. Place heaping teaspoonful ground beef mixture on each circle. Fold to enclose filling; moisten and seal edges with fork. Place on baking sheet; brush with egg yolks. Bake at 350 degrees for 15 minutes. Yield: 20 servings.

STUFFED SNOW PEAS

100 snow peas
1   8-oz. package cream cheese,
softened
1/4 c. Parmesan cheese
3 tbsp. catsup
2 tsp. dried dillweed
1 tsp. dry mustard
1 tsp. Worcestershire sauce
1/2 tsp. each salt and white
pepper

Arrange snow peas in shallow pan. Cover with boiling water. Let stand for 1 minute; drain. Cover with ice cold water; drain. Cut 1/4 inch from each stem end. Combine remaining ingredients in bowl; mix well. Pipe cream cheese mixture into pea pods using pastry bag. Arrange on serving tray. Chill until serving time.

BITE-SIZED CREAM PUFFS WITH SHRIMP

1/2 pkg. pie crust mix
2 eggs
5 oz. cooked shrimp, chopped
1 tbsp. finely chopped chives
1/4 tsp. salt
2 tsp. lemon juice
1/2 c. mayonnaise
Several drops of Tabasco sauce

Combine pie crust mix and 2/3 cup boiling water in saucepan. Cook until mixture leaves side of pan, stirring constantly. Remove from heat. Beat in eggs 1 at a time. Drop by tablespoonfuls 1 inch apart onto greased baking sheet. Bake at 400 degrees until brown. Combine remaining 6 ingredients in bowl; mix well. Fill cooled puffs with shrimp mixture. Heat filled puffs in hot oven for 3 minutes before serving. Yield: 3 dozen.

TANGERINE-SHRIMP COCKTAIL

1 lb. shrimp, shelled, cooked
1 orange, peeled, sliced
1 c. fresh tangerine sections
4 c. torn chicory
1/2 c. chili sauce
1/4 tsp. grated orange rind

Combine shrimp, orange slices, tangerine sections and chicory in bowl. Mix chili sauce and orange rind. Serve with shrimp mixture. Yield: 4 servings.

Photograph for this recipe above.

Appetizers

CRISP WON TONS

1/2 lb. ground pork
4 med. shrimp, cooked, chopped
4 water chestnuts, chopped
1 green onion, finely chopped
1/4 tsp. sugar
1/2 tsp. each salt, MSG
1 pkg. won ton wrappers
Oil for deep frying

Combine first 4 ingredients with seasonings in bowl; mix well. Place 1/2 teaspoonful on each won ton wrapper. Moisten edges with a small amount of water. Fold into triangle to enclose filling. Fold corners to center, pressing to seal. Deep-fry in oil until golden brown on both sides. Drain on paper towels. Serve hot.

SEVICHE

1 lb. fillet of sole, cut into
bite-sized pieces
Juice of 4 or 5 limes
Salt and pepper to taste
1/4 c. olive oil
1/2 tsp. oregano
1 tomato, peeled, seeded, chopped
1 onion, chopped
2 canned jalapeno peppers,
seeded, chopped
2 tbsp. chopped Chinese parsley
1 ripe avocado, peeled, cubed

Place fillets in deep glass bowl. Add enough lime juice to cover. Chill, covered, for 8 hours or longer; turn several times. Sprinkle with salt and pepper to taste. Add olive oil and oregano. Combine tomato, onion, peppers and parsley in bowl. Fold gently into fish mixture. Add pepper to taste. Fold in avocado. Chill, covered, until serving time.

ANTIPASTO SPREAD

1 med. eggplant, peeled, cubed
1/3 c. chopped green pepper
1 med. onion, chopped
3/4 c. sliced mushrooms
1/3 c. oil
1 c. tomato paste
2 cloves of garlic, crushed
2 tbsp. wine vinegar
1/2 c. green olives
1 1/2 tsp. sugar
1/2 tsp. oregano
Salt and pepper to taste

Combine eggplant, green pepper, onion, mushrooms and oil in saucepan. Simmer for 10 minutes. Add remaining ingredients and 1/2 cup water. Simmer for 30 minutes longer. Serve hot or cold with crackers. Yield: 10-12 servings.

21

Appetizers

CHICKEN LIVER PATE

1 lb. chicken livers
1/4 c. chopped onion
1/4 c. butter, softened
3 tbsp. mayonnaise
2 tbsp. lemon juice
8 drops of hot pepper sauce
1/2 tsp. dry mustard
1/2 tsp. salt
Dash of pepper

Saute livers and onion in 2 tablespoons butter in skillet for 5 minutes; stir occasionally. Drain, reserving 3 tablespoons drippings. Process livers, onion and drippings in blender container until finely ground. Add 2 tablespoons butter and remaining ingredients; mix well. Spoon into oiled 2-cup mold. Chill, covered, for 6 hours or longer. Unmold on serving plate. Garnish with chopped hard-boiled eggs, chopped chives or parsley. Serve with assorted crackers.

DILLED SHRIMP MOLD

1 1/2 env. unflavored gelatin
1 can shrimp soup
1 8-oz. package cream cheese, softened
2 4 1/4-oz. cans shrimp
Juice of 1 lemon
1 c. mayonnaise
Dash of cayenne pepper
1 tbsp. Worcestershire sauce
1/4 c. each finely chopped celery, green pepper
3 tbsp. grated onion
1 tbsp. dillweed

Soften gelatin in a small amount of cold water. Heat soup in double boiler; add cream cheese. Cook until melted, stirring constantly. Add gelatin; stir until dissolved. Rinse shrimp in cold water; drain. Combine with lemon juice in bowl; mash with fork. Add to cooled gelatin mixture with mayonnaise and remaining ingredients. Pour into 3-quart mold. Chill until firm. Serve with crackers.

FIESTA DIP

3 ripe avocados, mashed
2 tbsp. lemon juice
1/2 tsp. salt
1/4 tsp. pepper
1 c. sour cream
1 pkg. taco seasoning mix
1/2 c. mayonnaise
2 10 1/2-oz. cans jalapeno bean dip
1 lg. bunch green onions, chopped
3 med. tomatoes chopped
2 3 1/2-oz. cans ripe olives, sliced
8 oz. sharp Cheddar cheese, shredded

Combine first 4 ingredients in bowl; mix well. Mix sour cream, taco mix and mayonnaise in bowl. Spread bean dip on large serving platter. Top with avocado mixture. Spread sour cream mixture over top. Sprinkle with onions, tomatoes, olives and cheese. Chill, covered, until serving time. Serve with large round tortilla chips. Yield: 18-20 servings.

PARTY CHEESE DIP

1/4 to 1/2 tsp. Tabasco sauce
1 3-oz. package cream cheese,
softened
1 pt. sour cream
1 env. dry onion soup mix
1 2 1/4-oz. can deviled ham

Blend Tabasco with cream cheese in bowl. Blend in sour cream gradually. Add onion soup mix and deviled ham; mix well. Spoon into serving dish. Serve with artichoke hearts, mushrooms, cauliflowerets, scallions and cherry tomatoes. Yield: 2 2/3 cups.

Photograph for this recipe on page 14.

TANGY SPINACH DIP

1 10-oz. package frozen chopped
spinach, thawed, drained
1 c. sour cream
1 c. mayonnaise
1/2 c. minced fresh parsley
1/2 c. chopped green onions
1 tsp. salt
1 tsp. Beau Monde seasoning
1/2 tsp. dillweed
Juice of 1 lemon
1 loaf French bread

Pat spinach dry with paper towels. Combine spinach with remaining ingredients except bread in bowl; mix well. Scoop out center of bread to make shell. Fill shell with spinach mixture. Serve with bread chunks and fresh vegetables.

FRIED SHRIMP WITH CURRIED CONCORD DIP

1 c. yogurt
1/2 c. Concord grape jam
2 tsp. lemon juice
1 tsp. horseradish
1/2 tsp. curry powder
1 sm. clove of garlic, minced
1/8 tsp. ginger
1 c. flour
1 tsp. each baking powder, salt
1 egg
1 c. milk
1/4 c. oil
1 1/2 lb. fresh shrimp
Oil for deep frying

Combine yogurt, jam, lemon juice, horseradish, curry powder, garlic and ginger in bowl; mix well. Chill in refrigerator. Combine flour, baking powder, salt, egg, milk and 1/4 cup oil. Beat with a rotary beater until smooth. Remove shells from shrimp, leaving tails. Pat dry. Dust lightly with additional flour. Dip shrimp into batter; shake off excess batter. Deep-fry in 375-degree oil for about 4 minutes or until golden brown. Drain on paper towels. Serve with dip.

World of Cheese Chart

HOW MUCH TO BUY

If a recipe calls for 2 1/2 cups of Cheddar cheese, how much do you buy? If the recipe calls for 3 cups of cottage cheese, will one carton be enough? Use this table when buying cheese for cooking.

BUY:	IF YOU NEED:			
	Cottage Cheese	Shredded	Grated	Crumbled
3/4 ounce			1/4 cup	
1 ounce		1/4 cup	1/3 cup	1/4 cup
1 1/2 ounces			1/2 cup	
2 ounces	1/4 cup	1/2 cup	2/3 cup	1/2 cup
2 1/4 ounces			3/4 cup	
3 ounces		3/4 cup	1 cup	3/4 cup
4 ounces	1/2 cup	1 cup	1 1/3 cups	1 cup
8 ounces	1 cup	2 cups	2 2/3 cups	2 cups
12 ounces	1 1/2 cups	3 cups	4 cups	3 cups
1 pound	2 cups	4 cups		4 cups

CHEESE CHART

NATURAL CHEESE	CHARACTERISTICS AND USES
Bel Paese	A soft cheese often used in cooking to replace mozzarella. Although it is an Italian cheese, there is a very good American version bearing the same name that is made in Wisconsin.
Blue	A crumbly and sharp-flavored soft dessert cheese that is white and contains blue mold. French blue cheese is referred to as "bleu cheese."
Brie	A soft, creamy dessert cheese ranked as one of the world's great cheeses. It should be served at room temperature. At room temperature, good Brie is almost always runny.
Camembert	A soft, creamy, rich dessert cheese that is another of the world's great cheeses. Camembert that is shrunken in appearance or smells like ammonia is past its prime.

Charts

NATURAL CHEESE	CHARACTERISTICS AND USES
Cheddar	A variety of hard cheese that is the most popular American cheese. Cheddar is sold as mild, mellow, or sharp cheese. Mild has aged 2-3 months; mellow from 6-9 months; and sharp, from 12-15 months. Excellent for eating or cooking.
Cottage	The large or small drained curd of soured whole or skim milk. One of the few soft cheeses suitable for cooking.
Cream	An unripened American soft cheese that is popular for desserts. Like cottage cheese, cream cheese is a soft cheese suitable for cooking.
Edam	A mild, semihard cheese. It was originally Dutch cheese that now has several American versions. It has a bright red exterior rind and pale gold interior. Edam is primarily an eating cheese.
Feta	The most popular of Greek cheeses. White and crumbly, it has a unique flavor that is perfect for Hellenic cuisine.
Gorgonzola	A white and blue-veined Italian pressed cheese that may range from soft (very young) to semihard (aged). It is used in cooking, for desserts, or in sandwiches. An American gorgonzola is made in Wisconsin.
Gouda	Like gorgonzola, the mild-flavored gouda cheese becomes firmer with age. It was originally a Dutch cheese, that now has several American versions. Gouda is a popular dessert cheese.
Monterey	Also known as Monterey Jack, this California cheese is of two types: a semihard cheese and a hard cheese. Both are good cooking cheeses.
Mozzarella	A semisoft white cheese popular in Italian dishes. There are American versions but they lack the flavor of the Italian varieties.
Parmesan	A staple hard cheese of Italian cookery. American Parmesans, sold already grated, have only a fraction of the flavor of the original, ungrated cheese.
Provolone	An Italian cottage-type cheese. American cottage cheese can be substituted in appetizers or sandwiches. The American version has little of the flavor of the Italian cheese.
Ricotta	An Italian cottage-type cheese. American cottage cheese can be substituted in almost every recipe calling for ricotta.
Romano	A very hard Italian cheese grated like Parmesan and used for cooking. There is also an American Romano.
Roquefort	A soft dessert cheese that is white with a characteristic blue veining. The veining comes from the penicillin mold that gives this cheese its sharp flavor.
Swiss	The common United States term for any of the Emmentaler or Gruyere cheeses. Used in cooking. (Not to be confused with the process cheese of the same name.)
Touloumisso	A spicy Greek cheese that is very good.

Salads

I n this land, the variety of ingredients to choose for salads is practically unlimited. Colorful salads are a lovely accompaniment to almost any meal, while many salads stand on their own as satisfying, nutritious main courses. Accompanied by a soup or sandwich, they sparkle as the center of attention.

Practically every type of food can be the basis of a delicious salad. They can be hot or cold, crunchy or wilted, tossed or molded. They can be tossed with a sweet sauce or a tangy marinade. They can be sprinkled with spices or dusted with cheese. Salads offer a free reign to the imagination and the venturesome spirit of the cook.

This collection of favorite recipes brings you dozens of very special salads. There are recipes for wonderful concoctions of fruits to tempt your appetite — as well as several pasta specialties, today's all-purpose cuisine.

These pages are also packed with superb recipes starring seafood, poultry, cheese and meat. Many are family heirlooms; and each is guaranteed to please your family and friends!

CHEESE SALAD MOLDS, Recipe on page 28.

Salads

AMBROSIA MOLD

1 3-oz. package orange gelatin
1/2 c. sugar
1 8 1/2-oz. can crushed
pineapple
1 c. flaked coconut
1 8-oz. carton sour cream
1 can mandarin oranges
1 c. chopped pecans

Dissolve gelatin and sugar in 1 cup boiling water in bowl. Chill until partially set. Stir in remaining ingredients. Spoon into 9 x 13-inch dish. Chill until firm. Yield: 10-12 servings.

CHEESE SALAD MOLDS

1 env. unflavored gelatin
1 tsp. salt
2 c. creamed cottage cheese
1/4 c. crumbled Roquefort cheese
2 tbsp. chopped chives
1/2 c. whipping cream, whipped
1 c. sour cream
3 tbsp. honey
3 tbsp. lemon juice
1/2 tsp. grated lemon rind

Soften gelatin in 1/4 cup cold water. Heat in pan of boiling water until dissolved; add 1/2 teaspoon salt. Mix cheeses in bowl. Add gelatin; mix well. Fold in chives and whipped cream. Fill buttered individual molds. Chill until firm. Unmold on plate. Combine remaining ingredients with 1/2 teaspoon salt in bowl; mix well. Chill for 30 minutes. Arrange mandarin orange, banana, avocado and apple slices and strawberries around cheese molds. Spoon dressing over molded salads and fruit.

Photograph for this recipe on page 26.

CHERRY-YOGURT FREEZE

1 10-oz. carton whipped topping
1 8-oz. carton lemon yogurt
1/2 c. mayonnaise
1/2 c. chopped pecans
1 c. pineapple chunks, drained
1 can dark sweet cherries, drained

Fold whipped topping, yogurt and mayonnaise together in bowl. Add pecans, pineapple and cherries; mix gently. Pour into 9 x 12-inch dish. Freeze until firm. Cut into squares. Yield: 12 servings.

VERY BERRY SALAD

1 c. each blackberries, blueberries,
raspberries and boysenberries
3 oranges, peeled, thinly sliced
1 c. chopped walnuts
1 1/2 c. yogurt
1/3 c. orange juice, chilled
2 tbsp. honey

Combine berries, oranges and walnuts in bowl. Chill in refrigerator. Combine remaining ingredients in blender container. Process until smooth. Fold into fruit mixture. Spoon into chilled serving dishes.

PEACH-ALMOND CHIFFON SALAD

1 3-oz. package orange gelatin
2 tbsp. lemon juice
1/2 c. mayonnaise
1/4 tsp. salt
1 1/2 c. chopped peaches, drained
1 3-oz. package cream cheese, softened
1/4 c. toasted slivered almonds

Dissolve gelatin in 1 cup boiling water in large mixer bowl. Add 1/2 cup cold water, lemon juice, mayonnaise and salt. Beat at medium speed until well blended. Pour into freezing tray. Freeze for 20 minutes. Pour into chilled mixer bowl. Beat at high speed until thick and fluffy. Fold in peaches, cream cheese and almonds. Spoon into 1-quart mold. Chill until firm. Unmold on chilled serving plate. Yield: 6 servings.

SHERRIED FRUIT SALAD

1 pineapple
1 cantaloupe
1 papaya
3 apples, sliced
1 bunch seedless grapes
1 pt. strawberries
1 c. slivered almonds
1 3-oz. package cream cheese, softened
1 tbsp. lime juice
1 tbsp. sugar
3/4 c. Sherry
Dash of salt

Chill fruit overnight. Cut pineapple, cantaloupe and papaya into bite-sized pieces. Combine all fruit with almonds in serving bowl, reserving enough papaya and almonds to garnish. Toss gently. Chill in refrigerator. Blend cream cheese with remaining ingredients in bowl. Fold into fruit; toss gently. Garnish with remaining papaya and almonds. Serve with light crackers and white wine.

POLYNESIAN CHICKEN SALAD

6 whole chicken breasts, cooked, chopped
1 7-oz. can sliced water chestnuts, drained
1 c. slivered almonds, toasted
2 c. seedless white grape halves
1 c. chopped celery
1 lg. can pineapple chunks
1 1/2 c. salad dressing
1/4 tsp. curry powder
1 tsp. soy sauce
2 tbsp. pineapple juice

Mix first 6 ingredients in bowl. Combine salad dressing and remaining ingredients in small bowl; blend well. Pour over chicken mixture; toss lightly. Chill for 2 to 3 hours. Yield: 10 servings.

CURRIED PINEAPPLE-TURKEY SALAD

2 tsp. curry powder
1/2 c. cider vinegar
1 tbsp. sugar
1/2 tsp. garlic salt
1   20-oz. can pineapple chunks, drained
4 c. chopped cooked turkey
1/3 c. finely chopped green onions
1 c. thinly sliced celery
1/4 c. finely chopped green pepper
1 c. mayonnaise
Garlic-salted raisins
Chopped macadamia nuts
Chopped hard-boiled egg
Toasted coconut chips

Heat curry powder, vinegar, sugar and garlic salt to simmering in saucepan; cool. Combine with pineapple and turkey; mix lightly. Chill until serving time. Mix with onions, celery, green pepper and mayonnaise. Sprinkle with remaining ingredients.

Photograph for this recipe above.

Salads

MANDARIN ORANGE-HAM SALAD

3 c. chopped cooked ham
1 13-oz. can pineapple
chunks, drained
1 16-oz. can Bing cherries,
drained
1 11-oz. can mandarin oranges,
drained
1 1/2 c. miniature marshmallows
1 c. sour cream
1/3 c. mayonnaise
2 c. cooked rice

Combine ham, pineapple, cherries, oranges and marshmallows in bowl. Mix sour cream, mayonnaise and rice in bowl. Add to ham mixture; toss lightly. Spoon onto lettuce-lined plates. Garnish with toasted coconut or slivered almonds. Yield: 6 servings.

SALAD DE TACO

1 lb. ground beef
1 8-oz. can tomato sauce
1 tsp. oregano
1/2 tsp. each salt and pepper
1 head lettuce, shredded
1 onion, chopped
12 oz. Colby cheese, grated
2 or 3 tomatoes, chopped
1/4 c. taco sauce
1 bottle of creamy Caesar salad
dressing
1 lg. package Doritos, crushed

Brown ground beef in skillet, stirring until crumbly; drain. Add tomato sauce, oregano, salt and pepper. Simmer, covered, for 15 minutes. Cook uncovered, until thickened. Chill until serving time. Layer lettuce, onion, cheese, meat sauce, tomatoes, taco sauce, salad dressing and Doritos in large salad bowl. Toss to mix.

FLORIDIAN SALAD

1/2 c. olive oil
3 tbsp. red wine vinegar
2 tsp. Dijon mustard
3/4 tsp. salt
1/2 tsp. minced garlic
1/4 tsp. pepper
Romaine lettuce leaves
1 7-oz. can tuna, drained
4 hard-boiled eggs, sliced
3/4 c. green pepper rings
3/4 c. sliced cooked new red
potatoes, chilled
3/4 c. sliced cucumber
3/4 c. tomato wedges

Combine olive oil, vinegar, mustard, salt, garlic and pepper in jar; mix well. Line serving platter with romaine. Place tuna in center of platter. Arrange eggs, green pepper, potatoes, cucumber and tomatoes around tuna. Garnish with olives. Spoon dressing over salad. Yield: 4 servings.

Photograph for this recipe on page 35.

31

Salads

TANGY DITALINI SALAD

1 c. yogurt
2 tbsp. oil
1 tbsp. tarragon vinegar
2 tbsp. chopped onion
1 tbsp. chopped parsley
1/2 tsp. salt
1/4 tsp. each garlic powder,
oregano
1/8 tsp. white pepper
1 8-oz. package ditalini, cooked
2 c. chopped fresh cauliflower
1 c. each sliced carrots, celery

Combine yogurt, oil, vinegar, onion, parsley, salt, garlic powder, oregano and white pepper in blender container. Process at high speed for 2 minutes or until smooth and creamy. Chill for 2 hours or longer. Combine ditalini, cauliflower, carrots and celery in large bowl. Add dressing; toss lightly. Chill in refrigerator. Yield: 4-6 servings.

Photograph for this recipe above.

LIGHT ROTINI LUNCHEON SALAD

1 8-oz. package rotini, cooked
2 c. chopped cooked chicken
2 c. cherry tomato halves
2 c. green pepper strips
2 c. broccoli flowerets
1 8-oz. bottle of zesty reduced-
calorie Italian dressing
Salt and pepper to taste

Combine all ingredients in bowl; toss lightly. Chill until serving time.

Photograph for this recipe on opposite page.

LAMB AND MACARONI VINAIGRETTE

1/3 c. oil
1/3 c. vinegar
2 tbsp. grated onion
2 1/4 tsp. seasoned salt
1/2 tsp. crushed marjoram
Dash of cayenne pepper
2 c. elbow macaroni, cooked
1 10-oz. package frozen
French-style green beans,
cooked, drained
2 c. chopped cooked lamb
1 c. grated carrots

Blend oil, vinegar, onion, seasoned salt, marjoram and cayenne pepper in large bowl. Add macaroni and remaining ingredients; toss lightly. Chill in refrigerator. Yield: 6 servings.

GAZPACHO SALAD

1/2 c. chopped onion
2 tsp. minced garlic
2 tsp. Dijon mustard
1 tsp. grated lemon rind
1 tsp. salt
1/4 tsp. oregano
1/4 tsp. pepper
1/4 c. lemon juice
3/4 c. oil
1 c. soft bread crumbs
2 c. green peppers, cut in
1 1/2 x 1/4-in. strips
3 c. shredded cabbage
2 c. sliced cucumbers, halved
4 c. tomato chunks
1 c. diced celery

Combine onion, garlic, mustard, lemon rind, salt, oregano, pepper and lemon juice in blender container. Process until pureed. Add oil very gradually, blending until creamy. Spread half the bread crumbs in 3-quart straight-sided glass bowl. Cover with half the green peppers, cabbage, cucumbers, tomatoes, celery and dressing. Repeat layers with remaining ingredients. Chill, covered, for several hours. Garnish with chopped parsley. Yield: 8 servings.

Photograph for this recipe on page 35.

Salads

GOLDEN CARROT SALAD

3 1/4 c. shredded carrots
1 c. miniature marshmallows
1/2 c. crushed pineapple,
drained
1/2 c. golden raisins
1/2 c. shredded coconut
1 c. mayonnaise
1 c. whipped cream

Combine carrots, marshmallows, pineapple, raisins and coconut in bowl; toss lightly to mix. Add mayonnaise; mix well. Fold in whipped cream.

EL PEQUENO CORN SALAD

1 16-oz. can whole kernel corn,
drained
1 16-oz. can red kidney beans,
drained
1 green pepper, chopped
1 red pepper, chopped
1 tsp. sugar
1 c. wine vinegar
1 stalk celery, chopped
1/2 c. chopped green onions
2 cloves of garlic, minced
1 tsp. lemon juice
Salt and pepper to taste

Combine corn and beans in large bowl. Add remaining ingredients; mix well. Chill in refrigerator. Serve on lettuce-lined plates. Yield: 6-8 servings.

GARDEN POTATO SALAD

1/4 c. low-fat yogurt
1/4 c. low-fat cottage cheese
2 tsp. milk
1/2 tsp. cider vinegar
1/2 tsp. onion powder
1/4 tsp. crushed tarragon leaves
1/4 tsp. salt
Pinch of pepper
2 lb. new red potatoes, cooked
1 c. green beans, cut into 1-in.
pieces
1/2 c. corn
1/2 c. shredded carrots

Combine yogurt, cottage cheese, milk, vinegar, onion powder, tarragon, salt and pepper in blender container. Process at high speed until smooth. Cut potatoes into quarters. Place in large bowl. Cook beans in 1 inch boiling water in saucepan for 2 to 3 minutes or until tender-crisp; drain. Combine potatoes, beans, corn, carrots and yogurt mixture in bowl; mix lightly. Chill, covered, for 2 hours or longer. Yield: 7 cups.

Photograph for this recipe on page 35.

Recipes on pages 31, 33 and 34. →

Salads

ORIENTAL SPINACH SALAD

1 lb. fresh spinach, torn
5 slices crisp-fried bacon, crumbled
3 hard-boiled eggs, chopped
1 can bean sprouts, drained
1 can sliced water chestnuts, drained
1/2 c. oil
1/2 c. vinegar
1/3 c. catsup
1/2 c. chopped onion
2 tbsp. Worcestershire sauce

Combine spinach, bacon, eggs, bean sprouts and water chestnuts in bowl. Mix remaining ingredients in bowl. Chill salad and dressing for several hours. Pour dressing over salad just before serving. Yield: 12 servings.

EIGHT-LAYER SALAD

1 head lettuce, torn
1 head cauliflower, broken into flowerets
1 lb. bacon, crisp-fried, crumbled
1 lg. purple onion, sliced into thin rings
2 c. mayonnaise
1 c. Parmesan cheese
1/3 c. sugar
1 c. chopped walnuts

Layer lettuce, cauliflower, bacon and onion in large serving bowl. Spread mayonnaise over top, sealing to edge. Sprinkle Parmesan cheese and sugar over mayonnaise. Refrigerate overnight. Add walnuts. Toss just before serving.

SPRING GREEN SALAD

2 lb. fresh spinach, torn
1 head Boston lettuce, torn
1 head iceberg lettuce, torn
1 bunch watercress
1 cucumber, thinly sliced
1 10-oz. can mandarin oranges, drained
1 avocado, sliced
1/3 c. oil
2 1/2 tbsp. cider vinegar
1 1/4 tbsp. sugar
2 tsp. soy sauce
1 1/2 tsp. sesame seed

Combine spinach, lettuce, watercress, cucumber, oranges and avocado in salad bowl. Chill in refrigerator. Combine remaining ingredients in jar; shake to mix well. Pour over salad just before serving. Yield: 6-8 servings.

+ Recipes on pages 72 and 172.

Salad Dressings

BUTTERMILK SALAD DRESSING

1 pt. mayonnaise
1 pt. buttermilk
1/2 tsp. garlic salt
1/2 tsp. onion salt
1/2 tsp. MSG
1/8 tsp. pepper

Combine all ingredients in mixer bowl. Beat until well blended. Serve on tossed salad, baked potatoes or as dip. Store in refrigerator. Yield: 1 quart.

CELERY SEED DRESSING

1 c. oil
1 c. (scant) sugar
1/2 c. vinegar
1 tbsp. prepared mustard
1 tsp. celery seed
1 tsp. salt
1 sm. onion

Combine all ingredients in blender container. Process until well blended. Refrigerate for 24 hours or longer.

SWEET FRENCH DRESSING

1 can tomato soup
1 onion, chopped
1 clove of garlic, crushed
1 tsp. each salt and pepper
3/4 c. vinegar
1/2 tsp. paprika
1 1/2 c. oil
1/2 c. sugar
Dash of pepper

Combine soup, onion and garlic in blender container. Process until smooth. Add remaining ingredients. Process until well blended. Yield: 36 servings.

· GREEN GODDESS DRESSING

1 bunch parsley
1 bunch onions and tops
1 pt. mayonnaise
1/4 c. lemon juice
1 clove of garlic
1 can anchovies

Place all ingredients in blender container. Process until well blended. Store in refrigerator.

Salad Dressings

CREAMY ROQUEFORT DRESSING

1 pt. mayonnaise
1 pt. sour cream
2 tbsp. MSG
1 tbsp. garlic salt
1 tsp. lemon juice
1 pkg. blue cheese, crumbled

Combine first 5 ingredients in bowl; mix well. Stir in cheese. Store in refrigerator.

MICROWAVE SALAD DRESSING

2 tbsp. flour
1 tbsp. sugar
1/2 tsp. each salt, dry mustard
1 egg yolk, beaten
3/4 c. light cream
2 tbsp. vinegar
1 tbsp. butter

Mix flour, sugar, salt and dry mustard in 1-quart glass casserole. Mix egg yolk and cream. Stir into flour mixture gradually. Microwave on Medium for 1 1/2 to 3 minutes or until thickened, stirring once. Add vinegar and butter; mix with wire whisk until smooth. Store in refrigerator. Yield: 1 1/2 cups.

French Dressing:

Whisk in 1/2 teaspoon paprika and dash of cayenne pepper.

Creamy Italian Dressing:

Whisk in 1/2 teaspoon celery salt, 1/8 teaspoon garlic powder and dash of cayenne pepper.

Blue Cheese Dressing:

Stir 1/3 cup crumbled blue cheese and dash of cayenne pepper into cooled dressing.

SPECIAL RANCH DRESSING

1 c. mayonnaise
1/4 c. catsup
1 tbsp. lemon juice
1 tsp. Worcestershire sauce
Garlic powder to taste
1 tsp. sugar
1/2 tsp. paprika
1/4 tsp. MSG

Combine all ingredients in bowl; mix well. Store in refrigerator.

Herb and Spice Chart

Basil can be chopped and added to cold poultry salads. If your recipe calls for tomatoes or tomato sauce, add a touch of basil to bring out a rich flavor.

Bay leaf, the basis of many French seasonings, is nice added to soups, stews, marinades and stuffings.

Bouquet garni, a must in many Creole cuisine recipes, is a bundle of herbs, spices and bay leaf tied together and added to soups, stews or sauces.

Celery seed, from wild celery rather than our domestic celery, adds pleasant flavor to bouillon or stock.

Chervil is one of the traditional *fines herbes* used in French-derived cooking. (The others are tarragon, parsley and chive.) It is particularly good in omelets or soups.

Chives, available fresh, dried or frozen, can be substituted for raw onion in any poultry recipe.

Garlic, one of the oldest herbs in the world, must be carefully handled. When cooking, do not simmer until black or it will create an offensive odor. For best results, press or crush garlic clove against the kitchen table; then cook. If your recipe calls for sliced garlic, substitute grated or pressed garlic. The flavor will improve noticeably.

Marjoram is an aromatic herb of the mint family. It is good in soups, sauces, stuffings and stews.

Mustard (dry) brings a sharp bite to sauces. Sprinkle just a touch over roast chicken for a delightful flavor treat.

Oregano is a staple herb in Italian, Spanish and Mexican cuisines. It is very good in dishes with a tomato foundation; it adds an excellent savory taste.

Paprika, a mild pepper, adds color to many dishes, and it is especially attractive with poultry. The very best paprika is imported from Hungary — there is a world of difference between it and the supermarket variety.

Rosemary, a tasty herb, is an important seasoning in stuffing for duck, partridge and capon.

Sage, the perennial favorite with all kinds of poultry, adds flavor to stuffings. It is particularly good with goose.

Tarragon, one of the *fines herbes,* has wonderful flavor and goes well with all poultry dishes except one; it is too pungent for poultry soups.

Thyme is used in combination with bay leaf in soups and stews.

Allspice, a pungent, aromatic spice, comes in whole or powdered form. It is excellent in marinades, particularly in game marinade, or curries.

Cinnamon, ground from the bark of the cinnamon tree, is important in preparing desserts as well as savory dishes.

Coriander adds an unusual flavor to soups, stews, chili dishes, curries and some desserts.

Cumin is a staple spice in Mexican cooking. To use, rub seeds together and let them fall into the dish just before serving. Cumin also comes in powdered form.

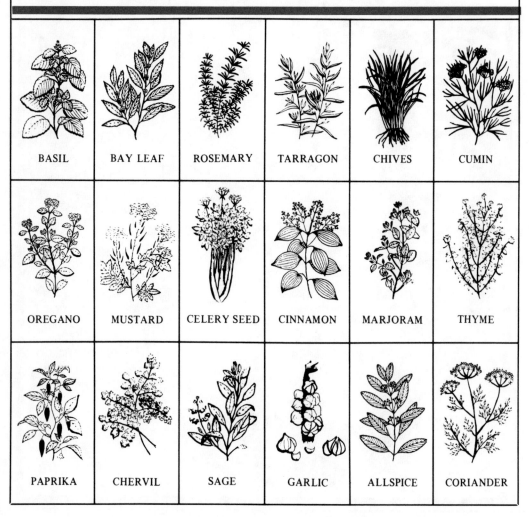

BASIL	BAY LEAF	ROSEMARY	TARRAGON	CHIVES	CUMIN
OREGANO	MUSTARD	CELERY SEED	CINNAMON	MARJORAM	THYME
PAPRIKA	CHERVIL	SAGE	GARLIC	ALLSPICE	CORIANDER

Soups and Stews

Soups and stews are among the most economical dishes you can serve to your family — and among the most nutritious. Both combine meats and vegetables in a liquid which is simmered over low heat for hours. This liquid draws nutrients and is a marvelous source of vitamins and minerals.

Thin, light soups make delicious first courses, but be sure to match your soup to your main course. Fruit soup such as the "Cold Fruit Soup" in this section is especially nice with chicken or veal while bouillon or consomme is a delightful beginning to a hearty beef dinner. Add a sandwich and a salad to one of these light soups and you'll have a perfect luncheon or supper. In summertime, substitute chilled or jellied soups for hot ones, and they'll cool off your family and guests wonderfully!

For meals in themselves, turn to the variety of thick soups and stews in the pages that follow. These include gumbos, kettles bubbling with meats and vegetables, and a variety of interesting chowders.

For your enjoyment there's a delicious selection of seafood soups in this chapter too, such as "Asparagus and Crab Bisque" and "Clam Vichyssoise." As you will see, there are both hot and cold recipes, so don't just think of soups as wintertime fare. They can be a delightful hot weather treat as well!

◆ MACARONI CHILI, Recipe on page 51.

Soups and Stews

ASPARAGUS AND CRAB BISQUE

1 can mushroom soup
1 can asparagus soup
1 c. cream
1 1/2 c. milk
1/4 tsp. seafood seasoning
1 c. crab meat
Salt to taste
1/2 c. Sherry
Chopped chives

Combine soups, cream, milk and seasoning in saucepan. Cook over low heat for several minutes, stirring frequently. Add crab meat. Heat to serving temperature. Stir in salt and Sherry. Top with chives.

CREAM OF BROCCOLI SOUP

1 1/2 c. broccoli, cooked
2 slices onion
2 tbsp. butter, melted
2 tbsp. flour
1/2 tsp. salt
1/4 tsp. pepper
1 c. milk

Puree broccoli in blender container; keep warm. Saute onion in butter in skillet until tender; discard onion. Blend flour and seasonings into onion butter. Stir in milk gradually. Cook until thick, stirring constantly. Add broccoli; mix well. Heat to serving temperature. Yield: 4 servings.

COLD CUCUMBER SOUP

1 can cream of mushroom soup
1 c. milk
1 c. sour cream
2 c. cubed peeled cucumbers
Salt and pepper to taste
Dill to taste
Tabasco sauce to taste

Blend first 3 ingredients in bowl. Fold in cucumbers; season to taste. Chill in refrigerator. Serve in glass bowls. Garnish with chopped walnuts. Yield: 4 servings.

COLD FRUIT SOUP

1 16-oz. can sliced peaches
in heavy syrup, chilled
1 16-oz. can pears, chilled,
drained
1 c. strawberries
1 c. apple juice
2 tbsp. lemon juice
Sliced strawberries
Sliced bananas

Puree first 5 ingredients in blender. Chill in refrigerator. Stir in sliced strawberries and bananas just before serving.

Soups and Stews

CLAM VICHYSSOISE

4 leeks, sliced
1/2 c. chopped onion
1 clove of garlic, minced
1 tbsp. butter
3 c. chopped potatoes
3 c. chicken broth
2 7-oz. cans minced clams
2 c. milk
1 c. coffee cream
Salt and pepper to taste

Saute leeks, onion and garlic in butter in skillet. Simmer potatoes in broth in saucepan until tender. Add leek mixture and clams to potatoes and broth. Puree in blender. Pour into large bowl. Add milk, cream and salt and pepper to taste; mix well. Chill in refrigerator. Serve cold. Garnish with chives. Yield: 8 servings.

ZUCCHINI SOUP

4 zucchini, sliced
Salt to taste
2 onions, finely chopped
1 clove of garlic, crushed
3 tbsp. butter, melted
3 1/2 c. chicken stock
1 1/2 tbsp. each finely chopped
fresh parsley, chives,
oregano and basil
1 tsp. lemon juice
1/3 c. heavy cream
Freshly ground pepper to taste
1 c. sour cream

Sprinkle zucchini with salt; let stand for 30 minutes. Place onions and garlic in butter in skillet; cover with waxed paper. Saute over low heat for 5 minutes. Rinse zucchini; pat dry. Add to skillet, reserving several slices for garnish. Cook over low heat for 5 minutes. Add chicken stock. Simmer for 15 minutes; remove from heat. Strain vegetables, reserving liquid. Puree vegetables, adding reserved liquid as necessary. Add herbs, lemon juice and cream; blend well. Season with salt and pepper. Chill until serving time. Garnish with sour cream and reserved zucchini slices. Soup may also be served hot.

BEAN SOUP DELUXE

1 16-oz. package Great Northern
beans
1/4 c. oil
1 lg. onion, chopped
1 c. chopped celery and leaves
1 c. chopped carrots
2 med. cloves of garlic, minced
1 tsp. oregano
1 c. chopped tomatoes
3 tbsp. minced parsley
2 tsp. salt
1/4 tsp. basil

Combine beans with 2 1/2 quarts water in large saucepan. Boil for 2 minutes; remove from heat. Let stand, covered, for 1 hour. Simmer, covered, for 1 1/2 hours, adding additional water if necessary. Heat oil in heavy skillet. Saute onion, celery, carrots, garlic and oregano for 10 minutes, stirring constantly. Add to beans. Stir in tomatoes, parsley, salt and basil. Cook for 1 hour longer or until beans are tender. Yield: 3 quarts.

Soups and Stews

MICROWAVE FRENCH ONION SOUP

2 onions, thinly sliced
2 tbsp. butter
2 cans beef broth
1 tsp. Worcestershire sauce
4 slices French bread, toasted
Parmesan cheese
4 oz. mozzarella cheese, shredded

Place onions and butter in 3-quart glass casserole. Microwave, covered, on High for 8 to 10 minutes or until onions are tender. Add broth, 1/2 cup water and Worcestershire sauce. Microwave, covered, on High for 5 to 7 minutes or until mixture boils. Sprinkle toast with Parmesan cheese. Top with mozzarella cheese. Microwave on Medium for 30 seconds or until cheese melts. Place one slice of bread in each serving bowl. Pour soup over bread.

OXTAIL SOUP

3 1/2 lb. oxtails, cut into 1-in. pieces
1/4 c. barley
1/2 c. each chopped onion, carrot
1 tbsp. salt
1/4 tsp. pepper
1 c. chopped potatoes
1 tbsp. chopped parsley
1 tbsp. Kitchen Bouquet

Combine oxtails with 2 1/2 quarts water in large saucepan. Bring to a boil. Add barley. Simmer for 2 hours. Add onion, carrot, salt and pepper. Cook for 20 minutes. Add potatoes. Cook until potatoes are tender. Remove oxtails; separate meat from bones. Return meat to soup. Add parsley and Kitchen Bouquet. Heat to serving temperature. Yield: 5-6 servings.

FAVORITE OYSTER STEW

1 pt. oysters with liquid
10 oz. clam juice
1/2 tsp. each salt, pepper
1/4 c. butter
1 pt. half and half
Paprika (opt.)

Combine oysters, clam juice, salt, pepper and butter in 2-quart saucepan. Cook over medium heat until edges of oysters begin to curl. Add half and half. Heat to serving temperature. Do not boil. Serve immediately sprinkled with paprika. Yield: 6 servings.

SPICY TOMATO SOUP

6 c. tomato juice
1 1/4 c. tomato puree
3 tbsp. sugar
2 whole cloves
Dash of ground cloves
1 slice onion, chopped
2 c. bouillon
1 1/4 tsp. salt
1 bay leaf
1/8 tsp. mixed herbs

Combine all ingredients in large saucepan. Bring to a boil, stirring occasionally. Simmer for 5 minutes. Yield: 4-6 servings.

MINESTRONE SOUP

1 1/2 lb. shin beef with bone
1/2 c. dried red kidney beans
1 tbsp. salt
2 bay leaves
3/4 tsp. Tabasco sauce
1 med. onion, sliced
1/4 c. chopped parsley
1/2 c. chopped celery
1 c. shredded cabbage
3 carrots, peeled, sliced
1 1-lb. can tomatoes
1 lg. zucchini, chopped
1 10-oz. package frozen peas
1/2 c. vermicelli
Parmesan cheese

Combine beef, 4 cups water, beans, salt and bay leaves in soup pot. Bring to a boil; skim. Simmer, covered, for 2 hours. Add Tabasco sauce, onion, parsley, celery, cabbage, carrots and tomatoes. Simmer for 25 minutes or until vegetables are tender. Add zucchini, peas and vermicelli. Simmer for 15 minutes. Remove bay leaves. Sprinkle with cheese. Yield: 6-8 servings.

Photograph for this recipe above.

Soups and Stews

CURRIED TURKEY SOUP

1 c. chopped celery
1 c. chopped peeled apple
1/2 c. chopped onion
1/4 c. butter
1/4 c. flour
2 tsp. curry powder
1 1/2 tsp. salt
1/8 tsp. pepper
4 c. milk
2 c. chopped cooked turkey

Saute celery, apple and onion in butter in saucepan until tender. Blend in flour, curry powder, salt and pepper. Stir in milk gradually. Simmer until thickened, stirring constantly. Add turkey. Heat to serving temperature.

SHRIMP AND CRAB MEAT SOUP

6 slices bacon
1 can tomato soup
1 4 1/2-oz. can shrimp
1 4 1/2-oz. can crab meat
2 cans split pea soup with ham
1 onion, chopped
1 tsp. Worcestershire sauce
1/4 tsp. garlic powder
Dash of hot sauce
1/4 tsp. thyme
1 tsp. parsley
Salt and pepper to taste

Saute bacon in skillet until crisp; drain and crumble, reserving drippings. Combine bacon, drippings and remaining ingredients with 6 cups water in large saucepan. Simmer for 30 minutes, adding additional water if necessary.

FISH CHOWDER

6 slices bacon, chopped
2 onions, chopped
6 potatoes, cubed
2 pkg. frozen haddock, thawed,
cut into pieces
1 c. light cream
4 c. milk
1 green pepper, chopped
3 or 4 carrots, chopped
3 stalks celery, chopped
1/4 c. minute rice
3 tbsp. butter
1/8 tsp. Tabasco sauce
1/8 tsp. each thyme, salt and
pepper

Cook bacon in large skillet until crisp. Add onions. Cook for 5 minutes, stirring frequently. Stir in potatoes and 2 cups boiling water. Cook for 5 minutes. Add haddock. Simmer, covered, for 10 minutes. Combine with remaining ingredients in soup pot; mix well. Simmer for 1 hour. Yield: 6 servings.

NEW ENGLAND CLAM CHOWDER

1/4 c. finely chopped salt pork
1/3 c. chopped onion
1/4 c. finely chopped celery
2 c. finely chopped potatoes
1 tsp. salt
1/8 tsp. white pepper
1 6 1/2-oz. can chopped clams
2 c. milk, scalded
1/4 c. butter
Paprika

Saute salt pork in skillet. Add onion. Saute until lightly browned. Add 1 cup boiling water and next 5 ingredients; mix well. Bring to a boil. Add hot milk. Ladle into bowls. Dot with butter; sprinkle with paprika. Yield: 6 servings.

HAM AND BEAN CHOWDER

2 c. dried Great Northern beans
2 c. finely chopped onions
1/2 c. finely chopped celery
2 tsp. minced garlic
3 tbsp. butter
3 cans chicken broth
1 1/2 lb. ham hocks
1 1-lb. can tomatoes
2 whole cloves
1 bay leaf
1 tsp. pepper
2 c. shredded Cheddar cheese

Cook beans in 2 quarts boiling water in 6-quart soup pot for 2 minutes; turn off heat. Let stand for 1 hour. Drain, reserving liquid. Saute onions, celery and garlic in butter in skillet for 5 minutes. Combine with beans, 4 cups reserved liquid, broth and 2 cups water in soup pot. Remove skin and excess fat from ham hocks. Add ham hocks to soup pot with remaining ingredients except cheese. Simmer for 2 hours or longer. Remove ham hocks, bay leaf and cloves. Chill in refrigerator. Skim. Cut ham from ham hocks. Add to soup with cheese. Heat until cheese melts, stirring constantly. Yield: 10 servings.

CHICKEN-HAM GUMBO

5 c. sliced okra
3 tbsp. bacon drippings
1/2 c. flour
1 c. chopped onion
1/2 c. chopped green pepper
2 cloves of garlic, chopped
2 c. chopped ham
1 16-oz. can tomato sauce
1 tsp. each pepper, parsley,
thyme, salt and red pepper
2 tbsp. file powder
4 bay leaves
4 c. chopped chicken
1 c. ham gravy

Saute okra in bacon drippings in skillet. Add flour; mix well. Add onion, green pepper, garlic, ham, tomato sauce and 1 sauce can water. Bring to a boil. Stir in seasonings. Add chicken, ham gravy and 3 quarts water. Simmer for 2 hours or longer. Yield: 16 servings

Soups and Stews

SEAFOOD GUMBO

2 qt. beef stock
1 lg. can tomatoes
1 6-oz. can tomato paste
1 bay leaf
1/2 c. flour
3 stalks celery, chopped
1 onion, chopped
1/2 green pepper, chopped
2 1-lb. packages sliced okra
1 lb. shrimp, cleaned
1 lb. crab meat
Salt and pepper to taste

Combine stock, tomatoes, tomato paste and bay leaf in large saucepan. Bring to a boil. Brown flour in a small amount of oil in saucepan. Add next 3 vegetables. Cook for 2 minutes. Add with okra to stock mixture. Simmer for 1 1/2 hours. Add shrimp. Cook for 30 minutes. Add crab meat and salt and pepper to taste. Cook for 30 minutes longer. Serve over rice. Yield: 8-10 servings.

MICROWAVE BURGUNDY BEEF STEW

1/2 c. red wine
2 tbsp. flour
1 tbsp. microwave browning sauce
1 bay leaf
1 tsp. salt
1/4 tsp. each pepper, marjoram
2 lb. stew beef
1 c. chopped carrots
1 c. chopped celery
1 lg. onion, chopped
4 potatoes, coarsely chopped

Combine 1 cup water, wine, flour, browning sauce and seasonings in 3-quart glass casserole; mix well. Add beef. Microwave, covered, on Medium for 11 to 13 minutes or until beef is no longer pink. Add vegetables. Microwave, covered, on Medium for 40 to 60 minutes or until beef and vegetables are tender, stirring once.

SAVORY MEATBALL STEW

1 egg, beaten
1 c. soft bread cubes
1/4 c. milk
2 tsp. seasoned salt
1/2 lb. ground beef
1/2 c. sliced carrots
1 28-oz. can tomatoes
1 1/2 c. chopped celery
1 c. finely chopped onions
1 c. diced potatoes
Dash of hot pepper sauce
1 c. shredded Cheddar cheese

Mix first 4 ingredients in bowl. Add ground beef; mix well. Chill for 1/2 hour. Combine remaining ingredients except cheese with 2 cups water in large saucepan. Simmer for 30 minutes. Shape ground beef mixture into 16 meatballs. Add to vegetable mixture. Simmer, covered, for 10 minutes. Ladle into bowls. Top with cheese. Yield: 8 servings.

MACARONI CHILI

2 lb. ground round
3 tbsp. oil
1 28-oz. can tomatoes
4 c. tomato juice
2 c. chopped onions
3 cloves of garlic, minced
4 tsp. salt
2 tbsp. chili powder
1/2 tsp. each cumin, oregano,
pepper
1 bay leaf
1 15-oz. can red kidney beans,
drained
1 c. sweet mixed pickles,
chopped
1 8-oz. package elbow macaroni,
cooked

Brown ground round in oil in skillet, stirring frequently. Add tomatoes, tomato juice, onions, garlic and seasonings. Simmer, covered, for 1 hour. Stir in kidney beans and pickles. Cook for 30 minutes. Remove bay leaf. Mix in macaroni. Heat to serving temperature. Yield: 10 servings.

Photograph for this recipe on page 42.

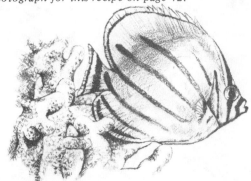

HUNGARIAN GOULASH

2 onions, sliced
1/3 c. oil
2 lb. stew beef
1 tbsp. paprika
2 tsp. salt
1/2 tsp. pepper
1 6-oz. can tomato paste
1 clove of garlic, minced
1/2 c. sour cream (opt.)

Saute onions in oil in skillet. Remove onions. Coat beef with mixture of paprika, 1 teaspoon salt and pepper. Brown in pan drippings. Add onions, tomato paste, garlic, 1 teaspoon salt and 1 1/2 cups water. Simmer for 1 1/2 to 2 hours or until tender, stirring occasionally. Stir in sour cream. Heat to serving temperature. Do not boil. Serve over noodles. Yield: 6 servings.

SAN FRANCISCO STEW

3/4 lb. ground beef
1/2 green pepper, chopped
4 onions, chopped
1 clove of garlic, minced
2 15-oz. cans pork and beans
2 tbsp. brown sugar
2 15-oz. cans tomatoes
1/2 tsp. mustard
3 slices crisp-fried bacon,
crumbled

Brown ground beef with green pepper, onions and garlic in Dutch oven, stirring until crumbly. Add remaining ingredients; mix well. Cook for several minutes. Pour into casserole. Bake, covered, at 325 degrees for 1 1/2 hours. Yield: 6 servings.

Game

It comes as no surprise that preparing game is the oldest cooking art we know. It demands special care and handling if it is to appear on your dining table as the epicurean delight it is.

You'll find a number of tempting recipes in this chapter, rare in most recipe collections. Take advantage of the tasty flavor of duck, the most popular game bird. For variety, some recipes offer creative sauces your family will surely enjoy — such as avocado-orange sauce and Brandied peach sauce. There's a number of venison recipes as well, such as the "Venison Stew" — not only economical but delicious. Or, try a favorite winter treat when the cold weather comes — "Venison Chili."

This chapter also treats you to the secrets of combining just the right spice with special cooking techniques to produce flavorful recipes for dove, elk, rabbit, quail, pheasant and goose.

← SPANISH-ROASTED GAME HENS, Recipe on page 55.

Game

CORNISH HENS A LA BOURBON

8 Cornish game hens
3/4 c. chopped onion
1 3/4 c. melted butter
4 1/2 c. cooked wild rice
2/3 c. chopped toasted almonds
1/2 tsp. thyme
Salt to taste
1/4 tsp. pepper
1/2 c. Bourbon
1/2 c. bouillon
1/2 c. currant jelly, melted

Wash Cornish hens; pat dry inside and out. Saute onion in 1/4 cup butter in skillet. Add wild rice, almonds, thyme and salt; mix well. Stuff Cornish hens with wild rice mixture. Place breast side up in shallow baking dish. Mix 1/2 cup butter, salt and pepper; pour over Cornish hens. Roast at 425 degrees for 20 minutes, basting with mixture of Bourbon and 1 cup butter every 5 minutes. Reduce temperature to 350 degrees. Roast for 30 minutes, basting twice. Turn Cornish hens breast side down. Roast for 15 minutes, basting several times; add bouillon if necessary. Turn Cornish hens; pour melted jelly over top. Roast for 30 minutes longer.

CORNISH HENS WITH BLUEBERRIES

8 Cornish game hens
Salt and pepper to taste
1/4 c. oil
1/4 c. lemon juice
4 c. fresh blueberries, rinsed, drained
4 tsp. sugar
1/2 c. butter, softened
8 bay leaves

Wash Cornish hens; pat dry inside and out. Sprinkle inside and out with salt and pepper. Mix oil and lemon juice in bowl. Brush inside and outside of Cornish hens. Fill each with 1/2 cup blueberries and 1/2 teaspoon sugar. Skewer opening; place in shallow baking pan. Spread butter over breasts of Cornish hens; place 1 bay leaf on each breast. Roast in 350-degree oven for 1 hour or until tender. Remove bay leaves. Garnish with additional blueberries. Yield: 8 servings.

CORNISH HENS WITH HERBED RICE

2 tbsp. honey
2 tbsp. unsalted margarine, melted
Orange juice
4 Cornish game hens
1/4 c. chopped celery
1/4 c. chopped onion
2 tbsp. chopped parsley
1 tsp. grated orange rind
1/8 tsp. each rosemary, thyme
1 c. dry-roasted unsalted peanuts
1 c. rice

Combine honey, margarine and 2 tablespoons orange juice in small bowl. Wash Cornish hens; pat dry inside and out. Place on rack in baking pan. Bake at 375 degrees for 1 hour or until tender, basting frequently with honey mixture. Saute celery and onion in saucepan until tender. Add remaining ingredients with 1/2 cup orange juice and 1 1/2 cups water; mix well. Simmer, covered, until rice is tender. Place Cornish hens on serving platter. Spoon rice around hens. Yield: 4 servings.

GLAZED CORNISH HENS

1/3 c. light corn syrup
1/4 c. prepared mustard
2 tsp. curry powder
1 clove of garlic, minced
2 Cornish game hens

Combine first 4 ingredients in bowl; mix well. Wash Cornish hens; pat dry inside and out. Place on rack in baking pan; brush with syrup mixture. Bake at 350 degrees for 1 1/2 hours, basting occasionally. Yield: 2 servings.

SPANISH-ROASTED GAME HENS

4 Cornish game hens
Salt and pepper to taste
1 lb. small fresh mushrooms
1 c. chopped pimento-stuffed olives
2 slices bacon
1/2 tsp. paprika
1/3 c. chopped filberts
1/4 c. melted butter
1/3 c. finely chopped onion
1 c. rice
2 c. chicken broth
1/2 c. grated Swiss cheese

Wash Cornish hens; pat dry inside and out. Sprinkle cavities with salt and pepper. Stuff with mixture of mushrooms and 2/3 cup olives. Secure with poultry pins; tie legs together. Place in roasting pan; place 1/2 slice bacon on each. Roast at 450 degrees for 20 minutes. Reduce temperature to 350 degrees. Remove bacon. Stir paprika into pan drippings. Brush over Cornish hens. Roast until browned and tender. Saute filberts in 2 tablespoons butter in skillet; remove filberts. Add remaining butter, onion and rice. Saute until rice is very lightly browned, stirring occasionally. Add broth. Simmer, covered, for 15 minutes or until rice is tender. Stir in cheese, remaining 1/3 cup olives and filberts. Spoon onto serving platter. Arrange Cornish hens on top. Garnish with whole stuffed olives. Serve with pan juices.

Photograph for this recipe on page 52.

BRAISED DOVE BREASTS

1 onion, chopped
6 tbsp. butter, softened
16 dove breasts
1 tsp. each salt and pepper
2 tsp. Worcestershire sauce
1/4 tsp. thyme
2 tsp. chopped parsley
1/2 c. red wine
1 c. beef bouillon
2 tbsp. flour

Saute onion in 1/4 cup butter in skillet until tender; add dove breasts. Brown on both sides. Add seasonings and herbs; reduce heat. Arrange breasts meaty side up. Add wine. Cook until sauce is reduced by half. Add bouillon. Cook, covered, for 45 minutes or until tender. Remove dove from skillet; place on heated platter. Mix flour and 2 tablespoons butter in small bowl. Add to sauce in skillet. Cook until thick, stirring constantly. Serve with dove.

Game

DOVE AND WILD RICE DRESSING

12 to 16 dove breasts
2 c. flour
Salt, pepper and paprika to taste
1/2 c. wild rice
1/4 lb. sausage
1 onion, chopped
1/2 tsp. sage
1/2 c. wine

Coat dove with flour seasoned with salt, pepper and paprika. Brown in shortening in skillet. Arrange in circle in casserole. Cook wild rice in 2 cups boiling salted water in saucepan until tender. Brown sausage with onion and sage in skillet; drain. Add to rice; mix well. Spoon into center of casserole. Pour mixture of wine and 3/4 cup water over all. Bake, covered, at 350 degrees for 1 hour or until dove breasts are tender. Yield: 4-6 servings.

WILD DUCK A LA FAUVETTE

4 wild duck halves
2 tbsp. butter
2 tbsp. Sherry
2 tbsp. tomato paste
2 tbsp. flour
1 1/2 c. bouillon
1/2 c. dry red wine
1 tsp. salt
1/4 tsp. pepper
1/2 lb. mushrooms, sliced
1 bay leaf
2 c. cooked wild rice

Wash ducks; pat dry. Brown ducks in butter in large skillet. Pour Sherry over ducks; remove ducks. Blend tomato paste and flour with pan juices. Stir in bouillon and wine gradually. Bring to a boil, stirring constantly. Add ducks, salt, pepper, mushrooms and bay leaf. Cook, covered, over low heat for 2 hours or until tender. Place ducks on warm serving platter. Pack hot wild rice into 4 individual molds; unmold. Alternate rice molds and duck halves on platter. Skim and strain pan juices. Serve with ducks.

WILD DUCK WITH ORANGE STUFFING

1 5-lb. duck
2 to 3 c. bread cubes, toasted
2/3 c. orange pulp
2 c. chopped celery
1/4 c. melted butter
1 egg, beaten
1/2 tsp. salt
Dash of pepper
1/4 tsp. poultry seasoning
2 tsp. grated orange rind
1/2 c. oil (opt.)

Wash duck; pat dry inside and out. Soak bread in 1/2 cup hot water in bowl for 15 minutes. Add remaining ingredients except oil; mix lightly. Stuff duck with bread mixture. Place in roasting pan. Roast at 325 degrees for 2 to 3 hours or until tender, basting occasionally with mixture of oil and 1 cup hot water.

WINE-SPICED WILD DUCK

1 c. white wine
1 clove of garlic
1 c. oil
1 tsp. each thyme, oregano,
seasoned salt and pepper
2 duck breasts
Bacon strips

Combine wine, garlic, oil and seasonings in bowl; mix well. Add duck breasts. Marinate in refrigerator for several days. Place duck with marinade in saucepan. Simmer, covered, for 2 hours or until tender, adding water if necessary. Place duck on rack in broiler pan. Top with bacon. Broil for 3 to 5 minutes or until bacon is crisp.

DUCK WITH BRANDIED PEACHES

1 4 to 5-lb. duck
1/2 tsp. each salt, pepper,
rosemary and basil
1 stalk celery, chopped
1 carrot, chopped
1 onion, chopped
1 c. beef broth
4 peach halves
1/4 c. Brandy
3 tbsp. sugar
1 tbsp. butter
1/3 c. vinegar
1 c. peach juice
1/2 tsp. cornstarch

Wash duck; pat dry inside and out. Rub duck with seasonings; prick skin in several places. Place on rack in roasting pan. Roast at 450 degrees for 1 1/2 hours. Drain excess drippings, reserving 2 tablespoons; split duck in half. Saute vegetables in reserved drippings in saucepan for 10 minutes. Add broth. Cook for 5 minutes; strain. Marinate peaches in Brandy in bowl. Cook sugar and butter in saucepan until brown; add vinegar. Cook until reduced by half. Add strained sauce, peach juice and cornstarch dissolved in 1 tablespoon water. Simmer for 10 minutes. Add peaches and Brandy. Simmer for 5 minutes longer. Place duck on serving platter. Arrange peach halves around duck; top with sauce.

SHERRIED SPICED DUCKLING

1 4 to 5-lb. duckling
Salt
2 leeks, sliced
1 c. dry Sherry
1/4 c. dark soy sauce
1 whole star anise
1 lg. piece of dried tangerine rind
1 tbsp corn syrup
1 tbsp. cornstarch

Wash duckling; pat dry inside and out. Sprinkle with salt. Place on rack in roasting pan. Roast at 350 degrees over pan of water until tender. Prick with fork. Place layer of leeks in saucepan. Stuff remaining leeks into duck cavity. Place duck breast side up over leeks. Add Sherry and soy sauce. Bring to a boil over high heat; add 2 1/2 cups hot water. Simmer for 1 hour, basting frequently. Add anise, tangerine rind and corn syrup. Simmer for 1 hour longer. Remove duckling to platter. Skim sauce; strain into saucepan. Add cornstarch blended with 1 tablespoon cold water. Cook until thickened, stirring constantly. Pour over duckling. Garnish with sliced fresh oranges and scallion.

HONEY-BAKED DUCK WITH MUSHROOM RICE

4 wild ducks, cut in half
Butter, softened
Salt and pepper to taste
3 tbsp. honey
2 tsp. soy sauce
1 c. rice
2 c. boiling chicken broth
1 c. sliced fresh mushrooms
1/2 c. chopped onion

Wash ducks; pat dry inside and out. Coat with butter. Sprinkle with salt and pepper. Place skin side up on rack in roasting pan. Roast at 350 degrees for 1 to 1 1/2 hours or until tender. Brush with mixture of honey and soy sauce. Roast for 15 minutes longer. Brush with remaining honey mixture. Combine rice and broth in shallow buttered 2-quart casserole; mix well. Bake, covered, at 350 degrees for 30 minutes or until rice is tender. Saute mushrooms and onion in butter in skillet for 5 minutes or until onion is tender. Stir into rice. Season with salt and pepper. Spoon onto serving platter. Arrange ducks over top.

Photograph for this recipe above.

DUCK WITH AVOCADO-ORANGE SAUCE

1 c. melted butter
1/2 tsp. ginger
1/2 tsp. salt
Dash of pepper
1 duck, cut up
1 tbsp. cornstarch
1 6-oz. can frozen orange
juice concentrate
1 tsp. soy sauce
1 avocado, sliced

Blend butter, 1/4 teaspoon ginger, salt and pepper in bowl. Brush duck with seasoned butter. Arrange in baking pan. Bake at 375 degrees for 1 hour, turning occasionally. Remove duck to warm platter. Stir cornstarch into pan drippings; add orange juice concentrate, soy sauce and 1/4 teaspoon ginger. Cook until thick, stirring constantly. Mix avocado slices into orange sauce quickly; pour sauce over duck. Serve with buttered rice. Yield: 4 servings.

CAJUN DUCK

4 to 6 mallard ducks
2 tsp. red pepper
1/4 c. salt
2 bunches celery, coarsely chopped
6 onions, coarsely chopped
2 green peppers, coarsely chopped
2 lb. lean mild pork sausage
2 1/2 c. wild rice, cooked

Wash ducks; pat dry inside and out. Sprinkle with mixture of red pepper and salt. Let stand for 20 minutes. Place in saucepan. Add celery, onions, peppers and 1/2 to 1 cup water. Simmer until ducks and vegetables are tender. Brown sausage in skillet, stirring frequently; drain. Place ducks on serving platter. Add sausage and wild rice to vegetables. Heat to serving temperature, stirring frequently. Serve with ducks. Yield: 6 servings.

GOLDEN STUFFED GOOSE

1 10 to 12-lb. goose
Salt
1 1/2 c. maple syrup
2 tbsp. lemon juice
1/2 c. chopped celery
1/2 c. chopped onion
1/4 c. butter, melted
3 c. bread cubes
1 c. chopped apples
1/4 c. chopped parsley
1/2 tsp. savory
Dash of pepper
16 sm. onions
8 potatoes, peeled, quartered

Soak goose in salted water to cover for 2 hours. Wash goose; pat dry inside and out. Combine maple syrup and lemon juice in small bowl. Brush cavity with 1/2 cup syrup mixture. Saute celery and onion in butter in skillet until tender. Add bread cubes, apples, parsley, 1/2 teaspoon salt, savory and pepper; mix well. Fill cavity loosely with stuffing; truss. Place breast side up on rack in roasting pan. Bake at 325 degrees for 1 1/2 hours. Pour off drippings. Place goose on bottom of pan. Arrange onions and potatoes around goose. Bake for 1 1/2 hours or until goose and vegetables are tender, basting frequently with remaining syrup mixture. Yield: 8-10 servings.

Game

HUNTSMAN-STYLE PARTRIDGE

2 or 3 young partridge, cut up
Seasoned flour
7 oz. Brandy
1 onion, chopped
2 carrots, sliced
1 tsp. mixed dry seasoning
1 c. canned consomme
1 can mushrooms

Wash partridge; pat dry. Coat with seasoned flour. Brown in oil in skillet. Add Brandy. Ignite. Add vegetables and seasoning; mix gently. Add consomme and mushrooms. Simmer, covered, for 45 minutes or until partridge is tender. Yield: 4-6 servings.

PHEASANT SUPREME

2 pheasant, cut into quarters
Salt and pepper to taste
1/2 tsp. MSG
8 thin slices Canadian bacon
1 can cream of mushroom soup
1 can sliced mushrooms

Wash pheasant; pat dry. Place skin side up in greased 9 x 12-inch baking dish. Sprinkle with salt, pepper and MSG. Place 1 piece of Canadian bacon on each quarter. Spread soup over pheasant. Top with mushrooms. Bake at 300 degrees for about 2 hours or until tender. Yield: 6-8 servings.

ROAST PHEASANT WITH WILD RICE

1 pheasant
Salt and pepper to taste
1 c. wild rice
1 c. apricot juice

Wash pheasant; pat dry inside and out. Rub cavity with salt and pepper. Place in baking pan lined with large piece of foil. Sprinkle wild rice over pheasant. Pour apricot juice over all. Seal foil. Bake at 325 degrees for 1 hour or until pheasant and rice are tender. Yield: 4 servings.

BAKED PHEASANT WITH OYSTER DRESSING

1 pheasant
1/2 c. chopped celery
1/2 c. chopped onion
1/4 c. margarine
3 c. chopped oysters
6 c. dry bread crumbs
2 eggs, beaten
Salt and pepper to taste

Cook pheasant in water in saucepan for 45 minutes or until tender. Drain, reserving 1 3/4 cups broth. Saute celery and onion in margarine in skillet. Add oysters, bread crumbs, eggs, seasonings and reserved broth; mix well. Stuff pheasant with bread crumb mixture. Place in roasting pan. Spoon any remaining dressing around pheasant. Bake at 350 degrees for 45 minutes. Yield: 4-6 servings.

Game

BAKED QUAIL SUPREME

6 quail
6 slices bacon
Salt and pepper to taste
1/2 lb. mushroom caps
1 bunch green onions, chopped
3 tbsp. butter, melted
2 tbsp. prepared mustard
1/2 tsp. dry ginger
1 c. orange marmalade

Wash quail; pat dry inside and out. Wrap with bacon. Arrange on large piece of foil. Sprinkle with salt and pepper. Saute mushrooms and onions in butter in skillet. Spoon over quail; seal foil. Place on baking sheet. Bake at 325 degrees for 1 hour or until quail are tender. Combine mustard, ginger and marmalade in saucepan. Heat to serving temperature, stirring frequently. Serve with quail.

SHERRIED QUAIL

6 quail
Salt
Flour
3/4 c. cooking Sherry
3 tbsp. Worcestershire sauce
1/3 c. lemon juice

Wash quail; pat dry inside and out. Sprinkle with salt. Coat with flour. Brown in oil in skillet. Place in casserole. Combine remaining ingredients in bowl; mix well. Pour over quail. Bake, covered, at 350 degrees for 1 hour. Yield: 6 servings.

OVEN-BARBECUED RABBIT

1 rabbit, cut up
1 onion, chopped
1/4 c. chili sauce
2 tbsp. each lemon juice,
Worcestershire sauce
1/2 c. each catsup, vinegar
1 tbsp. brown sugar

Wash rabbit; pat dry. Place in baking dish. Bake at 325 degrees for 30 minutes. Combine remaining ingredients in saucepan. Heat until sugar is dissolved. Pour over rabbit. Bake for 35 minutes longer or until tender, basting every 15 minutes. Yield: 4 servings.

SQUIRREL MULLIGAN

6 squirrels, cut up
1 lb. butter
1 tbsp. salt
6 potatoes, chopped
6 onions, chopped
1 c. chopped celery
4 c. tomatoes
1 can cream-style corn
1 tsp. red pepper
3 tbsp. sugar
1 c. bread crumbs

Combine first 3 ingredients and water to cover in large saucepan. Simmer until tender. Remove squirrel; cool. Remove meat from bones. Return to broth. Add potatoes, onions and celery. Cook over low heat until tender. Add tomatoes, corn, red pepper and sugar. Simmer until vegetables are very tender. Stir in crumbs. Cook until thick. Yield: 3-4 quarts.

Game

BARBECUED VENISON

3 lb. venison
1 c. catsup
1 tbsp. salt
2 tbsp. Worcestershire sauce
1/4 c. vinegar
1 tbsp. butter
1/8 tsp. cinnamon
3 slices lemon
1 onion, thinly sliced
1/8 tsp. allspice

Brown venison in oil in skillet; remove venison to roasting pan. Add remaining ingredients. Simmer for 10 minutes, stirring constantly. Pour sauce over venison. Roast at 350 degrees for 1 1/2 to 2 hours or until tender, turning occasionally. Yield: 6-8 servings.

SMOKED VENISON

1 onion, finely chopped
3 cloves of garlic, minced
1 5 to 6-lb. venison roast
Salt, pepper and red pepper
to taste
1 jar Italian salad dressing
1 c. wine vinegar

Place onion and garlic in 1 1/2-inch slits cut at 2-inch intervals in roast. Sprinkle with salt, pepper and red pepper. Place in bowl. Pour salad dressing and wine vinegar over roast. Marinate in refrigerator for 24 hours, basting every 4 hours. Drain. Place in smoker. Cook using manufacturer's directions for 3 to 4 hours or to desired degree of doneness. Yield: 15-20 servings.

VENISON STEW

3 lb. venison
1 clove of garlic, minced
1/2 tsp. salt
1/8 tsp. pepper
3 tbsp. butter
1 onion, grated
1 16-oz. can tomatoes
1/8 tsp. each soda, paprika
1/2 c. evaporated milk
3 tbsp. flour
3 tbsp. Sherry
1 tbsp. Worcestershire sauce
5 drops of angostura bitters
1 tbsp. chopped parsley

Cut venison into small pieces; trim. Coat with mixture of garlic, salt and pepper. Cook in butter in large skillet for 5 minutes. Add onion. Cook, covered, for 5 minutes. Add tomatoes, soda and paprika. Simmer for 15 minutes. Blend milk and flour in bowl. Stir in Sherry, Worcestershire sauce and bitters. Add to venison mixture; mix well. Cook for 5 minutes. Add parsley. Pour into 2-quart casserole. Bake, covered, at 375 degrees for 40 minutes. Serve immediately over rice or noodles. Yield: 6-8 servings.

VENISON CHILI

1/2 lb. ground beef suet
2 lb. ground venison
6 cloves of garlic, minced
1/4 c. paprika
1/4 c. chili powder
3 dried chili pepper pods, chopped
1 tbsp. cumin
2 tbsp. salt
1/4 c. Worcestershire sauce
1 tsp. white pepper
1 1/2 tsp. cayenne pepper
3 long sweet green chilies, chopped
1 tbsp. crushed red pepper
3 tbsp. flour
6 tbsp. cornmeal

Render suet in skillet. Add venison. Cook until no longer pink, stirring frequently. Add garlic, seasonings and 3 cups water. Simmer for 4 hours, adding additional water if necessary. Combine flour and cornmeal in bowl. Add enough water to make thin batter; mix well. Stir into venison mixture. Cook for 1 hour longer. Yield: 6-8 servings.

VENISON POT ROAST

1 venison pot roast
1/2 c. dry red wine
1 bay leaf
6 peppercorns
2 carrots, cut into halves
2 celery stalks
1 onion, cut in half
Juice and rind of 1 orange
3 tbsp. flour
1/3 c. bacon drippings
Salt and pepper to taste
2 tbsp. sour cream

Brown roast in oil in Dutch oven. Add 1 cup water, wine, bay leaf, peppercorns, carrots, celery and onion. Pour orange juice over roast. Place orange rind on roast. Bake, covered, at 350 degrees for 2 hours or until tender. Remove roast; discard rind. Skim and strain pan juices. Blend flour and bacon drippings in Dutch oven. Cook over low heat for several minutes, stirring constantly. Blend in pan juices. Cook until thick, stirring constantly. Add seasonings and enough water to make of desired consistency. Heat to serving temperature. Stir in sour cream. Serve with roast. Yield: 6 servings.

MONTEREY ELK PIE

1 elk round steak, cut into bite-sized pieces
1/2 stick butter
1 beef bouillon cube
Flour
1/2 green pepper, chopped
1 carrot, chopped
1/2 onion, chopped
1 recipe 2-crust pie pastry
Monterey Jack cheese, grated

Brown steak in butter in skillet. Add bouillon cube and 1 cup water. Simmer for 3 hours or until tender. Drain, reserving pan juices. Prepare a small amount of gravy using pan juices and flour. Add to steak with vegetables; mix well. Cook, covered, over low heat for 1 hour, stirring occasionally. Line 9-inch pie plate with half the pastry. Layer steak mixture and cheese alternately in prepared pie plate until all ingredients are used. Cover with remaining pie pastry. Seal and flute edge; cut vents. Bake at 450 degrees for 45 minutes. Yield: 5 servings.

Meats

Meat is the cornerstone of any meal. Whether it's a formal dinner or a backyard barbecue, your meat dish sets the pace and style for the occasion.

Through the years, families have developed favorite meat recipes that have been handed down from mother to daughter for generations. You'll sense a regional flavor that is unique in most of these traditional American favorites.

Many of our great meat recipes borrow secrets from European and Asian cooking. We have also developed special techniques that blend the whole world of meat cookery into a special taste that is uniquely American.

The pages that follow set forth a sparkling array of superb meat recipes. You will find unique ways to prepare cuts of beef, and delicious recipes for every variety of pork including ham, chops and ribs. You will learn how to perfectly season lamb and will discover the secrets of combining meats with spices for unusual taste treats. You'll also find new twists for old favorites such as "Peach-Glazed Corned Beef."

These exciting recipes offer you meat entrees that are seasoned with care and cooked to perfection!

← FESTIVE CROWN ROAST, Recipe on page 80.

Meats

BARBECUED BEEF BRISKET

1 lg. beef brisket
Garlic, onion and celery salts
to taste
1/3 bottle of liquid smoke
2 tbsp. brown sugar
2 tbsp. vinegar
2 tsp. Worcestershire sauce
1 c. catsup
5 drops of Tabasco sauce
Pinch of cayenne pepper
1/2 tsp. salt

Season brisket with garlic, onion and celery salts. Refrigerate, covered, overnight. Place in baking pan. Bake, covered, at 275 degrees for 1 hour per pound. Carve diagonally into thin slices. Arrange slices in baking pan. Combine remaining ingredients in bowl; mix well. Pour over brisket. Bake at 350 degrees for 1 hour. Yield: 8 servings.

PEACH-GLAZED CORNED BEEF

1 3-lb. corned beef brisket
4 apples, cut into halves
1/3 c. peach preserves
1/4 tsp. ginger

Rinse brisket in cold water. Place fat side up on rack in shallow roasting pan. Pour in 2 cups water. Bake, covered, at 325 degrees for 2 hours; drain. Arrange apples skin side up around brisket; add 1/2 cup water. Bake, uncovered, for 30 minutes. Blend preserves and ginger in bowl. Turn apples skin side down. Spoon preserves over brisket and apples. Bake for several minutes longer.

CHOP SUEY

2 lb. lean pork steak, cubed
2 lb. lean beef, cubed
Flour
3 tbsp. shortening
4 stalks celery, chopped
2 onions, chopped
1/2 tsp. pepper
2 tsp. salt
5 beef bouillon cubes
2 tbsp. Worcestershire sauce
1/4 tsp. each marjoram, thyme
1/2 tsp. garlic salt
1 tbsp. dry onion flakes
1/2 lb. mushrooms, sliced

Sprinkle meat with flour. Brown in shortening in skillet. Cook celery in 1 cup water in saucepan for 15 minutes; drain. Add to skillet with remaining ingredients except mushrooms. Cook until tender, stirring frequently. Add mushrooms. Serve with hot rice. Yield: 8 servings.

BEEF STROGANOFF

3 cloves of garlic, minced
2 onions, chopped
1/2 c. butter
2 lb. lean sirloin, cut into thin strips
2 tbsp. flour
1 bay leaf
2 tsp. soy sauce
1 1/2 c. tomato juice
1 lb. mushrooms, sliced
2 tsp. Worcestershire sauce
Salt, pepper and paprika to taste
2 pt. sour cream

Saute garlic and onions in butter in skillet until tender. Add sirloin. Cook until brown. Stir in remaining ingredients except sour cream. Cook until sirloin is tender. Stir in sour cream. Cook until heated through; cool. Chill overnight. Heat to serving temperature.

PEPPER STEAK WITH RICE

1 lb. 1/2-inch thick round steak
1 tbsp. paprika
2 tbsp. butter
2 cloves of garlic, crushed
1 1/2 c. beef broth
1 c. sliced green onions with tops
2 c. green pepper strips
2 tbsp. cornstarch
1/4 c. soy sauce
2 tomatoes, cut into eighths
3 c. cooked rice

Cut steak into 1/4-inch strips. Sprinkle with paprika. Let stand for several minutes. Brown steak in butter in skillet. Add garlic and broth. Simmer, covered, for 30 minutes. Add onions and green peppers; mix well. Cook for 5 minutes. Blend cornstarch with 1/2 cup water. Add soy sauce; mix well. Add to steak. Cook until thickened, stirring constantly. Add tomatoes; mix gently. Cook for 2 minutes. Serve over rice. Yield: 6 servings.

HUNGARIAN BEEF

1/2 lb. 1/2-inch thick boneless round steak
1 16-oz. can potatoes, drained, quartered
1/2 c. chopped onion
1 clove of garlic, minced
2 tsp. paprika
2 tbsp. oil
1 can golden mushroom soup
1/4 c. chopped sweet gherkins
2 tbsp. gherkin juice
1 tsp. dried parsley flakes

Freeze steak for 1 hour. Slice into very thin strips. Saute potatoes, onion and garlic with paprika in oil in skillet until potatoes are brown and onion is tender. Add steak. Cook until lightly browned, stirring frequently. Stir in remaining ingredients with 1/2 cup water. Cook until steak is tender. Yield: 4 servings.

Meats

STEAK FINGERS

1 1/2 lb. sirloin steak, cut
into strips
Flour
1/2 tsp. (about) salt
Pepper to taste
1 c. crushed cornflakes
1/2 c. chopped pecans
1/4 c. Parmesan cheese
1/2 tsp. paprika
1/4 tsp. nutmeg
1 stick margarine, melted
1 c. milk
1 5-oz. package sharp cheese,
grated
1 tsp. Worcestershire sauce

Coat steak with 2/3 cup flour seasoned with salt and pepper; arrange on waxed paper-lined plate. Chill in refrigerator. Combine cornflake crumbs with next 4 ingredients in bowl; mix well. Blend 2 tablespoons flour with 1/4 cup melted margarine in saucepan. Cook until bubbly, stirring constantly. Stir in milk, sharp cheese and Worcestershire sauce. Cook until cheese melts, stirring constantly. Dip steak in cheese sauce; coat with cornflake mixture. Place 1 inch apart on baking sheet greased with remaining butter. Bake at 400 degrees for 15 minutes or until deep golden brown. Cool slightly before removing to serving plate. Yield: 6 servings.

SWISS STEAK ROLLS

6 thin slices flank steak
Salt and pepper to taste
6 slices boiled ham
6 slices Swiss cheese
6 thin slices dill pickle
3 tbsp. margarine
2 tbsp. flour
2 tbsp. minced onion
1/4 tsp. basil
1 can consomme

Season steak with salt and pepper. Layer ham, cheese and pickle on steak. Roll as for jelly roll; secure with toothpicks. Brown lightly in margarine in skillet. Place in baking dish. Blend flour into pan drippings. Stir in onion, basil and consomme. Simmer for 5 minutes, stirring constantly. Pour over steak rolls. Bake, covered, at 350 degrees for 45 minutes. Slice steak rolls before serving.

BURGUNDY FILETS FOR TWO

2 filets mignons
Bacon slices (opt.)
2 tbsp. butter, melted
1/2 c. sliced mushrooms
1 env. dry onion soup mix
1 tbsp. finely chopped parsley
1 1/2 tsp. flour
1/4 c. Burgundy
1 tsp. lemon juice
1 tsp. Worcestershire sauce

Wrap filets with bacon; secure with string. Brown in butter in skillet for 2 minutes on each side. Add mushrooms. Cook until mushrooms are tender. Add soup mix, parsley, flour blended with 1/2 cup water, Burgundy, lemon juice and Worcestershire sauce. Simmer for 8 minutes or until tender, turning steaks occasionally. Serve with hot cooked julienned vegetables of choice. Yield: 2 servings.

Recipe on page 78. →

Meats

FLANK STEAK WITH MUSHROOM STUFFING

Salt
1/4 tsp. white pepper
1 2-lb. flank steak
2 tsp. Dijon mustard
3 onions, chopped
2 tbsp. oil
1 4-oz. can mushrooms, drained, chopped
1/4 c. chopped parsley
2 tbsp. chopped chives
3 tbsp. catsup
1/4 c. dried bread crumbs
1/4 tsp. pepper
1 tsp. paprika
3 slices bacon, chopped
1 c. hot beef broth

Sprinkle 1/2 teaspoon salt and white pepper on both sides of flank steak. Spread one side with 1 teaspoon mustard. Saute 1 chopped onion in oil in skillet for 3 minutes or until lightly browned. Add mushrooms. Cook for 5 minutes. Stir in parsley, chives, 1 tablespoon catsup and bread crumbs. Season with 1/4 teaspoon salt, pepper and paprika. Spread over mustard on flank steak. Roll as for jelly roll; tie with string. Fry bacon in large saucepan until partially cooked. Add steak. Cook for 10 minutes or until brown on all sides. Add 2 finely chopped onions. Saute for 5 minutes. Pour in broth. Simmer, covered, for 1 hour. Remove steak to heated platter. Season pan juices with 1 teaspoon mustard and salt and pepper to taste. Stir in remaining 2 tablespoons catsup. Serve gravy with steak. Yield: 6 servings.

FILET OF BEEF WITH BORDELAISE SAUCE

1 4-lb. filet of beef
1/2 c. butter, melted
1 tsp. salt
1/2 tsp. freshly ground pepper
2 tsp. crushed rosemary leaves
1 c. Burgundy
1 1/2 lb. mushrooms, sliced
Bordelaise Sauce

Brush filet with butter; sprinkle with salt, pepper and rosemary. Place on rack in broiler pan. Broil for 20 minutes or until brown on all sides. Pour Burgundy over beef. Roast at 300 degrees for 30 minutes. Saute mushrooms in remaining butter in skillet until tender. Place filet and mushrooms on serving platter; garnish with watercress. Serve with Bordelaise Sauce.

Bordelaise Sauce

1 onion, chopped
1 shallot, chopped
1 clove of garlic, chopped
1/2 carrot, grated
2 tbsp. chopped parsley
2 bay leaves
1/4 c. butter
3 tbsp. flour
1/4 tsp. each salt and pepper
1 can beef bouillon
1 c. Burgundy
Meat extract paste to taste

Saute onion, shallot, garlic, carrot, parsley and bay leaves in butter in skillet until onion is brown. Stir in flour, salt and pepper. Cook over low heat until flour is brown, stirring constantly. Stir in bouillon and 1/2 cup Burgundy. Simmer for 10 minutes, stirring frequently. Strain sauce; discard vegetables. Add meat extract and 1/2 cup Burgundy. Cook until heated through. Do not boil. Serve with filet.

+ Recipes on pages 146 and 152.

Meats

MARINATED EYE OF ROUND ROAST

1 5-lb. eye of round roast
1 clove of garlic, chopped
1 tsp. salt
1/2 tsp. pepper
1 tsp. thyme
1/2 c. Italian dressing
1 c. red wine
1 bay leaf, crumbled

Cut eight 1-inch deep slashes in roast. Insert garlic in slashes. Rub roast with mixture of salt, pepper and thyme. Place in shallow dish. Combine dressing, wine and bay leaf in small bowl. Pour over roast. Chill, tightly covered, overnight, turning several times. Place roast in shallow baking pan; reserve marinade. Roast at 450 degrees for 25 minutes. Pour marinade over roast. Roast for 25 minutes longer for rare. Yield: 8 servings.

POT ROAST WITH FRESH WINTER VEGETABLES

1/4 c. flour
1 clove of garlic, finely minced
3 tbsp. chopped fresh parsley
1 1/2 tsp. salt
1/2 tsp. celery salt
1/4 tsp. paprika
1/8 tsp. pepper
1 6 to 8 lb. middle chuck
roast, rolled, tied
2 tbsp. oil
6 c. sliced onions
4 med. carrots, cut into 2-in.
pieces
4 white turnips, peeled, cubed
3 med. potatoes, peeled, cubed
1 c. 1-inch pieces celery

Combine flour, garlic, 2 tablespoons chopped parsley, salt, celery salt, paprika and pepper. Coat roast with flour mixture. Brown in oil in Dutch oven. Remove roast. Arrange onions on bottom of Dutch oven. Place roast on onions. Add 1 cup water. Cover. Simmer, covered, for 3 hours. Add carrots, turnips, potatoes and celery. Simmer, covered, for 30 minutes longer or until roast and vegetables are tender. Place on heated platter. Sprinkle with 1 tablespoon chopped parsley. Yield: 6-8 servings.

Photograph for this recipe on page 36.

WEST BANK PIZZA LOAVES

1 lg. loaf unsliced French bread
Butter
1 1/2 to 2 c. cooked ground beef
1 6-oz. can tomato paste
2 tbsp. chopped onion
1/4 c. chopped olives
1/4 c. Parmesan cheese
1/2 to 1 tsp. salt
1/4 tsp. each pepper, oregano
14 thin tomato slices
7 slices Cheddar cheese

Split French bread lengthwise. Spread with butter. Combine remaining ingredients except tomatoes and Cheddar cheese. Spread on buttered bread. Arrange tomato slices over ground beef mixture. Place on baking sheet. Bake at 350 degrees for 20 minutes. Arrange Cheddar cheese over top. Bake for 5 minutes longer. Yield: 8 servings.

SWEET AND SOUR BEEF SHORT RIBS

2 1/2 lb. beef short ribs,
cut into serving pieces
1 c. sweet mixed pickles
1 8-oz. can pineapple chunks,
drained
1/2 c. sliced celery
1 med. onion, sliced
1 med. green pepper, cut into
rings
1 can beef broth
1 tbsp. soy sauce
1/4 c. flour

Trim ribs. Place in Crock-Pot with pickles, pineapple, celery, onion and green pepper. Add mixture of broth and soy sauce. Cook, covered, on Low heat for 8 1/2 hours or on High for 4 1/2 hours. Skim. Blend flour with 1/3 cup water. Stir into pan juices. Cook, covered, for 30 minutes longer. Serve with noodles.

Photograph for this recipe above.

Meats

MOZZARELLA MEAT LOAF

2 lb. ground beef
2 eggs, slightly beaten
3/4 c. soft bread crumbs
1/2 c. vegetable juice cocktail
1/2 tsp. each oregano, salt
Pepper
Garlic salt
6 oz. mozzarella cheese, chopped
3 tbsp. Parmesan cheese
1/2 c. tomato paste

Combine first 6 ingredients with 1/4 teaspoon pepper and 1/2 teaspoon garlic salt in bowl; mix well. Shape half the mixture into flattened oval in 9 x 13-inch baking dish. Spread chopped mozzarella and 2 tablespoons Parmesan cheese to within 1 inch of edge. Top with remaining ground beef mixture, sealing edges. Spread tomato paste over top. Sprinkle lightly with pepper and garlic salt. Bake at 350 degrees for 1 hour. Top with additional mozzarella cheese and 1 tablespoon Parmesan cheese. Bake until cheese melts.

GROUND BEEF-RICE RING

2 onions, chopped
1/2 green pepper, chopped
1 clove of garlic, minced
2 tbsp. butter
1 1/2 lb. lean ground beef
1   6-oz. can tomato paste
1 tsp. salt
1/2 tsp. chili powder
1/8 tsp. pepper
1 pimento, cut into strips
2 c. cooked rice
1   10-oz. package frozen peas,
cooked, drained
1 can tomato soup
2 hard-boiled eggs, chopped
2 tbsp. Parmesan cheese

Saute first 3 ingredients in butter in skillet until tender. Add ground beef. Cook until brown, stirring frequently. Stir in tomato paste and seasonings. Arrange pimento strips in bottom of buttered 2-quart ring mold. Layer rice, peas and ground beef mixture in mold, pressing each layer firmly with back of spoon. Place mold in shallow baking pan filled with hot water. Bake at 350 degrees for 30 to 40 minutes. Unmold on serving plate. Heat soup to serving temperature; stir in eggs. Spoon over mold; sprinkle with Parmesan cheese. Yield: 6 servings.

CHINESE EGG ROLLS

1/4 lb. ground beef
1 onion, chopped
3 c. shredded cabbage
1/2 c. shredded carrots
1 green onion, chopped
1 chicken bouillon cube
Dash each of salt and pepper
12 egg roll wrappers
Oil for deep frying

Brown ground beef in skillet, stirring until crumbly; drain. Add onion. Stir-fry for 3 minutes. Add next 4 ingredients. Stir-fry for 5 minutes. Season with salt and pepper. Place 1 spoonful on corner of each egg roll wrapper. Roll up diagonally, folding in corners to enclose filling. Deep-fry in hot oil until golden brown. Serve hot with sweet and sour sauce.

SPAGHETTI PIE

1 8-oz. package spaghetti,
broken, cooked
2 tbsp. butter, melted
1/3 c. Parmesan cheese
1/2 tsp. salt
1/4 tsp. pepper
1 egg, beaten
1 1/2 lb. ground chuck
1 onion, chopped
1/4 c. chopped green pepper
2 tbsp. oil
1 15-oz. jar spaghetti sauce
1 tsp. sugar
1/2 tsp. each oregano, garlic
salt
1 8-oz. carton cottage cheese
4 oz. mozzarella cheese, shredded

Combine first 6 ingredients in bowl; mix well. Spread over bottom and side of 10-inch pie plate. Saute ground chuck, onion and green pepper in oil in skillet until vegetables are tender, stirring frequently. Stir in spaghetti sauce and seasonings. Spread cottage cheese over spaghetti mixture. Top with sauce. Bake at 350 degrees for 30 minutes. Sprinkle with mozzarella cheese. Bake for 10 minutes longer. Let stand for 15 minutes before serving.

HAWAIIAN HAMBURGERS

1 1/2 lb. ground beef
1/2 c. chopped onion
2/3 c. evaporated milk
2/3 c. cracker crumbs
1 tsp. salt
1 13 1/2-oz. can pineapple chunks
2 tbsp. cornstarch
1/4 c. vinegar
1/4 c. packed brown sugar
2 tbsp. soy sauce
1 c. coarsely chopped green pepper

Combine first 5 ingredients in bowl; mix well. Shape into patties. Brown in skillet; drain. Drain pineapple, reserving juice. Combine reserved juice with enough water to measure 1 cup; pour into saucepan. Blend in cornstarch, vinegar, brown sugar and soy sauce. Cook until thick, stirring constantly. Add pineapple and green pepper. Spoon over patties. Simmer over low heat for 15 minutes.

APRICOT-GLAZED HAM

1/2 c. apricot jam
2 tbsp. prepared mustard
2 tsp. lemon juice
1 tsp. Worcestershire sauce
1 1 1/2-lb. 1-inch thick cooked
center cut ham slice

Heat first 4 ingredients in saucepan until jam is melted, stirring constantly. Slash fat edge of ham. Place in shallow dish. Pour apricot mixture over top. Marinate, covered, for 2 hours at room temperature or overnight in refrigerator. Drain, reserving marinade. Grill over medium coals for 10 to 15 minutes on each side, basting frequently with marinade. Serve with hot marinade.

Meats

SCALLOPED POTATOES AND HAM

7 or 8 potatoes, thinly sliced
1 onion, thinly sliced
5 tsp. salt
1/4 c. margarine, melted
5 tsp. (heaping) flour
Paprika
2 1/4 c. milk
1/2 tsp. pepper
Ham slices
Chopped parsley

Cook potatoes and onion with 1 tablespoon salt in boiling water to cover in saucepan for 5 minutes; drain. Blend margarine, flour and 1/4 teaspoon paprika in saucepan. Stir in milk gradually. Add remaining 2 teaspoons salt and pepper. Cook over low heat until thick, stirring constantly. Alternate layers of ham slices, potatoes and white sauce in greased casserole, sprinkling each layer with parsley and paprika. Bake at 400 degrees for 40 minutes. Yield: 8 servings.

HAM AND BROCCOLI PIE

1 bunch fresh broccoli
2 stalks celery, sliced
1 onion, coarsely chopped
2 tbsp. margarine, melted
2 tbsp. cornstarch
2 tsp. dry mustard
1/4 tsp. marjoram
1/4 tsp. grated lemon rind
1/8 tsp. pepper
2 c. milk
2 tbsp. lemon juice
2 c. chopped cooked ham
1 recipe pie pastry

Separate broccoli into flowerets. Place in large saucepan with 1/2 inch boiling water. Simmer, covered, for 5 minutes; drain. Saute celery and onion in margarine in skillet for 3 minutes. Combine cornstarch, mustard, marjoram, lemon rind and pepper in medium saucepan; stir in milk gradually. Add celery and onion mixture. Bring to a boil over medium heat, stirring constantly. Boil for 1 minute; remove from heat. Stir in lemon juice, broccoli and ham. Pour into 2-quart casserole. Roll out pastry; cut into strips. Arrange lattice-fashion over top; flute edge. Bake at 375 degrees for 35 minutes or until golden brown. Yield: 4-6 servings.

SAUCY HAM CASSEROLE

1 c. rice, cooked
2 10-oz. packages frozen broccoli, cooked
2 onions, finely chopped
6 tbsp. butter, melted
3 tbsp. flour
1/4 tsp. pepper
3 c. milk
1 1/2 lb. cooked ham, cubed
1 8-oz. package American cheese, melted
2 c. fresh bread crumbs

Layer rice and broccoli in 9 x 13-inch baking dish. Saute onions in 1/4 cup butter in saucepan. Stir in flour and pepper. Cook until bubbly. Stir in milk gradually. Cook until thick, stirring constantly. Add ham; mix well. Pour over broccoli. Pour cheese over sauce. Top with bread crumbs mixed with 2 tablespoons butter. Chill, covered, overnight. Bake at 350 degrees for 45 minutes. Yield: 8 servings.

Meats

BAKED HAM SANDWICHES

12 slices bread
3 c. chopped ham
1 med. onion
1 tbsp. prepared mustard
1/2 tsp. pepper
1 tsp. celery salt
1 to 2 c. grated sharp cheese
2 cans cream of mushroom soup
1 tbsp. Worcestershire sauce
4 eggs, beaten
1/4 c. milk

Trim bread; reserve bread crusts. Place 6 slices bread in buttered 9 x 13-inch baking dish. Grind ham, onion and reserved bread crusts together. Add mustard, pepper and celery salt; mix well. Spread over bread. Cover with cheese. Top with remaining bread. Combine remaining ingredients; blend well. Pour over sandwiches. Bake at 350 degrees for 1 hour.

HAWAIIAN LAMB CHOPS

6 1 1/2-in. thick loin lamb chops with pockets
White pepper
1 8 1/4-oz. can crushed pineapple
1/2 c. shredded coconut
1/4 c. coarsely chopped green pepper
1 tsp. ginger
1/2 tsp. mustard
Salt
1/2 c. orange juice
1 tbsp. brown sugar
1 1/2 tsp. orange rind
1/2 tsp. cornstarch

Sprinkle lamb chops with pepper. Drain pineapple, reserving liquid. Combine pineapple with coconut, green pepper, 3/4 teaspoon ginger and mustard in bowl; mix well. Let stand for 15 minutes. Toss gently. Stuff each chop with 1 tablespoon pineapple mixture; secure with toothpicks. Place on rack in broiler pan. Broil 3 to 4 inches from heat source for 6 to 8 minutes on each side or to desired degree of doneness; sprinkle with salt. Combine orange juice, brown sugar, orange rind, cornstarch, reserved pineapple juice and remaining 1/4 teaspoon ginger in bowl; mix well. Mix with remaining pineapple mixture in skillet. Cook until slightly thickened, stirring constantly. Season to taste. Place lamb chops on serving plate. Garnish with parsley. Serve with orange sauce.

LAMB SHISH KABOBS

1 lb. lamb, cubed
1/4 c. light olive oil
1/4 c. Claret
Juice of 2 fresh lemons
4 onions, quartered
2 green peppers, coarsely chopped
4 tomatoes, quartered
4 mushroom caps

Place lamb in large bowl. Combine olive oil, Claret and lemon juice in bowl; pour over lamb. Marinate for 2 hours or longer. Alternate onion quarters, lamb, green peppers and tomatoes on 4 skewers. Top with mushroom caps. Cook on grill over medium-low heat until lamb is medium-rare and vegetables are tender-crisp, turning frequently.

Meats

ROLLED LEG OF LAMB IN CITRUS SAUCE

1   4 to 5-lb. leg of lamb,
boned, rolled, tied
1/2 tsp. salt
1/4 tsp. pepper
2 tsp. ginger
1/4 c. soy sauce
2 cloves of garlic, minced
Several drops of hot pepper sauce
2 tbsp. brown sugar
1 1/2 c. grapefruit juice
1 tsp. grated grapefruit rind

Place lamb in large glass bowl. Mix remaining ingredients in bowl; pour over lamb. Marinate, covered, in refrigerator for several hours. Remove lamb, reserving marinade. Grill lamb over hot coals for 20 minutes per pound or to 145 degrees on meat thermometer for medium-rare, 160 degrees for medium or 170 degrees for well done, basting frequently with marinade. Yield: 6-8 servings.

MICROWAVE BRAISED LAMB SHOULDER

6 med. carrots, peeled
6 med. onions, peeled
1 tsp. dried basil or oregano
1 tsp. salt
1/2 tsp. pepper
1   3 1/2 to 5-lb. lamb shoulder,
boned, rolled, tied
1/2 c. chicken broth
1/2 c. dry red wine
2 tbsp. flour
1/2 c. cream
1 lb. cooked asparagus

Combine carrots, onions, basil, salt and pepper in 3-quart glass casserole; mix well. Place lamb shoulder, fat side down, on vegetables. Blend broth and wine in bowl. Pour broth mixture over lamb and vegetables. Cover with plastic wrap. Microwave on High for 12 to 15 minutes. Turn lamb, fat side up. Cover with plastic wrap. Microwave on Medium for 30 to 35 minutes or until temperature of lamb is 170 degrees on meat thermometer. Place lamb and vegetables on serving platter, reserving juices. Cover with foil. Blend flour and cream in 2-cup glass bowl. Stir in 1 cup hot pan juices. Microwave on High for 1 to 2 minutes or until gravy is thickened, stirring once or twice. Serve gravy with roast and asparagus.

Photograph for this recipe on page 69.

SWEET AND SOUR LAMB

2 lb. lamb, cubed
1   8 3/4-oz. can pineapple
tidbits
1 green pepper, sliced
1/2 c. diagonally sliced celery
1/2 c. vinegar
1/2 c. sugar
1 tsp. soy sauce
1 tbsp. cornstarch
1 whole pimento, sliced

Brown lamb in skillet. Drain pineapple, reserving juice. Combine green pepper, celery, reserved juice, vinegar, sugar and soy sauce in large saucepan; mix well. Bring to a boil. Blend cornstarch with 2 tablespoons water. Add to saucepan. Boil for 1/2 minute, stirring constantly. Add lamb, pineapple and pimento. Heat to serving temperature. Serve over rice. Yield: 6 servings.

APRICOT-MARINATED PORK CHOPS

6 1 1/4-in. thick pork chops,
butterflied
1/2 c. apricot nectar
1/2 tsp. paprika
2 tsp. honey
1 1/4 tsp. salt
1 1/4 c. catsup
1/2 c. packed brown sugar
1 1/4 tbsp. lemon juice
2 1/2 tbsp. Worcestershire sauce
1/2 tsp. soy sauce
1 tsp. pepper
1 tsp. onion powder
1/2 tsp. horseradish

Place pork chops in glass dish. Combine remaining ingredients and 2 cups water in saucepan. Bring to a boil. Cool. Pour over pork chops. Marinate in refrigerator for 6 to 8 hours, turning occasionally. Drain chops, reserving marinade. Place on grill 6 to 8 inches from heat source. Cook over low heat for 8 minutes; turn. Cook for 1 hour, turning and basting frequently.

SPICED PORK CHOPS

3 apples, peeled, sliced
Brown sugar
1/4 tsp. ground cloves
Juice of 1 lemon
6 1-in. thick pork chops with
pockets
2 tbsp. butter, melted
1/3 c. raisins
1/4 tsp. each cinnamon, ginger

Combine apples, 1/4 cup packed brown sugar, cloves and lemon juice in bowl; mix well. Stuff pork chops with apple mixture. Brown pork chops in butter in skillet. Add raisins, 1/3 cup packed brown sugar, spices and 1/2 cup water. Cook, covered, for 20 to 25 minutes or until chops are tender. Yield: 6 servings.

SWEET AND SOUR PORK

1 1/2 lb. lean pork shoulder,
cut into 2-in. strips
1 tbsp. oil
1 1-lb. can pineapple chunks
in syrup
1/4 c. packed brown sugar
2 tbsp. cornstarch
1/4 c. cider vinegar
1 tbsp. soy sauce
1/2 tsp. salt
1 green pepper, cut into strips

Saute pork in oil in skillet until brown. Add 1/2 cup water. Simmer, covered, for 45 minutes. Drain pineapple, reserving syrup. Blend reserved syrup with next 5 ingredients in small bowl. Add to pork. Cook until thick, stirring constantly. Add pineapple and pepper strips. Cook for 2 to 3 minutes longer. Yield: 4 servings.

Meats

SOUTHERN-STYLE BARBECUED SPARERIBS

2 1/2 c. catsup
1/2 c. packed brown sugar
1/2 c. vinegar
2 tbsp. pepper
1 tbsp. liquid smoke
1 tbsp. mustard
1 onion, grated
4 lb. spareribs
2 onions, sliced
Salt and pepper to taste

Combine first 7 ingredients in saucepan. Simmer for 30 minutes. Place spareribs in baking pan; add sliced onions. Sprinkle with salt and pepper. Pour sauce over spareribs. Bake, covered, at 350 degrees for 1 1/2 hours. Bake, uncovered, for 20 minutes longer. Serve with rice. Yield: 6 servings.

FESTIVE CROWN ROAST

1   6 to 7-lb. crown pork roast
Salt and coarsely ground pepper
to taste
3/4 c. dill pickle liquid
2/3 c. chopped onion
5 tbsp. butter
1/2 to 1 c. milk
1 pimento, chopped
1/2 c. chopped parsley
3 lb. potatoes, peeled, cooked,
mashed
1   16-oz. can tomatoes in puree
1 env. brown gravy mix
1/4 c. chopped dill pickle
1/4 tsp. each thyme, tarragon
2 tbsp. each honey, sugar
1 1/2 tbsp. Dijon mustard

Sprinkle roast with salt and pepper. Place on rack in shallow roasting pan. Roast at 325 degrees for 30 minutes per pound or to 170 degrees on meat thermometer, brushing occasionally with 1/2 cup pickle liquid. Saute onion in butter in skillet. Stir milk, half the sauteed onion, pimento, 1/4 cup parsley and salt to taste into potatoes. Pipe potatoes into center of crown roast 20 minutes before end of roasting time. Stir remaining 1/4 cup pickle liquid, 1/4 cup parsley, 3/4 cup water and remaining ingredients into sauteed onion in skillet. Cook, covered, over low heat for 20 to 30 minutes, stirring occasionally. Serve with roast.

Photograph for this recipe on page 64.

COUNTRY SAUSAGE CASSEROLE

1 lb. smoked sausage, sliced
1 onion, chopped
1 tbsp. oil
1 pkg. au gratin potatoes
1/4 tsp. pepper
4 carrots, sliced
1   10-oz. package frozen
broccoli, thawed
1 c. shredded Cheddar cheese

Saute sausage and onion in oil in skillet for 5 minutes or until onion is tender. Stir in potatoes, sauce mix, 2 1/2 cups water and pepper. Simmer, covered, for 10 minutes, stirring occasionally. Stir in carrots. Simmer, covered, for 10 minutes or until carrots are tender-crisp. Stir in broccoli and cheese. Cook, covered, for 5 to 10 minutes or until broccoli is tender and cheese is melted.

CHINESE VEAL CASSEROLE

1 lb. veal, cubed
2 tbsp. oil
1 c. finely chopped onion
1/2 c. rice
1 can chicken with rice soup
1/4 c. soy sauce
1 c. finely chopped celery
1 pkg. frozen peas
1/4 c. toasted almonds

Brown veal in oil in skillet. Add onion. Saute until onion is golden. Add 1 cup water, rice, soup and soy sauce; mix well. Spoon into 2-quart casserole. Bake, covered, at 425 degrees for 40 minutes. Stir in celery and peas. Bake, covered, for 20 minutes longer. Sprinkle with almonds. Yield: 10-12 servings.

VEAL CURRY

2 or 3 onions, chopped
1/4 c. butter
1 lb. ground veal
1/2 tsp. cinnamon
1 can peas, drained
1 sm. can tomato juice
Salt to taste
2 tsp. curry powder

Brown onions in butter in skillet. Add veal and cinnamon. Cook until brown and crumbly, stirring frequently. Add peas, tomato juice and salt; mix well. Simmer for several minutes. Add curry powder. Cook, covered, for 1 hour. Serve over cooked rice. Yield: 6 servings.

VEAL MARSALA

1 1-lb. veal cutlet
1 egg, beaten
1 c. fine bread crumbs
1/4 c. butter
1 pkg. brown gravy mix
1/3 c. Marsala
1 4-oz. can mushrooms, drained

Pound veal with meat mallet to 3/8-inch thickness. Cut into serving-sized pieces. Beat egg with 1/4 cup water in bowl. Dip veal into egg mixture; coat with bread crumbs. Brown in butter in skillet. Remove to serving platter; keep warm. Prepare gravy mix according to package directions using Marsala and 2/3 cup water. Add mushrooms. Heat to serving temperature. Pour over veal. Serve over noodles or rice. Yield: 2-3 servings.

VEAL SCALLOPS WITH LEMON

1 1/2 lb. veal scallops, pounded thin
Salt and pepper
1/2 c. flour
6 tbsp. butter
3 tbsp. olive oil
8 thin slices lemon
1/4 c. lemon juice
2 tbsp. minced fresh parsley

Season veal with salt and pepper; coat with flour. Cook veal, several pieces at a time, in hot butter and oil in heavy skillet for about 1 minute on each side. Pieces should not touch in skillet. Remove to warm serving platter. Add lemon slices and juice to pan drippings; mix well. Pour over veal. Sprinkle with parsley.

Poultry

Poultry is as traditionally American as the Thanksgiving turkey. A vital part of most families' weekly menu, poultry offers an economical yet delicious entree.

The subtle taste of poultry gives the cook an almost unlimited choice of seasonings and sauces. It blends beautifully with a vast array of vegetables, yet stands well on its own with no more seasoning than a dash of salt and a sprinkling of pepper.

Poultry can be fried, baked, broiled or stewed. It can be served hot or cold, sliced or whole. So versatile, it well deserves its widespread popularity!

The following group of poultry recipes is one of the most exciting collections ever assembled. Among them you will find combinations to please the most discriminating diner.

Steaming dishes of chicken breasts blended with colorful vegetables or heaped over mounds of seasoned rice; Cornish hens that taste as good as they look, bubbling casseroles developed over the years by proud family cooks; and several Oriental dishes that are a delightful change to your menu planning.

Your meals will be very special when you choose from these superb poultry entrees, side dishes and sandwiches.

← CHICKEN LIVERS IN PATTY SHELLS, Recipe on page 95.

Poultry

ALMOND-MUSHROOM CHOP SUEY

2 onions, chopped
2 stalks celery, chopped
1 tbsp. oil
1 green pepper, sliced
2 c. chopped cooked chicken
breast
1 c. bean sprouts
1/2 lb. fresh mushrooms, sliced
1 tbsp. cornstarch (opt.)
2 tbsp. soy sauce
Cooked brown rice
3/4 c. chopped almonds

Stir-fry onions and celery in oil in skillet for 1 minute. Add green pepper, chicken, bean sprouts and mushrooms; mix well. Cook, covered, until heated through. Add cornstarch mixed with soy sauce. Cook until thick, stirring constantly. Serve on hot rice. Sprinkle with almonds.

CHICKEN IN BRANDY SAUCE

5 to 6 lb. boned skinned
chicken breasts
2 c. chicken broth
2 c. heavy cream
1 c. Brandy
2 tbsp. Worcestershire sauce
1 c. chopped onion
2 cloves of garlic, minced
1 tsp. salt
Flour
1/4 c. melted butter
Paprika

Place chicken in large baking pan. Combine next 7 ingredients and 1 tablespoon flour in saucepan. Cook until bubbly, stirring constantly. Pour over chicken. Bake at 325 degrees for about 1 1/2 hours. Reduce temperature to 300 degrees. Place chicken in shallow baking pan, reserving sauce. Brush with butter; sprinkle with paprika. Bake for 30 minutes or until brown. Skim sauce; strain into large saucepan. Mix 1 cup water and 1/4 cup flour in bowl. Stir slowly into sauce. Heat to boiling point, stirring constantly. Boil for 1 minute, stirring constantly. Serve over chicken. Yield: 6 servings.

PARTY CHICKEN SPAGHETTI

8 chicken breasts
Salt and pepper to taste
1 1-lb. package spaghetti,
cooked
1 16-oz. carton sour cream
2 cartons mushrooms, cooked
4 pkg. broccoli, cooked, drained
1 sm. package slivered almonds
Chopped celery (opt.)
1 lg. jar chopped pimento
1 can cream of celery soup
Mozzarella cheese

Season chicken breasts with salt and pepper. Wrap in foil. Bake at 325 degrees for 1 hour. Remove skin and bones. Combine spaghetti, sour cream and mushrooms in large oblong casserole. Mix broccoli, almonds, celery, pimento and soup in bowl. Spread over spaghetti. Top with chicken and cheese. Chill in refrigerator. Bake at 350 degrees until heated through. Yield: 12-14 servings.

BAKED CHICKEN SUPREME

10 chicken breasts, boned,
skinned
10 slices bacon
1   2 1/2-oz. jar dried beef,
chopped
1 can mushroom soup
1   8-oz. carton sour cream

Roll chicken breasts; wrap each with bacon slice. Line bottom of baking dish with chopped beef. Top with chicken breasts. Combine soup and sour cream in bowl; mix well. Pour over chicken breasts. Bake at 275 degrees for 3 hours.

CASHEW CHICKEN

1/4 c. soy sauce
2 tbsp. cornstarch
4 lg. boned chicken breasts, cut
into bite-sized pieces
1/2 c. slivered cashews
Oil
1 onion, chopped
2 carrots, sliced diagonally
2 stalks celery, sliced diagonally
2 cloves of garlic, chopped
1 head cauliflower, cut into
flowerets
1 lb. mushrooms, sliced
1 c. bouillon

Blend soy sauce and cornstarch in shallow dish. Add chicken, turning to coat. Marinate for several minutes. Saute cashews in a small amount of oil in electric skillet at 375 degrees until golden brown; drain. Brown slightly drained chicken in oil in skillet; set aside. Add next 6 vegetables. Cook, covered, for 2 minutes. Add bouillon. Cook, uncovered, for 4 minutes. Stir in chicken and cashews. Serve with wild rice.

CRAB-STUFFED CHICKEN

4 lg. chicken breasts, boned
1/4 c. melted butter
1/4 c. flour
3/4 c. milk
3/4 c. chicken broth
1/3 c. dry white wine
1/2 c. chopped onion
2   7 1/2-oz. cans crab meat,
drained
1   6-oz. can mushrooms, drained
2 tbsp. parsley
1/2 tsp. each salt and pepper
1/2 c. coarsely crumbled
saltine crackers
1 c. shredded Swiss cheese
1/2 tsp. paprika

Flatten chicken with meat mallet. Blend 3 tablespoons butter, flour, milk, chicken broth and wine in saucepan. Cook until thick, stirring constantly. Saute onion in 1 tablespoon butter in saucepan until tender. Stir in crab meat, mushrooms, parsley, salt and pepper and crackers. Stir in 2 tablespoons sauce. Top each chicken piece with 1/4 cup crab mixture. Fold in sides; roll up. Place seam side down in buttered baking dish. Pour remaining sauce over top. Bake, covered, at 350 degrees for 1 hour. Sprinkle chicken with cheese and paprika. Bake until cheese is melted. Yield: 4 servings.

Poultry

CHICKEN CORDON BLEU

4 boned chicken breasts
4 slices boiled ham
4 slices Swiss cheese
1 egg
Bread crumbs
1/4 c. oil
2 tbsp. flour
Salt and pepper to taste
3/4 c. chicken broth
1/2 c. white wine

Pound chicken breasts with meat mallet until thin. Place 1 slice ham and 1 slice cheese on each chicken breast; roll up. Secure with toothpicks. Beat egg with 2 tablespoons water. Dip chicken rolls in egg mixture. Coat with bread crumbs. Brown in hot oil in skillet. Remove to platter; keep warm. Stir flour, salt and pepper into pan drippings. Cook until brown. Add broth and wine. Cook until thick, stirring constantly. Serve over chicken. Yield: 4 servings.

HONEY-GLAZED CHICKEN

1 orange, quartered
4 chicken breasts, skinned, boned
1/2 c. orange juice
1 tsp. salt
1/4 tsp. each pepper, ginger
1/2 c. honey
1/2 c. red wine
Grated rind of 1 orange

Arrange orange quarters in baking dish. Place 1 chicken breast over each. Mix orange juice, salt, pepper and ginger in small bowl. Pour over chicken. Bake at 375 degrees for 1 hour. Brush with honey. Bake until golden brown, basting frequently with mixture of wine and orange rind.

PARADISE CHICKEN

3 1/2 lb. boned chicken breasts
Salt and pepper to taste
Butter
2 tbsp. raisins
2 tbsp. cherry juice
8 sprigs of fresh mint
6 tbsp. sugar
6 tbsp. cider vinegar
2/3 can frozen orange juice concentrate
Cornstarch
1 c. sliced fresh mango
24 litchi nuts
3/4 c. pineapple chunks
24 maraschino cherries

Season chicken with salt and pepper. Brown in butter in skillet. Place chicken in baking dish; reserve drippings. Combine raisins, cherry juice, mint, sugar, vinegar and juice concentrate in saucepan. Bring to a boil. Stir in reserved drippings and enough cornstarch dissolved in cold water to make medium-thick sauce. Pour over chicken. Bake at 350 degrees for 25 minutes. Add mango, nuts, pineapple and cherries; stir lightly. Cook for 10 minutes longer. Turn off oven. Let chicken stand in hot oven for 10 to 15 minutes. Serve with buttered noodles.

CHICKEN BREASTS MONTEREY

1/2 c. chopped onion
1/2 c. butter
2 c. bread cubes
1 tsp. each oregano, dry mustard
2 tsp. parsley flakes
4 whole boned chicken breasts
1 tsp. seasoned salt
4 slices Monterey Jack cheese
1 can mushroom soup
Paprika

Brown onion in butter in skillet. Add next 4 ingredients. Sprinkle inside of breasts with seasoned salt. Top with cheese and 1 spoonful bread mixture. Fold breasts to enclose filling; secure with toothpicks. Arrange in baking dish. Spoon remaining bread mixture around edge. Mix soup and 1 soup can water in bowl. Pour over chicken. Sprinkle with paprika. Bake at 350 degrees for 1 hour. Yield: 4 servings.

CHICKEN PAELLA

4 oz. Italian sausage, sliced
4 chicken breasts
Salt and pepper to taste
1 green pepper, chopped
1 onion, chopped
1 clove of garlic, minced
3/4 c. brown rice
1 1/4 tsp. turmeric
4 carrots, cut into chunks
1 10-oz. package frozen peas
1 10-oz. package frozen artichokes
1/4 c. pitted ripe olives
6 cherry tomatoes, halved

Saute sausage in skillet for 10 minutes; remove sausage and drain. Season chicken with salt and pepper. Brown in pan drippings. Remove chicken. Add green pepper, onion and garlic. Cook until tender. Add rice, turmeric and 3 cups hot water. Bring to a boil. Add sausage, carrots and chicken. Simmer, covered, for 20 minutes. Rinse peas and artichokes in hot water to separate. Arrange with olives around chicken. Cook, covered, for 15 to 20 minutes or until chicken and rice are tender. Add tomatoes. Heat to serving temperature. Yield: 4 servings.

ROSEMARY CHICKEN

6 chicken breasts
1/4 c. flour
1 tsp. salt
1/4 c. butter
2 tsp. crushed rosemary
1/4 c. chopped green onions
4 oz. sliced mushrooms
1 7-oz. bottle of lemon-lime soda
1 c. sour cream
1/8 c. cream Sherry
1 tsp. MSG

Coat chicken with mixture of flour and salt. Brown chicken in butter in skillet. Sprinkle rosemary, onions and mushrooms over chicken. Add soda. Cook, covered, over low heat for 45 minutes or until chicken is tender. Remove chicken to 9 x 15-inch serving platter. Stir sour cream, Sherry and MSG into sauce. Heat to serving temperature. Do not boil. Spoon over chicken.

Poultry

CRUSTY PARMESAN CHICKEN

4 chicken breasts
1 stick butter, melted
1 1/2 c. bread crumbs
1/2 c. (or more) Parmesan cheese
Salt and pepper to taste

Coat chicken with butter. Roll in mixture of crumbs and Parmesan cheese. Place in baking dish. Season with salt and pepper. Bake at 350 degrees for 1 hour. Yield: 4 servings.

CHICKEN PARMIGIANA

1 c. bread crumbs
3/4 c. Parmesan cheese
6 boned chicken breasts
2 eggs, slightly beaten
1/4 c. oil
2 tbsp. butter
1 c. chopped onion
1 tsp. minced garlic
2 cans tomato sauce
1 can tomatoes
1 1/2 tsp. basil
1/2 tsp. thyme
1/2 tsp. each salt, onion salt
1/4 tsp. pepper
8 oz. mozzarella cheese, shredded

Mix bread crumbs with 1/4 cup Parmesan cheese. Dip chicken breasts in eggs; coat with bread crumb mixture. Brown in mixture of 2 tablespoons oil and butter in skillet. Place in baking dish. Saute onion and garlic in 2 tablespoons oil in skillet. Stir in tomato sauce, tomatoes and seasonings. Simmer, covered, for 15 minutes. Layer mozzarella cheese, sauce and 1/2 cup Parmesan cheese over chicken. Bake at 350 degrees for 20 to 30 minutes. Serve over spaghetti. Yields: 6 servings.

BAKED CHICKEN REUBEN

6 chicken breasts
1 can sauerkraut, drained
4 slices Swiss cheese
1 c. Thousand Island salad dressing

Place chicken breasts in 9 x 13-inch baking dish. Sprinkle sauerkraut over chicken. Place Swiss cheese over sauerkraut. Top with dressing. Cover dish with foil. Bake at 325 degrees for 1 hour. Yield: 6 servings.

CHICKEN SAUTERNE

8 to 10 chicken breasts
2 cans cream of mushroom soup
1 env. dry onion soup mix
1 sm. can sliced mushrooms, drained
2/3 c. Sauterne

Place chicken breasts skin side up in baking pan. Combine remaining ingredients in bowl; mix well. Spread over chicken. Refrigerate, covered, overnight. Bake, covered, at 425 degrees for 35 minutes. Bake, uncovered, for 20 minutes longer. Garnish with pimento.

CHICKEN SALTIMBOCCA

6 whole boned chicken breasts,
cut in half
Flour
1/3 c. clarified butter
12 thin slices prosciutto
6 1-oz. slices Monterey Jack
cheese, cut in half
1/4 c. chopped shallots
3 cloves of garlic, minced
1/2 lb. mushrooms, sliced
1/2 c. dry white wine
1 c. chicken broth
1 tsp. each fresh thyme, oregano
1/2 c. Sherry
1/2 c. cream
Salt and pepper to taste

Coat chicken with flour. Brown in butter in skillet. Arrange in buttered 9 x 13-inch baking dish. Top each piece with 1 slice prosciutto and 1/2 slice cheese. Saute shallots and garlic in skillet until tender. Add mushrooms, wine, broth and herbs. Bring to a boil. Cook for 10 minutes. Stir in 1 tablespoon flour blended with a small amount of Sherry. Stir in remaining Sherry and cream; season with salt and pepper. Pour sauce over chicken. Bake at 375 degrees for 20 minutes. Yield: 6 servings.

PLUM-GLAZED CHICKEN

1/2 c. plum preserves
Juice and grated rind of 1 orange
2 tbsp. light corn syrup
6 cooked chicken breasts
3 c. cooked rice

Heat preserves, 1/4 cup orange juice and corn syrup in large skillet. Add chicken. Cook over low heat until chicken is heated through and glazed, turning frequently to coat evenly. Combine rice with remaining orange juice and orange rind in saucepan. Heat to serving temperature. Arrange chicken over rice. Spoon plum mixture over top. Yield: 4 servings.

CROCK•POT SWEET AND SOUR CHICKEN

6 carrots, peeled, sliced
1/2 c. finely chopped green
pepper
1/2 c. finely chopped onion
6 chicken breasts
1/2 tsp. salt
1 10-oz. jar sweet and sour
sauce
1 15-oz. can pineapple chunks
3 tbsp. cornstarch

Place carrots, green pepper and onion in 4-quart Crock-Pot. Top with chicken breasts; sprinkle with salt. Pour sweet and sour sauce and pineapple over all. Cook on Low for 7 to 8 hours or on High for 3 1/2 to 4 hours. Remove chicken to warm serving platter. Blend cornstarch with 3 tablespoons water; stir into pan juices. Cook on High for 10 to 15 minutes or until thickened, stirring frequently. Serve over hot rice. Yield: 6 servings.

Poultry

CHICKEN CREPES AMANDINE

3 eggs, beaten
2 1/2 c. milk
1/2 c. pancake mix
Butter
1 c. sliced fresh mushrooms
1/4 c. flour
1/4 tsp. pepper
2 chicken bouillon cubes, crushed
2 c. chopped cooked chicken
Toasted sliced almonds

Combine eggs, 1/2 cup milk and pancake mix in bowl; beat until smooth. Heat a small amount of butter in 8-inch skillet until bubbly. Pour a small amount of batter into hot skillet; tilt to cover bottom. Brown lightly on both sides. Repeat with remaining batter. Stack crepes between waxed paper. Saute mushrooms in 2 tablespoons butter in skiller; set aside. Blend 4 tablespoons melted butter with flour and pepper in medium saucepan. Cook over low heat for 1 minute, stirring frequently. Stir in 2 cups milk and bouillon cubes. Cook until thick, stirring constantly. Add mushrooms and chicken. Cook until heated through. Spoon 1/3 cup chicken mixture onto each crepe; roll to enclose filling. Arrange in 10 x 15-inch baking dish. Sprinkle with almonds. Bake at 325 degrees for 10 minutes.

CRUNCHY CHICKEN CRESCENTS

Margarine
2 3-oz. packages cream cheese with chives, softened
1 1/2 c. chopped cooked chicken
1 pkg. refrigerator crescent dinner rolls
1 c. seasoned stuffing mix

Cream 2 tablespoons softened margarine and cream cheese together in bowl. Add chicken; mix well. Separate crescent rolls. Spoon 1/4 cup chicken mixture onto each roll. Wrap dough to enclose filling; seal well. Coat each roll with melted margarine then with stuffing mix. Place on baking sheet. Bake at 375 degrees for 20 minutes.

CHICKEN TETRAZZINI DELUXE

1 onion, chopped
6 tbsp. butter
1/4 c. flour
1 1/2 c. chicken broth
1 c. heavy cream
1 tsp. salt
1/8 tsp. pepper
1/2 c. dry vermouth
3/4 c. Parmesan cheese
1/2 lb. mushrooms, sliced
1 12-oz. package spaghetti, cooked
3 c. chopped cooked chicken

Saute onion in 4 tablespoons butter in skillet until tender-crisp. Blend in flour. Stir in broth and cream gradually. Bring to a boil, stirring constantly. Add salt, pepper, vermouth and 1/4 cup cheese; mix well. Saute mushrooms in 2 tablespoons butter in skillet until brown. Combine spaghetti, mushrooms and chicken in 2 1/2-quart casserole. Top with sauce and remaining 1/2 cup cheese. Bake at 375 degrees for 20 minutes or until bubbly. Yield: 6 servings.

CHICKEN-NOODLE RAMEKINS

1 1/2 c. sliced fresh mushrooms
1 tbsp. butter
1 c. chicken broth
12 sm. white onions
1 c. skim milk
1 tbsp. flour
1/4 tsp. thyme
1/8 tsp. pepper
1 1/2 c. chopped cooked chicken
1 8-oz. package fine egg
noodles, cooked

Saute mushrooms in butter in skillet for 3 minutes. Add broth and onions. Cook, covered, for 20 minutes or until onions are tender-crisp. Mix milk, flour, thyme and pepper in bowl. Stir into skillet. Cook until slightly thickened, stirring frequently. Stir in chicken. Spoon over noodles in ramekins. Bake, covered, at 375 degrees for 25 minutes. Yield: 4 servings.

Photograph for this recipe above.

91

Poultry

CHICKEN-FILLED RICE RING

1/2 c. finely chopped onion
1/2 c. finely chopped celery
1/4 c. shortening
1/3 c. flour
1 c. chicken broth
1 c. tomato juice
1/2 tsp. Worcestershire sauce
Salt and pepper to taste
1 tsp. curry powder
4 c. chopped cooked chicken
4 c. hot cooked rice

Saute onion and celery in shortening in skillet. Blend in flour. Add broth. Cook until thick, stirring constantly. Add tomato juice, Worcestershire sauce, seasonings and chicken. Heat to serving temperature. Pack rice into ring mold. Unmold on serving plate. Fill center with chicken mixture. Yield: 8 servings.

CHICKEN CACCIATORE

1 3-lb. chicken, cut up
2 tbsp. olive oil
1/4 c. butter
1/2 lb. mushrooms, sliced
1 onion, chopped
2 green peppers, chopped
2 cloves of garlic, minced
2 tbsp. chopped parsley
1/2 c. dry white wine
1 can tomato paste
1 1/2 tsp. salt
1/4 tsp. each oregano, thyme
1 tsp. basil
1 8-oz. package vermicelli, cooked

Brown chicken in mixture of olive oil and 2 tablespoons butter in skillet. Remove chicken; reserve 3 tablespoons pan drippings. Add vegetables and garlic. Saute until onion is tender, stirring constantly. Add parsley, wine, tomato paste, seasonings, 1/2 cup water and chicken. Simmer for 45 minutes, stirring occasionally. Toss vermicelli with remaining butter; place in deep serving dish. Arrange chicken over vermicelli. Spoon sauce over chicken.

SESAME-PECAN CHICKEN

1 c. biscuit mix
1 1/2 tsp. salt
2 tsp. paprika
1/2 tsp. poultry seasoning (opt.)
2 tbsp. sesame seed (opt.)
1/2 c. finely chopped pecans
1 4-lb. fryer, cut up
1/2 c. evaporated milk
1/2 c. melted butter

Combine biscuit mix, seasonings, sesame seed and pecans. Dip chicken pieces into evaporated milk. Coat with pecan mixture. Place in 9 x 13-inch baking pan. Pour butter over chicken pieces, covering completely. Bake at 375 degrees for 1 hour or until tender. Yield: 4-6 servings.

CRANBERRY CHICKEN

1 8-oz. can whole cranberry
sauce
1 1/2 tsp. melted butter
2 tbsp. brown sugar
1 13 1/2-oz. can pineapple
tidbits, drained
1 chicken, quartered

Combine cranberry sauce, butter, brown sugar and pine-apple in bowl; mix well. Place chicken in baking dish. Pour cranberry mixture over chicken. Bake at 350 degrees for 1 1/2 hours. Yield: 4 servings.

CRISPY OVEN-FRIED CHICKEN

3 lb. chicken pieces
3 c. self-rising flour
2 pkg. Italian salad dressing mix
2 env. dry tomato soup mix
1 tbsp. paprika
1 tsp. seasoned salt
Melted butter

Rinse chicken with cold water; drain. Combine dry in-gredients in bag; shake to mix. Place chicken in bag; shake to coat well. Arrange chicken in well-greased bak-ing pan. Drizzle with melted butter. Bake at 350 degrees for 1 hour. Yield: 5-6 servings.

LEMON CHICKEN

2 3-lb. chickens, quartered
Salt and pepper to taste
1 6-oz. can frozen lemonade
concentrate, thawed
6 c. cornflakes, crushed
1/2 c. butter

Season chicken with salt and pepper. Combine with lemonade concentrate in bowl; turn to coat. Marinate at room temperature for 1 hour; drain. Coat chicken with crumbs. Place in buttered baking dish. Bake at 350 de-grees for 1 hour or until brown and tender. Yield: 8 servings.

SHAMROCK CHICKEN

2 chickens, cut up
1 onion, sliced
4 celery tops
2 bay leaves
2 tsp. each MSG, salt
1/2 tsp. peppercorns
1/4 c. melted butter
1/4 c. flour
3 egg yolks
1/4 c. lemon juice
1/2 c. finely chopped parsley

Combine chicken, onion, celery tops, bay leaves, MSG, salt, peppercorns and 3 cups water in large saucepan. Simmer for 1 hour or until tender. Place on heated serv-ing platter. Strain broth, reserving 3 cups. Blend butter and flour in saucepan. Stir in reserved broth gradually. Bring to a boil, stirring constantly. Stir hot sauce into mixture of egg yolks and lemon juice; stir egg yolks into hot sauce. Heat to boiling point, stirring constantly. Stir in parsley. Serve over chicken.

Poultry

SAFFRON CHICKEN PILAF

2 onions, sliced
1 1/2 c. oil
2 sticks cinnamon
3 lb. chicken thighs
1 1/2 tsp. garlic powder
1 1/2 tsp. each ginger,
coriander
2 tsp. salt
1/4 tsp. turmeric
1 tomato, quartered
1 c. yogurt
3 lb. long grain rice, cooked
1/4 tsp. saffron
1/2 c. milk

Saute onions in oil in skillet until golden. Add cinnamon and chicken. Saute until lightly browned. Stir in next 5 seasonings and tomato. Simmer for 15 minutes or until chicken is tender. Stir in yogurt. Layer half the rice and chicken mixture in casserole. Spread remaining rice over chicken. Stir saffron into milk. Pour over layers. Bake, covered, at 350 degrees for 35 to 40 minutes.

SPICY SPANISH CHICKEN

1   2 1/2-lb. chicken, cut up
1/2 c. chopped onion
2 cloves of garlic, minced
2 tbsp. minced parsley
1 1/2 tsp. salt
1/4 c. oil
2 tbsp. margarine
2 onions, thinly sliced
2 green peppers, sliced
2 stalks celery, chopped
2   15-oz. cans tomatoes
1 3/4 c. rice
2 1/2 c. chicken broth
1 tsp. saffron

Brown chicken with chopped onion, 1 clove of garlic, parsley and salt in 3 tablespoons oil in skillet. Remove chicken. Add margarine, 1 clove of garlic, sliced onions, green peppers and celery. Saute until lightly browned. Add tomatoes. Simmer for 30 minutes. Saute rice in 1 tablespoon oil in saucepan for about 2 minutes or until cream colored, stirring constantly. Add chicken broth. Simmer, covered, for 20 minutes. Stir in saffron. Layer rice, chicken and tomato sauce in casserole. Bake, covered, at 350 degrees for 25 minutes. Garnish with green peas, pimentos and boiled egg slices. Yield: 6-8 servings.

CREAMED CHICKEN LIVERS

4 slices bacon
1/2 lb. chicken livers
2 tbsp. flour
Dash of pepper
1 tbsp. chopped onion
1 can cream of mushroom soup
1 c. hot cooked rice

Cook bacon in skillet until crisp. Remove from skillet. Drain, reserving drippings. Coat chicken livers with mixture of flour and pepper. Brown with onion in 2 tablespoons reserved bacon drippings. Cook, covered, over low heat for 8 to 10 minutes. Blend soup with 1/4 cup water; stir into liver mixture. Heat to serving temperature. Spoon over rice; top with bacon strips.

GOURMET CHICKEN LIVERS WITH MUSHROOMS

1/2 lb. chicken livers
2 tbsp. butter
1   16-oz. can sliced mushrooms,
drained
1/4 c. chopped green onions
1/2 c. sour cream
1 1/2 tsp. soy sauce
1 tbsp. chili sauce
Dash of pepper

Saute chicken livers in butter in covered skillet over medium heat for 5 minutes or until no longer pink, stirring occasionally. Add mushrooms and onions. Cook for several minutes longer. Combine remaining ingredients in bowl; mix well. Add to chicken livers. Heat to serving temperature. Serve on toast points. Yield: 4 servings.

CHICKEN LIVERS IN PATTY SHELLS

1 lb. chicken livers
1/4 c. finely chopped onion
1 tsp. salt
Dash of pepper
1/3 c. butter
1 c. sliced fresh mushrooms
1 tbsp. flour
1 c. half and half
2 tbsp. Cognac (opt.)
4 patty shells
4 crisp bacon curls

Saute chicken livers with onion, salt and pepper in butter in skillet for 5 to 6 minutes. Add mushrooms. Cook for 3 to 4 minutes longer. Remove livers from pan. Blend in flour. Stir in half and half. Cook over low heat until sauce is thickened, stirring constantly. Add Cognac and chicken livers. Serve in patty shells. Top with crisp bacon curls. Yield: 4 servings.

Photograph for this recipe on page 82.

TURKEY INDIENNE

1/2 c. chopped green pepper
2 tbsp. shortening
2 c. flour
1 can mushroom soup
1/2 tsp. curry powder
2 tbsp. dry onion soup mix
2 c. chopped cooked turkey
1/4 c. chopped almonds
1 c. bean sprouts (opt.)

Saute green pepper in shortening in skillet until tender. Blend flour with 1/2 cup water in bowl. Stir into skillet with next 3 ingredients. Cook until thick, stirring constantly. Add turkey, almonds and bean sprouts; mix well. Simmer for 10 minutes. Serve over rice. Yield: 4-6 servings.

Poultry

SMOKED TURKEY

1 13-lb. turkey
Dry white wine
2 c. melted margarine
1 c. lemon juice
1 c. Worcestershire sauce
1 tbsp. salt
Red pepper to taste
Tabasco sauce to taste
1 tbsp. paprika
1 tsp. MSG
1/4 c. dry Sherry

Place turkey in deep roasting pan. Fill cavity with 1/2 inch white wine. Combine remaining ingredients except Sherry in saucepan. Bring to a boil. Stir in Sherry; mix well. Cook turkey over hot coals and hickory chips in barbecue grill with hood closed for 4 to 6 hours or until turkey tests done. Baste frequently with Sherry sauce during cooking.

TURKEY CRESCENT AMANDINE

3 c. chopped cooked turkey
1 can cream of mushroom soup
1 8-oz. can sliced water chestnuts, drained
1 4-oz. can sliced mushrooms, drained
1/2 c. each chopped celery, onion
2/3 c. mayonnaise
1 can refrigerator crescent dinner rolls
2/3 c. shredded Swiss cheese
1/2 c. slivered almonds
1/4 c. melted margarine

Combine turkey, soup, vegetables and mayonnaise in saucepan; mix well. Cook over medium heat until bubbly, stirring frequently. Spoon into 9 x 13-inch baking dish. Unroll crescent roll dough. Place over turkey mixture. Sprinkle mixture of cheese, almonds and margarine over top. Bake at 375 degrees for 25 minutes or until golden brown. Yield: 6-8 servings.

FANTASTIC TURKEY CASSEROLE

1 lb. mushrooms, sliced
1 onion, chopped
3 tbsp. butter
2 tsp. salt
1/4 tsp. pepper
1 pkg. white and wild rice mix with seasoning packet
3 c. diced cooked turkey
1/2 c. chopped blanched almonds
3 c. chicken broth
1 1/2 c. heavy cream

Saute mushrooms and onion in butter in skillet for 10 minutes. Combine with remaining ingredients in order listed in large greased casserole; mix well. Bake at 350 degrees for 1 1/2 hours. Yield: 6-8 servings.

ORIENTAL TURKEY

1 onion, sliced
1 4-oz. can mushrooms, drained
1/8 tsp. ground ginger
1 tsp. oil
1 can cream of celery soup
1 c. chopped cooked turkey
1 5-oz. can sliced water chestnuts, drained
1/3 c. cooked chopped spinach
1 tbsp. soy sauce

Saute onion, mushrooms and ginger in oil in skillet until onion is tender. Stir in soup, 2/3 cup water, turkey, water chestnuts, spinach and soy sauce. Cook over low heat for 10 minutes, stirring frequently. Serve with rice. Yield: 4 servings.

OVERNIGHT TURKEY AND DRESSING

1 pkg. herb-seasoned stuffing mix
1 stick margarine, melted
3 c. chopped cooked turkey
1/2 c. chopped onion
1/2 c. mayonnaise
3 eggs, beaten
1 1/2 c. milk
2 cans cream of celery soup

Combine stuffing mix, margarine and 1 cup water in bowl; mix well. Combine turkey, onion and mayonnaise in bowl; mix well. Layer half the stuffing mixture, all the turkey mixture and remaining stuffing in 9 x 13-inch baking dish. Mix eggs with milk; pour over layers. Chill, tightly covered, overnight. Let stand at room temperature for 1 hour. Bake, uncovered, at 350 degrees for 25 minutes. Spread soup over top. Bake for 40 minutes longer. Yield: 6 servings.

TURKEY TWISTER

1 c. chopped celery
1/2 c. chopped green pepper
1/2 c. chopped onion
1 1/2 c. bouillon
1 8-oz. package macaroni twists, cooked
1 can cream of mushroom soup
1/2 c. milk
1 c. shredded cheese
3 c. chopped cooked turkey
1 sm. jar pimentos, drained
1 tsp. salt
1/4 tsp. pepper
1/2 c. cracker crumbs
2 tbsp. butter
Paprika

Combine celery, green pepper, onion and bouillon in saucepan. Simmer until tender. Stir in macaroni, soup, milk, cheese, turkey, pimentos and seasonings. Pour into large casserole. Top with crumbs; dot with butter. Sprinkle with paprika. Bake at 350 degrees for 30 minutes or until golden brown. Yield: 12 servings.

Seafood

The lakes, rivers and seas are very generous to America. Our expansive waters yield a large and varied supply of fish and shellfish for our dining pleasure.

Modern developments in packaging and transportation have made it possible for every section of America to have a plentiful supply of fish and shellfish readily available. Homemakers everywhere can now bring to their family and friends the delicious seafood dishes for which coastal areas have long been famous.

Your cooking can become just as legendary with the following collection of recipes that make the most of the flavor of fish. You'll find superb recipes for fish fillets of many types and tastes. From flounder to snapper, salmon to sole — discover perfect seasoning combinations and cooking directions! Plus, the varied collection of shellfish recipes make excellent company fare, like the "Tipsy Crab Casserole" or "Lobster Cantonese." And crepe specialties which look so elegant yet are so easy to prepare, will whet the appetite of everyone.

Whether you fry your fish, bake or stuff it with a wonderful mixture, then serve it elegantly whole, you will be guaranteed success with these spectacular recipes.

← GRAPEFRUIT SAUCE FOR SEAFOOD, Recipe on page 111.

Seafood

FLORENTINE FISH FILLETS

1 1/2 tbsp. flour
1/2 tsp. salt
1/8 tsp. pepper
1 1/2 tbsp. melted butter
1 c. milk
1/2 c. grated cheese
2 pkg. frozen chopped spinach,
cooked, drained
2 lb. fish fillets

Blend flour and seasonings into melted butter in sauce-pan. Stir in milk gradually. Cook until thick, stirring constantly. Add cheese. Cook over very low heat until cheese is melted, stirring constantly. Spread spinach over bottom of 9 x 13-inch baking dish. Cover with sauce. Top with fillets. Bake at 375 degrees for 30 minutes. Yield: 6 servings.

BAKED FLOUNDER IN WINE SAUCE

3 c. thinly sliced cooked
potatoes
1 4-oz. can sliced mushrooms,
drained
1 tsp. paprika
1/2 tsp. salt
1/4 tsp. pepper
1 c. sour cream
1/2 c. dry white wine
2 tbsp. flour
1 tbsp. grated onion
2 lb. flounder fillets

Layer potatoes and mushrooms in greased casserole. Sprinkle half the combined seasonings over vegetables. Mix sour cream, wine, flour and onion in bowl. Spread half the mixture over mushrooms. Arrange flounder over top. Sprinkle with remaining seasonings. Spread remaining sour cream mixture over flounder. Bake at 350 degrees for 35 to 45 minutes or until flounder flakes easily. Let stand for 10 minutes before serving. Yield: 6 servings.

SAUCY FLOUNDER

1 to 1 1/2 pkg. frozen flounder
fillets, thawed
1 lg. can artichoke hearts,
drained
1 can mushroom soup
1 c. heavy cream
Sherry to taste
2 8-oz. packages shredded
Cheddar cheese
1 8-oz. package herb-seasoned
stuffing mix

Roll up each piece of flounder; place in casserole. Arrange artichoke hearts around flounder. Blend soup, cream and Sherry in bowl. Cover flounder completely with soup mixture. Sprinkle with cheese. Top with stuffing mix. Bake, covered, at 350 degrees for 30 minutes. Bake, uncovered, for 30 minutes longer. Yield: 6 servings.

BROILED FISH FILLETS

2 lb. fish fillets
2 tbsp. lime juice
3 tbsp. mayonnaise
1/2 c. Parmesan cheese
1/4 c. butter
3 tbsp. chopped green onion
Dash of Tabasco sauce

Arrange fillets in 10 x 15-inch broiler pan. Brush with lime juice. Broil for 6 to 8 minutes or until fish flakes easily. Combine remaining ingredients in bowl; mix well. Spread over fillets. Broil for 2 to 3 minutes longer. Yield: 6 servings.

FILLETS ELEGANTE

1 lb. frozen fish fillets, partially thawed
Pepper
2 tbsp. butter
1 10-oz. can frozen cream of shrimp soup, thawed
1/4 c. Parmesan cheese
1/2 tsp. paprika

Arrange fillets in buttered 9-inch round baking dish. Season with pepper; dot with butter. Spread soup over top. Sprinkle with cheese and paprika. Bake at 400 degrees for 25 minutes or until fish flakes easily.

BAKED GROUPER FILLETS

1 lemon, sliced
1 onion, sliced
Salt and pepper to taste
2 lb. fresh grouper fillets
1 c. sour cream
1 tsp. prepared mustard
1/4 tsp. paprika

Arrange lemon and onion slices in greased baking pan. Sprinkle with salt and pepper. Top with grouper fillets. Bake, covered, at 400 degrees for 20 minutes. Combine sour cream, mustard, paprika and salt in bowl; mix well. Spread over fillets. Broil 3 inches from heat source until brown. Yield: 4 servings.

SEAFOOD-STUFFED SALMON

1/2 lb. crab meat, flaked
1/2 lb. cooked shrimp, chopped
2 tbsp. parsley flakes
1/2 c. chopped celery
1/4 c. chopped onion
4 c. bread crumbs
3/4 c. melted butter
1/2 c. (or more) chicken bouillon
1 4 to 6-lb. salmon
1/4 c. fresh lemon juice

Combine first 6 ingredients with 1/2 cup butter and enough bouillon to moisten in bowl; mix well. Fill salmon cavity; fasten with skewers. Place in baking pan. Bake at 300 degrees for 2 hours, basting several times with mixture of lemon juice and 1/4 cup butter. Yield: 8-10 servings.

Seafood

PARTY SALMON CREPES

1 c. pancake mix
3 1/2 c. milk
5 tbsp. melted butter
1 egg, slightly beaten
1/4 c. minced onion
1/2 c. chopped celery
1/4 c. flour
1/2 tsp. salt
2/3 c. grated Parmesan cheese
2 c. cooked salmon
1 8-oz. can peas, drained

Combine pancake mix, 1 1/4 cups milk, 1 tablespoon butter and egg in bowl; mix until just moistened. Pour 1/3 cup batter at a time onto hot griddle. Bake until browned on both sides. Saute onion and celery in 1/4 cup butter in skillet until tender. Blend in flour and salt to make smooth paste. Add 2 1/4 cups milk gradually, stirring constantly. Cook until thick, stirring constantly. Add cheese. Cook until cheese is melted, stirring constantly. Set aside 1 1/3 cups sauce; keep warm. Add salmon and peas to remaining sauce. Cook until heated through, stirring constantly. Spread pancakes with salmon mixture; roll up. Place in 9 x 11-inch baking dish. Bake at 350 degrees for 15 to 20 minutes or until heated through. Serve with reserved sauce.

CRAB-STUFFED SOLE

1/4 c. melted butter
1/2 tsp. seasoned salt
1 tbsp. lemon juice
1/4 tsp. horseradish
5 drops of Tabasco sauce
1/3 c. heavy cream
1 can crab meat
4 sole fillets

Combine 2 tablespoons butter, seasoned salt, 1 teaspoon lemon juice, horseradish and Tabasco sauce in small saucepan. Stir in cream. Heat just to boiling point, stirring constantly. Do not boil. Remove from heat. Add crab meat; mix well. Place 2 fillets in greased shallow casserole. Spread crab meat mixture over top. Top with remaining fillets. Mix remaining 2 tablespoons butter and 2 teaspoons lemon juice in small bowl. Drizzle over fillets. Bake at 350 degrees for 30 minutes.

FILLET OF SOLE WITH DILL SAUCE

1 lb. fillet of sole
1 med. carrot, cut into julienne strips
1 sm. zucchini, cut into julienne strips
2 green onions, cut into julienne strips
1/2 tsp. salt
2 tsp. cornstarch
1/4 c. sour cream
1/4 tsp. dillweed

Cut fillets into serving pieces. Arrange in shallow greased baking dish. Bake at 400 degrees for 10 minutes or until fish flakes easily. Stir-fry vegetables with salt in large saucepan for 2 minutes. Add 1 cup water. Simmer, covered, for 5 minutes. Remove vegetables to bowl with slotted spoon. Blend cornstarch with 1 tablespoon water; stir into vegetable pan juices. Cook until thick, stirring constantly; remove from heat. Stir in sour cream and dillweed. Spoon half the dill sauce into serving plate; arrange fish over sauce. Top with vegetables. Stir fish pan juices into remaining dill sauce. Spoon over vegetables. Yield: 4 servings.

Recipes on pages 160, 170, 171, 172 and 173. →

KEY LIME RED SNAPPER

4 med. red snapper fillets
1 c. Key lime juice
1 1/2 c. Italian bread crumbs
Dash of salt
Dash of lemon-pepper seasoning
1 egg, slightly beaten
4 cloves of garlic, crushed
1/2 lb. butter, melted

Marinate fillets in lime juice in covered glass bowl in refrigerator for 1 hour. Mix bread crumbs, salt and lemon-pepper. Dip fillets in beaten egg; coat with bread crumb mixture. Saute garlic in butter in skillet until browned; remove garlic. Cook fillets in garlic butter until browned and easily flaked. Yield: 4 servings.

TROUT FARCIE

1 green onion, finely chopped
6 tbsp. butter
1 lb. crab meat
2 c. half and half
1 c. crushed saltines
2 egg yolks
Salt and pepper to taste
4 trout fillets
1/2 c. grated Swiss cheese

Saute onion in 1 tablespoon butter in skillet until tender-crisp. Stir in crab meat and half and half. Simmer for 3 minutes. Add saltines, egg yolks, salt and pepper; mix well. Cook until heated through. Brown trout in remaining 5 tablespoons butter in skillet. Season with salt and pepper. Place in 9 x 9-inch baking dish. Pour warm crab mixture over top. Sprinkle with cheese. Broil until cheese is melted and browned. Yield: 4 servings.

TUNA WITH CURRIED ALMOND RICE

1/2 tsp. curry powder
1 c. blanched slivered almonds
6 tbsp. butter
2 c. hot cooked rice
1 tomato, peeled, chopped
4 peppercorns
1 clove of garlic, crushed
1 tsp. Worcestershire sauce
1/2 tsp. salt
1/4 tsp. paprika
1/4 c. flour
2 c. milk
1 7-oz. can tuna, drained

Saute curry powder and almonds in 2 tablespoons butter in saucepan until almonds are golden brown, stirring constantly. Blend into rice lightly; set aside and keep warm. Melt 4 tablespoons butter in saucepan. Add tomato, peppercorns, garlic, Worcestershire sauce, salt and paprika. Cook, covered, over low heat for 5 minutes or until tomato is soft. Remove peppercorns and garlic. Blend in flour. Stir in milk. Cook until thickened, stirring constantly. Add tuna. Cook until heated through. Serve over hot Curried Almond Rice. Yield: 4 servings.

+ Recipes on pages 158, 160 and 168.

Seafood

CLAM LINGUINE

2 onions, chopped
1 lb. mushrooms, sliced
6 to 8 cloves of garlic, minced
4 tsp. olive oil
2 10-oz. cans baby clams
2 6-oz. cans minced clams
1 can clam juice
Salt and pepper to taste
1/2 tsp. oregano
1 pkg. linguine, cooked
Parmesan cheese

Saute onions, mushrooms and garlic in olive oil in skillet until golden. Stir in clams, clam juice and seasonings. Simmer, covered, for 20 minutes. Serve over linguine. Top with Parmesan cheese. Note: Thicken with mixture of cornstarch and a small amount of water if desired. Yield: 6-8 servings.

BAKED STUFFED QUAHOGS

1 c. seasoned bread crumbs
Juice of 1 lemon
1 tsp. garlic powder
1 tbsp. parsley flakes
1/4 tsp. cayenne pepper
1/3 c. olive oil
Salt and pepper to taste
12 quahogs
1/4 c. bread crumbs
Butter

Mix first 6 ingredients and salt and pepper in bowl. Put quahogs through food grinder; reserve liquid. Add reserved liquid and a small amount of water to seasoned bread crumb mixture; stir until crumbly. Stir in quahogs and 1/4 cup bread crumbs. Spoon into quahog shells. Dot with butter. Bake at 400 degrees for 30 minutes. Yield: 6-8 servings.

SPAGHETTI WITH CLAM SAUCE

1 clove of garlic, chopped
1/2 c. chopped green pepper
2 tbsp. margarine, melted
1/2 c. clam juice
2 7 1/2-oz. cans minced clams, drained
2 8-oz. cans tomato sauce
1/8 tsp. pepper
3/4 tsp. celery salt
Italian seasoning to taste
1 lb. spaghetti, cooked

Saute garlic and green pepper in margarine in skillet until tender. Add clam juice, clams, tomato sauce and seasonings. Cook over low heat for 10 minutes, stirring frequently. Serve over hot spaghetti. Yield: 8 servings.

Seafood

NEW ENGLAND CLAM FRITTERS

2 eggs, lightly beaten
1 c. chopped clams
1 tsp. salt
1/8 tsp. pepper
1/2 c. milk
1/2 c. clam juice
2 c. flour
1 tbsp. baking powder
Oil for deep frying

Combine all ingredients except oil in order given in bowl; mix well after each addition. Drop by spoonfuls into deep 375-degree oil. Fry until dark brown. Drain on paper towels.

DELICIOUS DEVILED CRAB

1/4 c. flour
Butter
2 c. milk
1 lb. white crab meat
1 lb. crab claw meat
8 hard-boiled eggs, mashed
Bread crumbs
3 stalks celery, finely chopped
1 onion, grated
3 tbsp. catsup
Juice of 1 lemon
3 tbsp. Worcestershire sauce
1 tsp. each pepper, cayenne pepper
Salt to taste

Blend flour and 1/4 cup melted butter in saucepan. Stir in milk. Cook until thick, stirring constantly. Add crab meat, eggs, 1 cup bread crumbs, celery, onion, catsup, lemon juice and seasonings; mix well. Spoon into baking shells. Sprinkle with bread crumbs; dot with butter. Bake at 450 degrees until browned. Yield: 12 servings.

TIPSY CRAB CASSEROLE

6 tbsp. butter, melted
2 tbsp. flour
1/2 c. cream
1/2 tsp. each salt and pepper
Dash of red pepper
1/2 tsp. dry mustard
Dash each of Tabasco sauce, Worcestershire sauce
2 tbsp. Sherry
2 tbsp. Bourbon
1 lb. back fin crab meat
1/2 c. bread crumbs

Blend 1/4 cup butter and flour in saucepan. Stir in cream. Cook until thick, stirring constantly. Stir in next 6 seasonings, Sherry and Bourbon. Add crab meat; mix well. Spoon into buttered baking dish. Toss bread crumbs with 2 tablespoons butter. Sprinkle over casserole. Bake at 350 degrees until browned.

Seafood

SHERRIED CRAB CASSEROLE

1/4 lb. mushrooms, sliced
1/2 c. butter
1/4 c. flour
1/2 tsp. salt
1/8 tsp. pepper
2 1/2 c. milk
1/2 c. Parmesan cheese
1 lb. fresh crab meat
3 tbsp. Sherry
1/4 c. cracker crumbs

Saute mushrooms in 1 tablespoon butter in skillet for 10 minutes. Blend 1/4 cup melted butter with flour, salt and pepper in saucepan. Stir in milk gradually. Cook until thick, stirring constantly. Add cheese, mushrooms, crab meat and Sherry; mix well. Spoon into buttered casserole. Sprinkle with cracker crumbs. Dot with remaining 3 tablespoons butter. Bake at 350 degrees for 15 minutes. Garnish with paprika. Yield: 6 servings.

CRAB IMPERIAL

1 lb. back fin crab meat
1/4 c. melted margarine
2 tbsp. flour
1 c. cream
2 egg yolks, beaten
1/4 tsp. each cayenne pepper,
salt
1 tsp. horseradish
2 tbsp. Sherry
Paprika

Place crab meat in shallow baking dish. Blend margarine and flour in saucepan. Stir in cream. Bring to a boil over low heat, stirring constantly. Simmer for 2 minutes, stirring constantly. Stir a small amount of hot mixture into egg yolks; stir egg yolks into hot mixture. Add cayenne pepper, salt and horseradish. Cook for 3 minutes, stirring constantly. Remove from heat; stir in Sherry. Spoon over crab meat. Sprinkle with paprika. Bake at 350 degrees for 15 minutes. Yield: 6-8 servings.

LOBSTER CANTONESE

2 tbsp. preserved black beans,
washed, drained
2 cloves of garlic, finely chopped
4 tsp. soy sauce
1 c. ground pork
1 1/2 tsp. salt
1/2 tsp. sugar
2 tbsp. oil
1/8 tsp. pepper
2 lb. large lobster tails,
cut into 1/2-in. slices
2 green onions, cut into
1-in. pieces
1 c. chicken broth
2 tbsp. cornstarch
2 eggs, beaten

Mash black beans and garlic together in bowl; add 1 tablespoon soy sauce. Combine pork with 1/2 teaspoon salt, sugar and 1 teaspoon soy sauce in bowl; marinate for 15 minutes. Heat oil in skillet. Add remaining 1 teaspoon salt and pepper; add pork. Stir-fry for 4 minutes. Add lobster. Stir-fry for 2 minutes or until heated through. Add green onions and black bean mixture; mix well. Add broth. Cook, covered, for 10 minutes. Thicken sauce with cornstarch blended with 2 tablespoons water. Remove from heat. Stir in eggs. Season with remaining soy sauce. Yield: 6-8 servings.

LOBSTER CREPES

3 eggs
Salt
Flour
3/4 c. milk
1/2 c. butter
6 4-oz. frozen rock lobster
tails
1/2 lb. mushrooms, sliced
1 clove of garlic, crushed
1/4 c. each minced fresh
parsley, spinach
1 can chicken broth
1 c. light cream
Pepper

Beat eggs and 1/4 teaspoon salt together in medium bowl. Add 3/4 cup flour gradually; beat until smooth. Add milk and 1/4 cup melted butter; beat well. Chill, covered, for 1 hour or longer. Place lightly oiled 8-inch crepe pan over medium heat. Pour in enough batter to cover bottom of pan with very thin layer. Cook until batter is set and edges turn golden brown. Turn over gently with spatula. Cook for several seconds longer. Repeat with remaining batter. Stack crepes between waxed paper. Cook rock lobster tails in boiling salted water in large saucepan for 2 minutes. Drain; rinse with cold water. Remove shells and dice meat. Saute mushrooms and garlic in 1/4 cup butter in skillet for 5 minutes; stir in parsley, spinach and 1/3 cup flour. Stir in broth and cream gradually. Cook over low heat until sauce bubbles and thickens, stirring constantly. Stir in lobster. Season with salt and pepper to taste. Heat until bubbly. Heat crepes in 250-degree oven for 5 minutes. Spoon sauce onto each crepe; roll up. Place on oven-proof platter; keep warm. Garnish with chopped parsley. Yield: 6 servings.

LOBSTER NUGGETS

6 to 8 lobster tails
Lime juice
2 eggs, beaten
2 c. cracker meal
Oil for deep frying

Remove lobster meat from shells; split lengthwise. Cut each piece into thirds. Marinate lobster in lime juice in glass bowl in refrigerator for 1 hour. Drain. Dip lobster in egg. Coat with cracker meal. Deep-fry in hot oil for 1 to 2 minutes until golden. Do not overcook. Yield: 4 servings.

BOTANY BAY OYSTERS

4 doz. oysters
1/4 c. dry Sherry
6 tbsp. butter
1 clove of garlic, crushed
1 1/3 c. fresh white bread crumbs
1 1/2 tbsp. freshly chopped parsley
2 tsp. finely grated lemon rind
Salt and freshly ground pepper
to taste

Arrange oysters on 4 oyster plates; drizzle with Sherry. Heat butter in skillet until bubbly; add garlic. Saute until golden. Add remaining ingredients. Saute until bread crumbs are golden. Spoon over oysters. Bake at 400 degrees for 5 minutes or until heated through. Garnish with lemon slices. Serve immediately.

Seafood

DEVILED OYSTERS

2 tbsp. melted butter
2 tbsp. (heaping) flour
3/4 c. milk
1/2 tsp. salt
Pepper to taste
1 tsp. Worcestershire sauce
1 egg yolk, beaten
1 pt. fresh oysters
Paprika
Buttered bread crumbs

Blend butter and flour in top of double boiler. Add milk and seasonings. Cook until thick, stirring constantly. Stir a small amount of hot mixture into egg yolk; stir egg yolk into hot mixture. Parboil oysters in oyster liquor until curled; drain and cut into bite-sized pieces. Add to sauce. Spoon into buttered casserole. Sprinkle with paprika; top with bread crumbs. Bake at 350 degrees until brown. Yield: 4 servings.

COQUILLE ST. JACQUES

6 tbsp. butter
3 tbsp. flour
1 tsp. salt
1/8 tsp. white pepper
2 c. light cream
1/4 c. finely chopped onion
1/2 lb. scallops, sliced
1/2 c. sliced mushrooms
3/4 lb. cooked shrimp
1/2 lb. crab meat
2 tbsp. Sherry
5 tbsp. bread crumbs

Blend 1/4 cup butter with flour, salt and white pepper in skillet; stir in cream gradually. Simmer until sauce is smooth and thickened, stirring constantly. Saute onion in remaining 2 tablespoons butter in small skillet. Add scallops. Saute for 5 minutes; remove onion and scallops. Add mushrooms. Saute for 3 minutes. Combine onion, scallops, mushrooms, shrimp, crab meat, Sherry and sauce; mix lightly. Spoon into individual baking dishes; sprinkle with bread crumbs. Bake at 400 degrees for 15 minutes or until heated through.

SCALLOPS VERMICELLI

1 lb. mushrooms, quartered
3/4 c. unsalted butter
Salt and pepper to taste
4 shallots, minced
2 cloves of garlic, minced
6 scallions, minced
1 lb. bay scallops
6 tbsp. vermouth
1 tbsp. minced parsley
1 lb. vermicelli

Saute mushrooms in half the butter in skillet. Season with salt and pepper; remove mushrooms. Add remaining butter to skillet. Saute shallots, garlic and scallions lightly. Add scallops and vermouth. Cook until heated through. Add parsley and mushrooms. Cook vermicelli in boiling salted water in saucepan for about 5 minutes; drain. Add to scallop mixture. Cook for 3 or 4 minutes or until liquid is absorbed, stirring constantly. Serve with Parmesan cheese and hot pepper flakes.

SCALLOPS AMANDINE

3/4 lb. fresh scallops,
thickly sliced
1/3 c. flour
1/4 tsp. salt
1/4 c. butter
3 tbsp. slivered almonds
1 tbsp. lemon juice
1 tbsp. snipped parsley

Coat scallops with flour seasoned with salt. Saute in 2 tablespoons butter in skillet until golden brown. Remove to warm platter. Saute almonds in 2 tablespoons butter until golden brown. Stir in lemon juice and parsley. Serve over scallops. Yield: 4 servings.

SHRIMP CREOLE

1/2 c. flour
1/2 c. oil
2 16-oz. cans tomatoes
1 c. chopped onion
1 c. chopped green pepper
1 c. chopped celery
2 cloves of garlic, crushed
3 tbsp. parsley flakes
4 tsp. salt
3 lb. shrimp

Brown flour in oil in skillet, stirring constantly. Stir in remaining ingredients except shrimp. Cook for 20 minutes, stirring frequently; reduce heat. Add shrimp. Simmer until shrimp are pink. Serve over rice. Yield: 10 servings.

GRAPEFRUIT SAUCE FOR SEAFOOD

1 c. butter
6 tbsp. frozen grapefruit juice
concentrate, thawed
1 tsp. grated grapefruit rind
1/4 c. chopped parsley
2 tbsp. chopped dillweed
2 tbsp. chopped chives
1/4 tsp. salt

Melt butter in small saucepan. Stir in remaining ingredients. Heat to serving temperature. Serve with oysters, clams and shrimp. Yield: 4-6 servings.

Photograph for this recipe on page 98.

SHRIMP ALOUETTE

1 lb. shrimp, shelled
2 tbsp. butter
4 oz. Alouette cheese
Salt and pepper to taste

Saute shrimp in butter in skillet until just pink. Add cheese. Cook until melted. Season with salt and pepper. Serve hot over rice or noodles. Garnish with parsley and lemon wedges.

Seafood

SHRIMP WITH SPAGHETTI AND MUSHROOMS

2 cloves of garlic, minced
6 lg. mushrooms, chopped
1 lb. shrimp, shelled, chopped
1/2 c. butter
1 tsp. salt
1 tsp. MSG
1/4 tsp. pepper
1 8-oz. package spaghetti,
cooked
1/4 c. Parmesan cheese

Saute garlic, mushrooms and shrimp in butter in large skillet over low heat for 5 minutes or until shrimp turn pink. Sprinkle with seasonings. Add spaghetti and cheese; toss gently. Cook until heated through. Garnish with chopped parsley. Serve with additional cheese.

Photograph for this recipe above.

ELEGANT SHRIMP WITH PASTA

1/4 c. heavy cream
1 1/2 c. sour cream
1 tbsp. soy sauce
1/2 tsp. Worcestershire sauce
1/2 tsp. dry mustard
1 tsp. dillweed
1/4 tsp. white pepper
1/2 lb. small shrimp
1 lb. fresh pasta, cooked

Combine cream, sour cream and seasonings in saucepan. Heat until very warm. Add shrimp. Cook until shrimp turn pink. Serve over hot pasta. Yield: 4 servings.

SHRIMP A LA GRECQUE

2 onions, chopped
1 clove of garlic, minced
3 tbsp. olive oil
2 2-lb. cans Italian tomatoes
1 can tomato paste
3 doz. shrimp, shelled
1 stick butter
3/4 c. ouzo
Chopped parsley
Feta cheese

Saute onions and garlic in olive oil in skillet until tender. Stir in tomatoes and tomato paste. Cook until thickened. Saute shrimp in butter in skillet until pink. Pour ouzo over shrimp; ignite. Add shrimp to tomato sauce. Cook for 5 minutes. Pour into serving dish. Top with parsley and feta cheese. Serve with rice. Yield: 4-6 servings.

SHRIMP CACCIATORE

1/2 c. each minced onion, green pepper
2 cloves of garlic, minced
1/3 c. olive oil
1 20-oz. can tomatoes
1 8-oz. can tomato sauce
1/2 c. red wine
2 tsp. salt
1/4 tsp. pepper
1/2 tsp. allspice
1 bay leaf, crumbled
1/4 tsp. thyme
Dash of cayenne pepper
2 lb. shrimp, shelled, cooked

Saute onion, green pepper and garlic in olive oil in skillet until onion is tender. Add remaining ingredients except shrimp. Simmer for 20 minutes. Add shrimp. Heat just to serving temperature.

Seafood

GULF SHRIMP AND CRAB AU GRATIN

3/4 c. butter
6 tbsp. flour
3 c. milk
1 lb. lump crab meat
1 lb. shrimp, cooked
3 oz. sharp cheese, shredded
Salt and pepper to taste
1/2 c. cracker crumbs
1/2 c. Romano cheese
1 tbsp. paprika

Mix 6 tablespoons melted butter and flour in medium saucepan. Cook for 1 minute. Stir in milk. Cook until thick, stirring constantly. Saute crab meat and shrimp in 3 tablespoons butter in saucepan. Add white sauce, sharp cheese, salt and pepper. Cook until heated through, stirring constantly. Spoon into casserole. Top with cracker crumbs, Romano cheese and paprika. Dot with remaining 3 tablespoons butter. Bake at 350 degrees until golden brown. Yield: 6 servings.

SHRIMP AND LOBSTER FIESTA

1/2 c. chopped onion
1 clove of garlic, minced
1 tbsp. butter
1 can cream of mushroom soup
2 tbsp. dry white wine
1 c. chopped cooked shrimp
1/2 c. tomatoes, drained
3 tbsp. chopped parsley
1/8 tsp. marjoram
2 c. cooked noodles
2 lobster tails, cooked, sliced

Saute onion and garlic in butter in skillet until tender. Combine with 1/2 cup water and remaining ingredients except lobster in 1 1/2-quart casserole; mix well. Arrange lobster on top. Brush with additional butter. Bake at 350 degrees for 30 minutes or until bubbly. Yield: 4 servings.

SHRIMP AND SCALLOPS GRUYERE

1 lb. fresh scallops
1 tbsp. lemon juice
1/2 lb. mushrooms, sliced
2 tbsp. chopped green pepper
Butter, melted
3/4 c. flour
3 c. milk
12 oz. Gruyere cheese, cubed
1/2 c. dry white wine
1/4 tsp. each garlic powder, MSG
1/4 tsp. white pepper
1/4 tsp. dry mustard
2 tsp. tomato paste
1 lb. cooked shrimp

Poach scallops in salted water with 1 teaspoon lemon juice in saucepan for 10 minutes; drain. Saute mushrooms and green pepper in 2 tablespoons butter in skillet until tender; set aside. Combine 3/4 cup melted butter and flour in top of double boiler. Stir in milk gradually. Cook until thick, stirring constantly. Add cheese. Cook until cheese is melted, stirring constantly. Stir in wine. Add seasonings, 2 teaspoons lemon juice, tomato paste, mushrooms and green pepper; mix well. Add scallops and shrimp; mix well. Cook over low heat for 10 to 15 minutes. Serve over rice. Yield: 6-8 servings.

Seafood

HOT SEAFOOD SALAD

1 lb. crab meat
1 lb. cooked shrimp
1 lb. lobster
2 c. mayonnaise
1/4 c. chopped onion
1/2 c. chopped green pepper
1 1/2 c. chopped celery
1/2 tsp. salt
1 tbsp. Worcestershire sauce
2 c. crushed potato chips
Paprika

Combine seafood, mayonnaise, vegetables and seasonings in bowl; mix well. Spoon into buttered 3-quart casserole. Top with potato chips. Sprinkle with paprika. Bake at 400 degrees for 20 to 25 minutes or until bubbly. Serve over rice. Yield: 12 servings.

MEDITERRANEAN SEAFOOD

4 cloves of garlic
1/2 c. olive oil
12 shrimp in shells
3 lobster tails, cut into 1-in. pieces
1 c. white vermouth
2 c. Italian tomatoes, drained
2 bay leaves
1/2 tsp. oregano
Salt and pepper to taste
12 clams, scrubbed

Saute garlic in olive oil in skillet over medium-high heat for 1 minute. Add shrimp and lobster. Saute for 1 minute. Add vermouth. Simmer for 2 to 3 minutes. Remove lobster and shrimp; set aside. Add tomatoes, bay leaves, oregano, salt, pepper and clams. Simmer for 2 to 4 minutes or until clams open. Discard bay leaves. Add lobster and shrimp. Heat to serving temperature. Spoon over hot rice in serving bowl. Garnish with parsley. Yield: 6 servings.

FROGS' LEGS GRUYERE

18 sm. frogs' legs
1/4 c. lemon juice
1/4 c. light cream
Salt and white pepper to taste
1/2 c. butter
2 tsp. minced shallots
1 tbsp. minced onion
1 c. dry white wine
1/2 c. Marsala
3 lg. oysters, minced
1/2 c. sliced sauteed mushrooms (opt.)
Dash of cayenne pepper
1/2 c. grated Gruyere cheese

Soak frogs' legs in very cold water for 3 hours; drain on cloth. Dip in mixture of lemon juice and cream. Sprinkle with salt and pepper. Melt butter in medium skillet; stir in shallots and onion. Add frog's legs. Saute over low heat for 3 minutes on each side. Add white wine and 1/4 cup Marsala. Poach gently for 15 minutes or until tender, turning once. Remove frogs' legs to ovenproof platter; strain pan juices into small saucepan. Add oysters, mushrooms and remaining 1/4 cup Marsala. Simmer for 10 minutes. Season with cayenne pepper and salt to taste. Pour sauce over frogs' legs; sprinkle with cheese. Bake at 400 degrees for 3 to 5 minutes until cheese is bubbly and lightly browned. Garnish with lemon wedges. Serve immediately. Yield: 6 servings.

Vegetables

Fresh vegetables with their rainbow of colors can be a treasure chest of different tastes. Our land offers her bounty beautifully in the wide array of vegetables that make their way to our dining tables.

No longer is the gentle art of vegetable cookery ignored or under-rated. Rather, it has become an area that good cooks love to explore.

Vegetables now come alive. They appear with intriguing sauces, nuts, mushrooms and subtle herbs and spices.

An exciting array of excellent recipes for a wide variety of vegetables appears on the following pages. Be bold; pick a vegetable you have never tried. Or learn new ways for preparing old favorites.

Choose a cauliflower specialty like "Cauliflower Puff;" perhaps a squash fritter, a corn casserole, or a blend of bright red beets. Mix bacon and beans, spinach and cottage cheese, or celery with pecans. Simmer asparagus with sesame seed . . . prepare barbecued beans the old-fashioned way . . . or explore elegant artichoke cookery. Within these pages, you'll see how cooking vegetables can become an adventure!

No matter what you choose for your entree, you can add excitement to every meal with this fabulous collection of favorite vegetable recipes.

◆ SEASONED STUFFED ZUCCHINI, Recipe on page 126.

Vegetables

ARTICHOKES ELEGANTE

1 can artichoke hearts, drained
3 hard-boiled eggs, sliced
1/2 c. sliced stuffed olives
1/4 c. sliced water chestnuts
1/2 c. grated American cheese
1 can mushroom soup
1/4 c. milk
1/2 c. buttered bread crumbs

Cut artichoke hearts in half; arrange in casserole. Layer eggs, olives, water chestnuts and cheese over artichokes. Blend soup with milk in small bowl. Pour over layers. Top with crumbs. Bake at 350 degrees until brown and bubbly. Yield: 8 servings.

SESAME ASPARAGUS

1 lb. fresh asparagus, sliced
1/4 c. unsalted butter
2 tbsp. lemon juice
2 tbsp. toasted sesame seed
2 tsp. sesame oil
Salt and pepper to taste

Cook asparagus in boiling salted water in saucepan for 3 to 4 minutes or until tender-crisp; drain. Rinse under cold water; pat dry. Melt butter in large skillet over medium heat. Stir in remaining ingredients. Add asparagus. Heat to serving temperature, stirring frequently.

SASSY LIMA BEANS

1 lb. dried baby lima beans
2 tsp. salt
1 14-oz. bottle of catsup
1 c. packed brown sugar
1 tbsp. vinegar
2 onions, chopped
4 slices bacon, chopped

Soak beans in salted water in Dutch oven overnight; drain. Add enough cold water to cover. Simmer for 1 hour. Add remaining ingredients; mix well. Bake, covered, at 325 degrees for 2 hours. Yield: 8 servings.

WESTERN-BARBECUED BEANS

1/2 lb. ground beef
1/2 lb. bacon, chopped
1/2 onion, chopped
1/4 c. each catsup, barbecue
sauce
1/2 tsp. each salt, pepper
2 tbsp. each mustard, molasses
1/2 tsp. chili powder
1 16-oz. can red kidney beans
1 16-oz. can pork and beans
1 16-oz. can lima beans

Brown ground beef, bacon and onion in skillet, stirring frequently; drain. Add remaining ingredients except beans; mix well. Stir in beans. Pour into casserole. Bake at 350 degrees for 1 hour. Yield: 12 servings.

GREEN BEANS DELUXE

3/4 c. chopped onion
1/2 c. chopped green pepper
3 tbsp. bacon drippings
2 tsp. flour
2 tbsp. brown sugar
1 tsp. Worcestershire sauce
1/4 tsp. pepper
1/2 tsp. salt
1/4 tsp. dry mustard
1 1/2 c. chopped tomatoes
2 16-oz. cans French-style
green beans, drained
6 slices crisp-fried bacon,
crumbled

Saute onion and green pepper in bacon drippings in skillet until tender. Blend flour with next 5 ingredients in saucepan. Stir in tomatoes and sauteed vegetables. Cook until thickened, stirring constantly. Pour over green beans in 1 1/2-quart casserole. Top with bacon. Bake at 350 degrees for 20 to 30 minutes or until bubbly. Yield: 8 servings.

SWEET AND SOUR GREEN BEANS

3 slices bacon
1 tbsp. minced onion
1/4 tsp. pepper
1/2 tsp. sugar
1/2 tsp. dillweed
1 tbsp. vinegar
2 15-oz. cans green beans,
drained, rinsed

Saute bacon in skillet until crisp; remove bacon, crumble and reserve. Mix remaining ingredients except beans into drippings. Add beans; mix gently until coated. Heat to serving temperature. Top with crumbled bacon.

CREOLE RED BEANS AND RICE

1 lb. dry red beans
1 meaty ham bone
1 lb. hot sausage, thinly sliced
2 c. chopped onion
2 stalks celery, chopped
1 bunch green onions, chopped
1 green pepper, chopped
4 bay leaves
Pinch of thyme
Salt and freshly ground pepper
to taste
Hot pepper sauce to taste

Soak beans in water to cover overnight; drain. Combine beans, 2 quarts water and next 8 ingredients in soup pot. Simmer for 3 hours or longer. Mash about 1/3 of the beans against side of pot with spoon; mix well. Season with salt, pepper and hot pepper sauce. Serve over rice.

Vegetables

BEETS IN SOUR CREAM

1 20-oz. can whole baby
beets
2 tbsp. butter
1/4 tsp. allspice
1 c. sour cream
2 tbsp. chopped parsley

Place beets and liquid in saucepan. Heat through; drain liquid. Add butter, allspice and sour cream. Heat to serving temperature, mixing gently. Do not boil. Sprinkle parsley over top.

GOLDEN BROCCOLI STIR FRY

2 10-oz. packages frozen
broccoli spears, thawed
2 tbsp. sesame seed
1/3 c. oil
1 head romaine, torn
1 tsp. salt
1/2 tsp. MSG (opt.)
3 c. grapefruit sections

Cut broccoli spears in half lengthwise. Brown sesame seed in oil in large skillet. Remove from skillet; set aside. Add broccoli. Stir-fry until tender. Add next 3 ingredients. Stir-fry for 2 minutes. Remove from heat. Add sesame seed and grapefruit. Yield: 8 servings.

CRUNCHY BROCCOLI CASSEROLE

1 sm. jar sliced mushrooms
1 can sliced water chestnuts,
drained
1 env. dry onion soup mix
2 tbsp. butter
2 pkg. frozen broccoli, cooked,
drained
1/4 c. bread crumbs
1/2 c. grated cheese

Saute mushrooms and water chestnuts with soup mix in butter in skillet. Mix with broccoli in casserole. Top with bread crumbs and cheese. Bake at 325 degrees for 20 to 25 minutes or until bubbly. Yield: 6 servings.

CARROT SOUFFLE

3 tbsp. butter, melted
3 tbsp. flour
1/4 tsp. salt
1 c. hot milk
3 eggs, separated
2 c. mashed cooked carrots

Blend first 3 ingredients in saucepan. Cook until bubbly, stirring constantly. Stir in milk gradually. Cook until thick, stirring constantly. Stir a small amount of hot mixture into beaten egg yolks; stir egg yolks into hot mixture. Add carrots; mix well. Cool. Fold in stiffly beaten egg whites. Pour into greased 1 1/2-quart casserole. Place in pan of hot water. Bake at 350 degrees for 40 to 50 minutes. Yield: 6 servings.

CAULIFLOWER PUFF

1 head cauliflower, separated
into flowerets
1/2 c. grated Swiss cheese
1/2 c. mayonnaise
1 egg white, stiffly beaten
1 tsp. lemon juice
1 tbsp. Parmesan cheese

Blanch cauliflower for 10 minutes; drain. Place in shallow baking dish. Mix Swiss cheese and mayonnaise in bowl. Fold in egg white and lemon juice. Spread over cauliflower. Sprinkle with Parmesan cheese. Broil 6 inches from heat source for 5 to 10 minutes or until golden brown.

CREAMED CELERY WITH PECANS

4 c. diagonally sliced celery
2 tbsp. melted butter
2 tbsp. flour
2 c. milk
1 tsp. salt
3/4 c. pecan halves
Buttered bread crumbs

Cook celery in water to cover in saucepan until tender; drain. Blend butter and flour in saucepan. Stir in milk gradually. Cook until thick and smooth, stirring constantly. Add salt and celery; mix well. Pour into greased 1 1/2-quart casserole. Top with pecans. Cover with buttered crumbs. Bake at 400 degrees for 15 minutes.

SOUFFLED FRESH CORN CASSEROLE

3 c. cooked fresh corn
3 tbsp. unsalted butter, melted
3 tbsp. flour
1 c. warm milk
1 c. warm heavy cream
Salt and freshly ground black
pepper
5 eggs, separated

Place corn in food processor container. Turn machine on and off 2 or 3 times until corn is lightly crushed and milky. Blend butter and flour in saucepan. Stir in warm milk gradually. Cook until thickened, stirring constantly. Stir in warm cream and corn with corn liquid. Season with salt and pepper to taste. Add beaten egg yolks. Beat egg whites with pinch of salt until stiff. Fold into corn mixture. Do not overmix. Pour into buttered and floured casserole. Bake at 400 degrees for 12 to 15 minutes or until puffed and golden brown.

EGGPLANT SAUTE

1 green pepper, chopped
1 onion, chopped
1 eggplant, cubed
4 tomatoes, chopped
2 tsp. salt
1/4 tsp. pepper
1/4 c. oil
1/4 c. (or more) Parmesan cheese

Saute vegetables with seasonings in oil in ovenproof skillet until tender. Top with cheese. Broil until cheese melts. Yield: 4 servings.

Vegetables

CREAMED ONIONS WITH MUSHROOMS AND CARROTS

24 sm. white onions, peeled
1 1/2 c. diagonally sliced
carrots
3 tbsp. butter
2 tbsp. flour
1 c. milk
3/4 tsp. salt
1/4 tsp. thyme
1/8 tsp. pepper
1/2 lb. mushrooms, thickly sliced

Cook onions in lightly salted boiling water in saucepan for 8 to 10 minutes or until just tender. Add carrots. Cook for 3 minutes or until just tender. Drain, reserving 1/2 cup liquid. Melt butter in saucepan. Blend in flour. Cook over medium heat for 2 minutes, stirring constantly. Stir in cooking liquid, milk, salt, thyme and pepper. Bring to a boil, stirring constantly. Simmer for 3 minutes. Add mushrooms. Cook over low heat for 5 minutes. Add onions and carrots. Cook, covered, for 3 to 4 minutes, or until heated through. Yield: 6-8 servings.

Photograph for this recipe on page 1.

PEAS VINCENTA

1   16-oz. can peas, drained
1/2 c. pea liquid
1 1/2 tsp. seasoned chicken
stock
1/4 tsp. ginger
1 tbsp. oil
1   5-oz. can sliced water
chestnuts
1   3-oz. can sliced mushrooms
1 1/2 tsp. cornstarch
1 tbsp. soy sauce

Combine first 7 ingredients in saucepan. Heat, covered, to boiling point. Blend cornstarch and soy sauce in small bowl. Stir into vegetable mixture. Cook over low heat until thickened, stirring constantly.

HASHED BROWN CASSEROLE ✓

2 lb. frozen hashed brown
potatoes, thawed
1/2 c. melted margarine
1 tsp. salt
1/4 tsp. pepper
1 can cream of mushroom soup
2 c. grated cheese
1/2 c. chopped onion
2 c. sour cream
Bread crumbs

Combine all ingredients except bread crumbs in large bowl; mix well. Spread in 9 x 13-inch baking pan. Top with bread crumbs. Bake at 350 degrees for 1 hour.

CRUNCHY POTATO BAKE

1/3 c. instant nonfat dry
milk powder
2 c. mashed potatoes
1/4 c. finely chopped onion
1 egg, beaten
1 tsp. salt
Dash of cayenne pepper
1 c. cornflakes
1/2 c. Parmesan cheese
3 tbsp. melted butter

Whip instant nonfat dry milk with 1/3 cup water in mixer bowl until thick. Mix in potatoes, chopped onion, egg, salt and pepper. Beat until light and fluffy. Spoon into greased 8 x 8-inch baking dish. Mix cornflakes, Parmesan cheese and butter in small bowl. Spread over top. Bake at 375 degrees for 20 to 25 minutes or until golden brown. Yield: 6 servings.

Photograph for this recipe above.

Vegetables

PARTY POTATO CASSEROLE

5 lb. potatoes, peeled, chopped
2 3-oz. packages cream cheese,
softened
1 c. sour cream
1/4 c. butter
2 tsp. onion salt
1 tsp. salt
1/4 tsp. pepper

Cook potatoes in boiling, salted water until tender; drain and mash. Add remaining ingredients; beat until light and fluffy. Store, covered, in refrigerator for 2 weeks or less. Place desired amount of potato mixture in greased casserole; dot with additional butter. Bake at 350 degrees until heated through. Yield: 12 servings.

NEW POTATO CASSEROLE

1 c. each grated sharp Cheddar
cheese, Colby cheese
7 new red potatoes, boiled, sliced
1 tsp. salt
Pepper to taste
1/2 lb. bacon, chopped
1/2 stick margarine, melted

Combine cheeses in small bowl; mix well. Alternate layers of potatoes, seasonings and cheese in buttered 9 x 13-inch casserole until all ingredients are used. Partially cook bacon in skillet; drain. Sprinkle over casserole. Drizzle margarine evenly over top. Bake at 325 degrees for 25 to 30 minutes. Yield: 8 servings.

SOUR CREAM-CHEDDAR POTATOES

6 med. potatoes
2 c. shredded Cheddar cheese
6 tbsp. butter
1 8-oz. carton sour cream
3 green onions, chopped
1 tsp. salt
1/4 tsp. pepper

Cook potatoes in boiling water for 30 minutes. Cool slightly. Peel and coarsely shred potatoes. Combine cheese and 1/4 cup butter in saucepan. Cook over low heat until cheese melts. Combine potatoes, cheese mixture, sour cream, onions, salt and pepper in shallow 2-quart casserole. Dot with 2 tablespoons butter. Bake, covered, at 300 degrees for 25 minutes.

SPINACH DIANA

2 pkg. frozen chopped spinach
1/4 c. melted butter
2 tbsp. flour
2 tbsp. chopped onion
1/2 c. evaporated milk
3/4 tsp. each celery salt,
garlic powder
1/2 tsp. each salt and pepper
1 tsp. Worcestershire sauce
Red pepper
1 6-oz. roll jalapeno cheese, sliced
Buttered crumbs

Cook spinach using package directions. Drain, reserving 1/2 cup liquid. Blend butter and flour in double boiler. Add onion. Cook until tender, stirring constantly. Add spinach liquid and evaporated milk. Cook until thickened, stirring constantly. Stir in seasonings and cheese. Add spinach; mix well. Spoon into casserole; top with buttered crumbs. Bake at 350 degrees for 30 minutes.

SERBIAN SPINACH

1 16-oz. carton cottage cheese
6 eggs, beaten
1 stick butter, chopped
1/2 lb. Cheddar cheese, chopped
1 pkg. frozen spinach, thawed, drained
6 tbsp. flour

Combine all ingredients in bowl; mix well. Spoon into greased 9 x 13-inch baking dish. Bake at 350 degrees for 1 hour. Yield: 10 servings.

SQUASH CASSEROLE SUPREME

1 stick margarine
1 pkg. herb-seasoned stuffing mix
2 c. mashed cooked squash
1 can cream of chicken soup
2 carrots, grated
1 sm. jar pimento
1 onion, chopped
1 c. sour cream
Salt and pepper to taste

Melt margarine in casserole. Add stuffing mix. Reserve 3/4 cup for topping. Spread stuffing mixture evenly over bottom of casserole. Combine remaining ingredients in large bowl; mix well. Spread squash mixture over stuffing mixture. Top with reserved stuffing. Bake at 350 degrees for 30 minutes.

SQUASH FRITTERS

2 eggs, beaten
2 c. grated squash
6 tbsp. flour
2 tsp. sugar
2 tbsp. melted margarine
1 onion, grated
Salt and pepper to taste
Oil for deep frying

Combine eggs and squash with flour, sugar, margarine, onion and seasonings in large bowl; mix well. Drop by spoonfuls into hot oil. Fry until brown.

MAPLE-WALNUT SWEET POTATOES

8 med. sweet potatoes
1/4 c. maple syrup
1/4 c. butter
1/2 tsp. salt
Pinch of cloves
1/2 c. chopped walnuts

Bake potatoes at 400 degrees for 50 minutes or until soft. Cut into halves. Cool slightly; peel. Press through sieve into bowl. Beat in syrup, butter, salt and cloves. Turn into buttered casserole. Sprinkle with walnuts. Bake at 400 degrees for 20 minutes. Yield: 6-8 servings.

Photograph for this recipe on page 1.

Vegetables

ORANGE-GLAZED SWEET POTATOES

2 lb. sweet potatoes, peeled
2/3 c. sugar
1 tbsp. cornstarch
1 tsp. salt
1/2 c. grated orange rind
1 c. orange juice
2 tbsp. butter

Cut sweet potatoes in half lengthwise. Arrange in ungreased 1 1/2-quart casserole. Combine sugar, cornstarch, salt and orange rind in saucepan; mix well. Blend in orange juice. Add butter. Cook until thick, stirring constantly. Boil for 1 minute, stirring constantly. Pour over sweet potatoes. Bake, covered, at 400 degrees for 1 hour, basting occasionally. Yield: 4-6 servings.

BOURBON-BAKED TOMATOES

2 cans stewed tomatoes
3 slices white bread, torn
2 tbsp. margarine, melted
2 c. sugar
1 tsp. nutmeg
1/8 tsp. cinnamon
1/2 c. Bourbon

Combine all ingredients in casserole; mix well. Bake at 350 degrees for 30 minutes, stirring once. Yield: 6-8 servings.

ZUCCHINI AU GRATIN

4 c. thinly sliced zucchini
1 onion, sliced
2 tomatoes, peeled, sliced
1/4 c. melted butter
1 tsp. salt
1/8 tsp. pepper
1/2 c. shredded sharp cheese

Layer zucchini, onion and tomatoes in butter in skillet. Sprinkle with salt and pepper. Cook, covered, over low heat for 15 minutes. Top with cheese. Heat until cheese melts.

SEASONED STUFFED ZUCCHINI

3 med. zucchini
1 6-oz. package stuffing mix
for beef
1/4 c. butter, chopped
1/4 c. grated Cheddar cheese

Cut zucchini in half; scoop out seeds. Parboil for 3 to 4 minutes; drain, reserving 1 1/2 cups liquid. Scoop out pulp, reserving shells. Combine stuffing seasoning packet, butter and reserved liquid in bowl. Stir in stuffing crumbs and reserved pulp. Let stand for 5 minutes. Spoon into zucchini shells in baking pan. Sprinkle with cheese. Bake at 400 degrees for 20 minutes.

Photograph for this recipe on page 116.

BUFFET VEGETABLE BAKE

2 10-oz. packages frozen
mixed peas and carrots
1 9-oz. package frozen green
beans
1 5-oz. can sliced water
chestnuts, drained
1 3-oz. can broiled sliced
mushrooms, drained
1 can cream of mushroom soup
3 to 4 tbsp. Sherry
1 tsp. Worcestershire sauce
Dash of hot pepper sauce
2 c. shredded sharp cheese
1/4 c. buttery cracker crumbs

Cook frozen vegetables using package directions until
tender-crisp; drain. Combine cooked vegetables, water
chestnuts and mushrooms. Combine remaining ingredients except crumbs in bowl; mix well. Add to vegetables;
toss to mix. Turn into 2-quart casserole. Bake at 350
degrees until bubbly, stirring occasionally. Sprinkle with
crumbs. Bake for 5 minutes longer. Yield: 10-12
servings.

RATATOUILLE

1 zucchini, sliced
1 onion, sliced
2 yellow squash, sliced
1/2 green pepper, sliced
10 mushrooms, sliced
1 tsp. garlic salt
1 tbsp. margarine
4 tomatoes, chopped
2 c. grated mozzarella cheese

Combine first 5 ingredients with garlic salt and margarine in skillet. Cook, tightly covered, over low heat until
tender. Spread tomatoes over vegetables. Cook, covered,
until tomatoes are tender. Cook, uncovered, for 2 to 3
minutes longer or until juices are reduced to desired
consistency. Top with cheese. Let stand, covered, until
cheese melts. Yield: 6 servings.

VEGETABLE MEDLEY AMANDINE

1 12-oz. can Shoe Peg
corn, drained
1 16-oz. can French-style green
beans, drained
1/2 c. chopped celery
1 12-oz. jar pimento, drained
1/2 c. chopped onion
1/2 c. sour cream
1/2 c. shredded Cheddar cheese
1 can cream of celery soup
1/2 c. slivered almonds

Combine all ingredients except almonds in bowl; mix
well. Pour into casserole. Sprinkle with almonds. Bake at
350 degrees for 45 minutes. Yield: 8-10 servings.

Side Dishes

Side dishes are the "other foods" that go on the dinner plate with meats and vegetables. They include a number of delicious dishes from the simple baked potato with butter to the most enjoyable combinations of cheeses, spices, eggs, rice or pasta.

Fruit is also an important side dish — whether fresh, canned, cooked with the meal or as a garnish. A baked ham decked with pineapple slices and cherries, baked chicken surrounded by golden peach slices, or any cut of pork accompanied by applesauce or apple slices all make appetizing and eye-pleasing dishes. Cranberry sauces or spiced pears, peaches and crabapples, are not only pretty at Christmas, but make delicious complements for fowl and poultry dishes. For an elegant touch, serve frosted grapes or strawberries with the entree. And what makes a more appreciated hostess gift than a colorful jar of pepper jelly?

Side dishes can be simple or elegant. But because they are usually cereals, pastas or fruits (often with the addition of cheese and eggs) they are always nutritious. Sometimes, they may take a little extra time to prepare, but the difference in interest and taste appeal at your next dinner will be well worth the effort.

◄ MACARONI WITH SAUSAGE-EGGPLANT SAUCE, Recipe on page 134.

Side Dishes

BARLEY-MUSHROOM CASSEROLE

1 c. quick-cooking fine barley
1 med. onion, chopped
Melted butter
1/2 c. slivered almonds
1 env. dry onion soup mix
2 c. chicken broth
3/4 to 1 c. sliced mushrooms
1 5-oz. can water chestnuts,
   drained, sliced

Saute barley and onion in butter in skillet until light golden. Mix in almonds, soup mix and broth. Saute mushrooms in a small amount of butter in small skillet. Stir into barley mixture with water chestnuts. Spoon into 2-quart casserole. Bake, covered, at 350 degrees for 1 hour. Yield: 6 servings.

CUERNAVACA CASSEROLE

1 c. yellow cornmeal
3/4 tsp. salt
1/2 tsp. baking powder
1 c. milk
2 eggs, slightly beaten
1/4 c. oil
2 c. cooked rice
2 c. shredded Cheddar cheese
1 17-oz. can cream-style corn
1 3 1/4-oz. can sliced olives
1 med. onion, chopped
1 can chopped green chilies
4 drops of Tabasco sauce

Combine cornmeal, salt and baking powder in large bowl; mix well. Add remaining ingredients; stir until just mixed. Pour into well-greased 12-inch casserole. Bake at 350 degrees for 40 to 50 minutes or until set. Yield: 8-10 servings.

ACAPULCO OMELET

3 soft corn tortillas, sliced
Butter
1 onion, finely chopped
6 eggs, beaten
1/2 green pepper, chopped
1/4 c. grated cheese
1 tomato, chopped
1 tbsp. sunflower seed
1 tbsp. bacon bits
2 tbsp. alfalfa sprouts

Brown tortillas in a small amount of butter in skillet. Add onion. Saute until tender-crisp. Pour eggs over top. Sprinkle with green pepper and cheese. Cook over low heat until partially set. Top with remaining ingredients. Cook until set.

GRITS SOUFFLE

1 c. grits *1 1/2 tsp. salt* *4 eggs, beaten* *1/4 c. margarine, melted* *3/4 lb. Cheddar cheese, grated* *1 c. milk*	Cook grits in 3 cups boiling water in saucepan; add salt. Combine eggs, margarine, cheese and milk in bowl; mix well. Stir into grits. Pour into 2-quart baking dish. Bake at 325 degrees for 45 minutes. Yield: 12 servings.

OVEN BRUNCH OMELET

18 eggs, beaten *1 c. sour cream* *1 c. milk* *2 tsp. salt* *1/4 c. chopped green onions* *1/4 c. butter, melted*	Combine first 4 ingredients in large bowl, beating well. Stir in onions. Pour over butter in 9 x 13-inch baking dish. Bake at 325 degrees for 35 minutes or until eggs are set but moist. Serve immediately with Canadian bacon and sweet rolls. Yield: 12 servings.

EASY EGG AND CHEESE SOUFFLE

3 c. croutons *1 1/2 c. shredded Cheddar cheese* *6 eggs, slightly beaten* *3 c. milk* *3/4 tsp. salt* *1/4 tsp. onion salt* *Dash of pepper* *4 slices crisp-fried bacon,* *crumbled*	Mix croutons and cheese in 6 x 10-inch baking dish. Mix remaining ingredients except bacon in bowl; pour over cheese mixture. Chill, covered, overnight. Sprinkle bacon over top. Bake at 325 degrees for 50 to 60 minutes or until set. Yield: 8 servings.

CONFETTI RICE BAKE

1 c. rice *1 can consomme* *1/2 c. margarine* *1/2 can mushrooms* *1/4 tsp. salt* *1 onion, chopped* *1/2 green pepper, chopped* *2 tbsp. chopped pimento* *1/2 c. sliced almonds (opt.)*	Combine all ingredients with 1 consomme can water in 2-quart casserole. Bake, covered, at 250 degrees for 1 1/2 hours, stirring every 30 minutes. Serve with beef or chicken. Yield: 8 servings.

Side Dishes

FESTIVE RICE

1/2 c. chopped onion
2 tbsp. butter
1 c. rice
1 chicken bouillon cube
1 tsp. salt
1/8 tsp. pepper
1/2 tsp. thyme
1 10-oz. package frozen peas,
thawed, drained
1 1/2 c. orange sections

Saute onion in butter in skillet until tender. Add rice. Cook until golden, stirring frequently. Stir in next 4 ingredients and 2 cups water. Simmer, covered, for 15 minutes. Add peas. Cook for 5 minutes longer or until rice is tender and water is absorbed. Add orange sections. Cook until heated through. Yield: 6 servings.

SHRIMP-FRIED RICE

1/2 lb. small shelled shrimp
1 tbsp. each Sherry, soy sauce
1 tsp. sugar
2 tsp. cornstarch
4 c. cold cooked rice
1/2 c. chopped green onions
1 stalk celery, finely chopped
1 c. mushrooms (opt.)
1 can sliced water chestnuts
(opt.)
1 tsp. chopped gingerroot
2 tbsp. oil
2 eggs, lightly beaten
Salt and pepper to taste

Combine first 5 ingredients in bowl. Marinate for 1 hour. Drain. Stir-fry rice, vegetables, water chestnuts and gingerroot in 1 tablespoon oil in skillet until tender-crisp. Add shrimp. Stir-fry until pink. Remove vegetable mixture and shrimp; add 1 tablespoon oil. Add eggs and seasonings. Cook until set, stirring frequently. Add vegetable mixture and shrimp; mix well.

WILD RICE WITH MUSHROOM SAUCE

1 c. wild rice, rinsed
1/2 c. slivered almonds
2 tbsp. chives
2 8-oz. cans mushrooms,
drained
1/4 c. butter
3 c. chicken broth
2 cans cream of mushroom soup
3/4 soup can milk

Saute wild rice, almonds, chives and 1 can mushrooms in butter in large skillet until almonds are golden brown. Pour into 1 1/2-quart casserole. Heat chicken broth to boiling point; stir into rice mixture. Bake, covered, for 1 1/2 hours or until liquid is absorbed and rice is tender. Mix soup, milk and remaining mushrooms in saucepan. Heat to serving temperature. Pour over baked wild rice.

ORANGE RICE

1/2 c. orange juice
1 tbsp. grated orange rind
1 tsp. salt
1 c. rice

Combine first 3 ingredients with 2 cups water in saucepan. Bring to a boil; add rice. Reduce heat. Simmer, covered, for 25 minutes or until liquid is absorbed. Yield: 6 servings.

ORIENTAL RICE

3 tbsp. butter, melted
1/4 tsp. curry powder
4 c. hot cooked rice
1/3 c. finely chopped parsley
1 tsp. salt
1/4 c. finely chopped peanuts

Blend butter and curry powder in skillet. Stir in remaining ingredients. Heat to serving temperature.

Photograph for this recipe above.

133

Side Dishes

MACARONI WITH SAUSAGE-EGGPLANT SAUCE

3/4 lb. each Italian hot
sausage, Italian sweet
sausage
1 tbsp. olive oil
1/2 c. chopped onion
2 cloves of garlic, crushed
1 lg. eggplant, peeled, chopped
1 28-oz. can plum tomatoes
2 8-oz. cans tomato sauce
1 tsp. basil
Salt and pepper to taste
4 c. elbow macaroni, cooked

Remove casing from sausage links; break into chunks. Cook sausage, tightly covered, in 1/3 cup water in skillet for 10 minutes, stirring occasionally. Pour off water. Saute sausage until lightly browned; remove sausage. Add olive oil, onion and garlic. Saute until lightly browned. Add sausage, eggplant, tomatoes, tomato sauce and basil. Simmer, covered, for 45 minutes, stirring occasionally. Simmer, uncovered, for 15 minutes. Season to taste with salt and pepper. Serve over macaroni. Yield: 8 servings.

Photograph for this recipe on page 128.

HUNGARIAN NOODLES

1 16-oz. carton sour cream
1 12-oz. carton large curd
cottage cheese
1 16-oz. package wide egg
noodles, cooked
1/2 tsp. Hungarian paprika
Salt and pepper to taste

Combine sour cream and cottage cheese with hot drained noodles in saucepan. Stir in paprika, salt and pepper. Cook over low heat until heated through. Do not boil. Yield: 8-10 servings.

SPAGHETTI PRIMAVERA

1 bunch broccoli, coarsely
chopped
2 zucchini, sliced
1/2 lb. asparagus, sliced
Salt
1 clove of garlic, chopped
2 c. cherry tomato halves
1/4 c. oil
1 tsp. basil
1/2 lb. mushrooms, thinly sliced
1/2 c. frozen peas
1/4 c. chopped parsley
1/2 tsp. pepper
1/4 c. butter
3/4 c. cream
2/3 c. Parmesan cheese
1 lb. thin spaghetti, cooked

Cook first 3 ingredients in boiling salted water in saucepan until tender-crisp; drain. Stir-fry garlic and tomatoes in oil in large skillet for 2 minutes. Add basil and mushrooms. Stir-fry for 3 minutes. Add peas, parsley, 1 1/2 teaspoons salt and pepper. Stir-fry for 1 minute. Add to zucchini mixture. Melt butter in pan juices. Stir in cream and cheese. Cook over medium heat until smooth, stirring constantly. Add spaghetti; mix well. Add vegetable mixture. Cook until heated through. Yield: 8 servings.

SKILLET FETTUCINI

*1/2 c. coarsely chopped
green pepper
1 tbsp. bacon drippings
1 pkg. spaghetti sauce mix
1 6-oz. can tomato paste
1 8-oz. package egg noodles,
cooked
6 slices crisp-fried bacon,
crumbled
3 to 4 slices American cheese*

Saute green pepper in bacon drippings in skillet until tender but not brown. Add spaghetti sauce mix, tomato paste and 1 3/4 cups water. Bring to a boil, stirring occasionally; reduce heat. Simmer for 10 minutes. Stir in cooked noodles and bacon. Heat to serving temperature. Cut cheese into strips; arrange over noodles. Yield: 4 servings.

TORTELLINI WITH GORGONZOLA SAUCE

*3/4 c. dry white vermouth
1 c. heavy cream
Freshly ground pepper and
nutmeg to taste
1/3 to 1/2 lb. Gorgonzola cheese
1 tbsp. Parmesan cheese
1/2 lb. tortellini, cooked*

Boil vermouth in saucepan until reduced by 1/2. Stir in cream, pepper and nutmeg. Simmer until reduced by 1/3. Remove from heat. Stir in cheeses until melted. Pour over drained tortellini in saucepan. Cook for 5 minutes or until thick. Serve immediately.

ULTIMATE BREAD DRESSING

*1 pkg. dry onion soup mix
1 loaf bread, toasted, crushed
1 bunch celery with leaves,
chopped
6 eggs, beaten
2 cans chicken-rice soup
1 4-oz. can mushrooms
1 can sliced water chestnuts
(opt.)
1 5 3/4-oz. can mushroom
steak sauce
3 tbsp. parsley flakes
1/2 c. melted butter
1 tsp. thyme
Seasoned salt and pepper to
taste
Turkey giblets, cooked, chopped
Turkey stock*

Mix soup mix with 1/2 cup water in bowl. Let stand for several minutes. Combine with remaining ingredients except stock in large bowl; mix well, moistening with stock as necessary. Stuff turkey and roast as usual or bake in buttered casserole.

Side Dishes

BASIC BREAD STUFFING AND VARIATIONS

1 c. butter
4 c. chopped celery
1 c. chopped onion
16 c. soft bread cubes
1 tbsp. salt
1 1/2 tsp. poultry seasoning
1/2 tsp. rubbed sage
1/2 tsp. pepper
Hot broth

Melt butter in large skillet. Add celery and onion. Saute until tender. Combine with bread cubes, salt, poultry seasoning, sage and pepper in bowl; mix lightly. Add enough broth to moisten. Yield: 16 cups or enough for 14 to 18-pound turkey.

Giblet Stuffing

Add chopped cooked giblets.

Apple Stuffing

Add 1 cup peeled chopped apple to celery and onion. Saute for 3 to 5 minutes or until apple is tender.

Chestnut Stuffing

Add 4 cups chopped boiled chestnuts. Substitute milk for broth.

Mushroom Stuffing

Saute 1/2 pound sliced mushrooms with celery and onion.

Photograph for this recipe on page 1.

OYSTER DRESSING

3/4 c. chopped onions
1 c. butter
3 c. oysters
1/2 c. oyster liquid
12 c. fresh bread crumbs
1 tbsp. salt
1 tsp. pepper
1/2 tsp. poultry seasoning

Saute onions in butter in saucepan until tender. Stir in oysters and remaining ingredients; mix well. Pour into greased 9 x 13-inch baking pan. Bake, lightly covered with foil, at 325 degrees for 40 minutes. Bake, uncovered, for 20 minutes or until lightly browned.

FRESH CRANBERRY SAUCE

4 c. fresh cranberries
2 c. sugar

Mix cranberries, sugar and 2 cups water in large saucepan. Cook over medium heat until sugar dissolves. stirring constantly. Boil for 5 minutes or until cranberries begin to pop. Serve warm or cold. Yield: 4 cups.

Photograph for this recipe on page 1.

STRAWBERRY BAKED APPLES

6 med. apples, cored
1/4 c. sugar
1/4 c. strawberry jam
1/2 c. chopped pecans

Place apples in buttered baking dish. Spoon sugar into each. Bake at 375 degrees for 30 minutes or until apples are tender but firm. Combine jam and pecans in bowl. Fill centers of apples with jam mixture. Yield: 6 servings.

FRUIT COMPOTE

1 can pitted Bing cherries
1 can peach halves, drained
1 pkg. dried apricots, pitted
Juice and grated rind of 1
lemon
Juice and grated rind of 1
orange
1/2 to 3/4 c. packed brown sugar

Drain cherries, reserving juice. Combine peaches, cherries and apricots in 1-quart casserole. Mix remaining ingredients with reserved cherry juice in bowl. Pour over fruit. Bake, covered, at 350 degrees for 1 hour. Bake, uncovered, for 1 hour longer. Serve hot or cold with whipped cream.

SOUR CHERRY JAM

5 c. sour cherries, pitted
5 c. sugar
2 tbsp. lemon juice

Heat cherries slowly in covered saucepan until skins soften slightly. Add sugar and lemon juice; mix well. Cook for 15 minutes or to 218 degrees on thermometer. Chill in refrigerator overnight. Bring to a boil. Boil for 1 minute. Pour into hot sterilized 1/2-pint jars leaving 1/2-inch headspace; seal. Process in water bath for 5 minutes. Yield: 4 or 5 jars.

PEPPER JELLY

1 c. chopped green peppers
1/4 c. chopped jalapeno peppers
1 1/2 c. cider vinegar
6 1/2 c. sugar
4 or 5 drops of green food
coloring
1 bottle of Certo

Process peppers and 1/3 cup vinegar in blender container. Combine with sugar and remaining vinegar in saucepan. Boil mixture for 5 minutes. Stir in food coloring and Certo. Pour into hot sterilized jars leaving 1/2-inch headspace. Seal with paraffin. Serve over cream cheese with crackers. Yield: 3 pints.

Breads

Fill your kitchen with the tempting aroma of home-baked breads and treat your family to old-fashioned goodness. There's nothing quite as special as breads baked with love in your own oven.

Bread making is one of the oldest of the culinary arts. Through the centuries, outstanding recipes have emerged as people around the world have learned to bake their own special breads.

The shapes and sizes of breads are as varied as their tastes. Some are sweet; others spicy. Some are filled with nuts; others are fried in a pan. There are flaky breads, hard breads, casserole breads, frosted breads. There are quick breads and yeast breads. There are breads with ingredients by the dozens; and there are those that include no more than meal and water.

The pages that follow present you with wonderful recipes for buns, biscuits, loaves and rolls. You will find very special holiday breads, coffee cakes, as well as everyday favorites to store in the refrigerator and bake at your convenience.

Among this superb collection are breads to accompany any meal. There are also dessert breads that crown your main course with distinction.

If you have not already added the art of baking to your cooking repertoire, by all means begin today. If you are already a regular baker, these pages will add exciting new recipes to your collection.

← COCONUT PRALINE COFFEE CAKE, Recipe on page 149.

Breads

FRUIT COFFEE CAKE

2 sticks margarine, softened
1 c. sugar
3 eggs
2 tbsp. milk
1 tsp. vanilla extract
2 c. flour
2 tsp. baking powder
1 can fruit pie filling
Confectioners' sugar

Combine first 7 ingredients in bowl; mix well. Spread 3/4 of the batter in greased and floured 9 x 13-inch baking pan. Layer pie filling and remaining batter over top. Sift confectioners' sugar over layers. Bake at 350 degrees for 45 minutes. Yield: 18 servings.

QUICK COFFEE CAKE

3/4 c. sugar
Flour
2 1/4 tsp. baking powder
3/4 tsp. salt
2 eggs, well beaten
1/2 c. oil
1/2 c. milk
1/3 c. packed brown sugar
1 tsp. cinnamon
2 tbsp. margarine, softened
1/2 c. pecans

Sift sugar, 2 cups sifted flour, baking powder and salt into small bowl. Combine eggs, oil and milk in bowl. Stir into dry ingredients. Pour into greased and floured 9-inch square baking pan. Combine brown sugar, 2 tablespoons flour and cinnamon in small bowl. Cut in margarine until crumbly. Add pecans. Spoon over batter. Bake at 400 degrees for 25 to 30 minutes or until cake tests done.

APPLESAUCE DOUGHNUTS

2 c. thick unsweetened applesauce
1/2 c. frozen orange juice concentrate, thawed
2 eggs, beaten
1 tsp. lemon extract
1 1/2 c. sugar
1 c. dry milk powder
5 c. sifted flour
1/2 tsp. nutmeg
2 tsp. soda
1 tsp. each salt, baking powder
Oil for deep frying

Combine applesauce, orange juice, eggs and lemon extract in large bowl. Sift dry ingredients into applesauce mixture; mix well. Roll 1/2 inch thick on floured surface; cut into doughnuts. Deep-fry at 360 degrees for 1 minute on each side or until brown; drain. Glaze or frost as desired.

Breads

BUTTERMILK CORN STICKS

1 1/2 c. cornmeal
1/2 c. sifted flour
1 tsp. each soda, salt and
baking powder
2 tsp. sugar
2 eggs, well beaten
2 c. buttermilk
3 tbsp. melted butter

Sift dry ingredients together. Combine eggs, buttermilk and butter in bowl. Add dry ingredients; mix well. Fill greased corn stick pans 2/3 full. Bake at 425 degrees for 20 to 25 minutes or until browned.

Photograph for this recipe on page 144.

MEXICAN CORN BREAD

1 c. self-rising cornmeal
1/2 c. self-rising flour
1 onion, chopped
2 hot peppers, finely chopped
1/2 c. oil
1 c. cream-style corn
1/2 c. grated Cheddar cheese
2 eggs
1 c. buttermilk

Combine dry ingredients in large bowl; mix well. Mix remaining ingredients in bowl. Add to dry ingredients; mix until just moistened. Pour into greased 8-inch square baking pan. Bake at 350 degrees for 45 minutes.

FRENCH BREAKFAST PUFFS

1 1/2 c. self-rising flour
1/4 tsp. nutmeg
1 c. sugar
1/2 c. milk
1 egg, beaten
6 tbsp. butter, melted
1 tbsp. cinnamon

Combine flour, nutmeg and 1/2 cup sugar in bowl. Add milk and egg; mix well. Spoon into greased muffin cups. Bake at 350 degrees until golden brown. Blend butter, cinnamon and remaining 1/2 cup sugar in bowl. Spread over puffs. Yield: 1 dozen.

GINGERBREAD WAFFLES

2 c. sifted flour
3/4 tsp. soda
1/2 tsp. salt
2 tsp. ginger
2 eggs, separated
1 c. molasses
1/2 c. buttermilk
1/2 c. melted shortening

Combine dry ingredients in large mixer bowl. Mix beaten egg yolks, molasses, buttermilk and shortening in medium bowl until well blended. Pour into well in flour mixture. Stir until just moistened. Fold in stiffly beaten egg whites. Bake in medium-hot waffle iron until waffles test done.

Breads

HUSH PUPPIES

1 3/4 c. cornmeal
3/4 tsp. salt
1 1/2 tsp. baking powder
1 c. milk
1 egg
1/4 c. chopped green onions
Oil for deep frying

Combine first 3 dry ingredients in bowl. Stir in next 3 ingredients. Drop by spoonfuls into 3-inch deep 350-degree oil. Fry until golden brown; drain. Yield: 24 servings.

APPLE-CARROT MUFFINS

2 eggs
3/4 c. sugar
1/4 c. oil
2 c. chopped Granny Smith apples
1/2 c. shredded carrots
2 c. sifted flour
2 tsp. baking powder
1 tsp. cinnamon
1/2 tsp. salt

Combine eggs, sugar and oil in mixer bowl. Beat until well blended. Stir in apples, carrots and sifted dry ingredients. Fill greased muffin cups 2/3 full. Bake at 325 degrees for 20 to 25 minutes or until brown. Yield: 1 1/4 dozen.

BLUEBERRY MUFFINS

1/2 c. butter, softened
1 1/4 c. sugar
1 egg
Flour
2 tsp. baking powder
1/2 tsp. salt
1/2 c. milk
2 c. blueberries
1/2 tsp. cinnamon

Cream 1/4 cup butter and 3/4 cup sugar in bowl. Beat in egg. Add mixture of 2 cups sifted flour, baking powder and salt alternately with milk, beating well after each addition. Fold in blueberries. Fill greased muffin cups 2/3 full. Combine remaining 1/4 cup butter, 1/2 cup sugar, 1/3 cup flour and cinnamon in small bowl; mix well. Sprinkle over batter. Bake at 400 degrees for 20 to 25 minutes or until golden brown. Yield: 1 1/2 dozen.

PEANUT-BACON MUFFINS

2 tbsp. margarine, softened
1 c. milk
1 egg, beaten
1/2 c. chopped peanuts
1/4 c. crumbled crisp-fried bacon
1 3/4 c. flour
1/4 c. packed light brown sugar
1 tbsp. baking powder

Combine margarine, milk and egg in bowl; mix well. Add peanuts and bacon. Sift in dry ingredients. Stir until just mixed. Fill greased muffin cups 2/3 full. Bake at 400 degrees for 25 minutes or until golden brown. Yield: 10 servings.

PEAR-YOGURT MUFFINS

2 c. sifted flour
1/2 c. sugar
1 1/2 tsp. baking powder
1 tsp. soda
1/2 tsp. salt
1 c. yogurt
1 egg, slightly beaten
1/4 c. oil
1 16-oz. can pears, drained, chopped

Sift dry ingredients into bowl. Blend yogurt, egg and oil in small bowl. Add to flour mixture with pears; stir until just moistened. Fill greased muffin cups 2/3 full. Bake at 400 degrees for 20 to 25 minutes or until golden brown. Yield: 1 dozen.

PROTEIN-PLUS MUFFINS

1 1/4 c. soy flour
2/3 c. dry milk powder
2 tsp. baking powder
1/2 tsp. salt
2 eggs, beaten
1 tsp. grated orange rind
3/4 c. orange juice
2 tbsp. honey
2 tbsp. oil
1/2 c. chopped dates
1/4 c. chopped pecans

Combine flour, milk powder, baking powder and salt in bowl. Combine eggs, orange rind, juice, honey and oil in small bowl. Add to dry ingredients; stir until just moistened. Fold in dates and pecans. Fill greased muffin cups 2/3 full. Bake at 350 degrees for 30 minutes or until brown. Yield: 1 dozen.

BANANA-PECAN BREAD

1/2 c. oil
1 c. sugar
2 eggs, beaten
3 ripe bananas, mashed
2 c. flour
1 tsp. soda
1/2 tsp. baking powder
1/2 tsp. salt
3 tbsp. milk
1/2 tsp. vanilla extract
1/2 c. chopped pecans

Beat oil and sugar together in bowl. Add eggs and bananas; beat well. Add sifted dry ingredients, milk and vanilla; mix well. Stir in nuts. Pour into greased and floured loaf pan. Bake at 350 degrees for 1 hour. Cool. Let stand overnight before cutting.

Breads

BUTTERMILK-WALNUT BREAD

1 1/4 c. sifted flour
3/4 tsp. salt
3/4 tsp. soda
1 1/2 tsp. baking powder
1 c. whole wheat flour
1 c. chopped walnuts
2 eggs, well beaten
1/2 c. sugar
2 tbsp. butter, melted
1/3 c. molasses
1 c. buttermilk

Sift flour, salt, soda and baking powder into bowl. Add flour and walnuts. Mix eggs, sugar, butter, molasses and buttermilk in bowl. Stir into dry ingredients; beat until smooth. Pour into greased loaf pan. Bake at 350 degrees for 50 to 60 minutes or until bread tests done.

Photograph for this recipe above.

FRESH BLUEBERRY BREAD

2/3 c. shortening
1 1/3 c. sugar
4 eggs, beaten
1/2 c. milk
1 1/2 tsp. lemon juice
1 c. drained crushed pineapple
3 c. flour
2 tsp. baking powder
1 tsp. soda
2 c. blueberries
1 c. chopped pecans
1/2 c. flaked coconut

Cream shortening in large bowl until fluffy. Beat in sugar gradually. Stir in eggs and next 3 ingredients. Beat in flour, baking powder and soda. Fold in blueberries, pecans and coconut. Pour into 4 greased and floured loaf pans. Bake at 350 degrees for 45 minutes. Turn onto wire rack to cool. Store, tightly wrapped, in freezer for 6 months or less. Yield: 4 loaves.

CRANBERRY-ORANGE BREAD

1 c. whole wheat flour
1 c. all-purpose flour
1 1/2 tsp. baking powder
1/2 tsp. soda
1 c. sugar
Juice of 1 orange
2 tbsp. butter
1 egg, well beaten
1 c. chopped cranberries
1 c. chopped walnuts

Combine first 5 ingredients in bowl. Add enough boiling water to orange juice to measure 3/4 cup liquid. Stir in butter until melted. Add to dry ingredients; mix well. Add egg; beat until smooth. Fold in cranberries and walnuts. Spoon into greased and floured loaf pan. Bake at 350 degrees for 50 to 55 minutes or until bread tests done.

GUMDROP BREAD

3 c. applesauce
1 c. shortening
2 c. sugar
5 c. flour
4 tsp. soda
1 tsp. each nutmeg, allspice and salt
2 1/2 tsp. cinnamon
1/2 tsp. cloves
3 pkg. small gumdrops
1 1/2 c. raisins

Heat applesauce in saucepan. Add shortening and sugar; mix well. Let stand, covered, overnight. Combine dry ingredients in large bowl; mix well. Blend in applesauce mixture. Remove and discard licorice gumdrops; stir remaining gumdrops and raisins into batter. Pour into greased and floured loaf pans. Bake at 250 degrees for 2 hours.

Breads

MINI CHIP CRANBERRY-NUT BREAD

2 c. flour
1 c. sugar
1 1/2 tsp. baking powder
1 tsp. salt
1/2 tsp. soda
3/4 c. orange juice
1 tsp. grated orange rind
2 tbsp. shortening
1 egg
1 c. chopped fresh cranberries
3/4 c. chopped nuts
1 c. semisweet miniature
chocolate chips
1 c. confectioners' sugar
1 tsp. butter
1 tbsp. milk
1/2 tsp. vanilla extract

Combine flour, sugar, baking powder, salt and soda in large bowl. Add orange juice, orange rind, shortening and egg; mix well. Stir in cranberries, nuts and chocolate chips. Pour into greased loaf pan. Bake at 350 degrees for 60 to 65 minutes or until bread tests done. Cool. Combine confectioners' sugar, butter, milk and vanilla in bowl; mix well. Drizzle over bread.

Photograph for this recipe on page 70.

SPICY GINGERBREAD

3 eggs
1 c. sugar
1 c. oil
1 c. molasses
1 tsp. each cloves, ginger
and cinnamon
2 tsp. soda
2 c. flour

Combine first 7 ingredients in bowl; mix well. Stir in soda dissolved in 2 tablespoons hot water. Add flour; mix well. Mix in 1 cup boiling water. Pour into greased and floured 9 x 13-inch baking pan. Bake at 350 degrees for 45 minutes. Yield: 6 servings.

EASY ORANGE BREAD

2 tbsp. butter, softened
3/4 c. sugar
1 egg, beaten
2 c. flour
2 tsp. baking powder
Milk
Juice and grated rind of 1
orange

Cream butter and sugar in mixing bowl. Add egg and sifted dry ingredients; mix well. Add enough milk to orange juice and rind to measure 3/4 cup. Stir into flour mixture. Spoon into well-greased loaf pan. Bake at 375 degrees for 45 minutes or until bread tests done. Yield: 12 servings.

Breads

PINEAPPLE-DATE BREAD

2 8-oz. cans crushed
pineapple
2 c. bread flour
2 pkg. dry yeast
2/3 c. milk
1/3 c. packed brown sugar
6 tbsp. oil
1/2 tsp. salt
4 to 4 1/2 c. whole wheat flour
8 oz. dates, chopped
1 c. chopped pecans

Drain pineapple, reserving 1/3 cup juice. Combine bread flour and yeast in large mixer bowl. Heat reserved juice, milk, brown sugar, oil and salt in saucepan until warm. Add to flour mixture; mix well. Beat at high speed for 2 minutes. Add pineapple and enough whole wheat flour to make moderately stiff dough. Stir in dates and pecans. Knead on floured surface until smooth and elastic. Place in greased bowl, turning to grease surface. Let rise, covered, in warm place until doubled in bulk. Shape into 2 loaves. Place in loaf pans. Let rise, covered, until doubled in bulk. Bake at 375 degrees for 25 minutes.

PUMPKIN-PECAN LOAVES

4 eggs
1 1/2 c. packed brown sugar
1 c. oil
1 16-oz. can pumpkin
3 c. flour
2 tsp. soda
2 tsp. baking powder
1 tsp. each cinnamon, nutmeg
1 c. chopped pecans

Combine first 4 ingredients in bowl; beat well. Add combined dry ingredients; stir until just moistened. Stir in 2/3 cup pecans. Spread in 2 greased loaf pans. Sprinkle with remaining pecans. Bake at 350 degrees for 1 hour or until loaves test done.

ZUCCHINI-BANANA BRUNCH BREAD

1 1/2 c. flour
1 tbsp. baking powder
1 tsp. salt
3/4 tsp. cinnamon
1 c. oats
2 bananas, mashed
1 1/2 c. (scant) sugar
2/3 c. oil
2 eggs
3/4 c. shredded zucchini
1/2 c. chopped walnuts

Combine first 5 ingredients in bowl; mix well. Beat bananas with sugar, oil and eggs. Stir into flour mixture until just mixed. Fold in zucchini and walnuts. Pour into greased and floured 9-inch square pan. Bake at 350 degrees for 40 minutes. Yield: 9 servings.

147

Breads

HONEY-RYE QUICK BREAD

2 c. rye flour
1/2 tsp. salt
2 tsp. baking powder
2/3 c. instant nonfat dry milk
powder
1 tbsp. honey
2 tbsp. oil

Combine flour, salt, baking powder and dry milk in bowl. Mix honey, 1 cup water and oil in small bowl. Add to flour mixture; mix well. Spoon into greased and floured 10-inch cast iron skillet. Press to 1/2-inch thickness. Prick dough with fork. Bake at 350 degrees for 10 minutes or until well browned.

ANISE BREAD

1 tbsp. salt
2 sticks margarine
1 c. sugar
1 pkg. yeast
6 eggs
3/4 c. white wine
2 to 3 tbsp. aniseed
5 lb. (or less) bread flour

Heat first 3 ingredients with 2 cups water in saucepan until margarine melts and sugar dissolves; cool. Dissolve yeast in 1/3 cup warm water in large bowl. Add eggs, wine and aniseed; mix well. Add cooled sugar mixture. Stir in flour gradually; mix until dough forms ball. Knead on floured surface until smooth. Place in greased bowl, turning to grease surface. Let rise, covered, until doubled in bulk. Shape into 4 loaves. Place in greased loaf pans. Let rise until doubled in bulk. Bake at 300 degrees for 1 hour or until bread tests done. Remove from pans to cool on wire rack. Brush with additional margarine while warm.

CREAM CHEESE-FILLED COFFEE CAKES

1 c. sour cream
1 1/8 tsp. salt
1/2 c. margarine, melted
1 1/4 c. sugar
2 pkg. yeast
3 eggs
4 c. flour
1 lb. cream cheese, softened
4 tsp. vanilla extract
2 c. confectioners' sugar
1/4 c. milk

Scald sour cream in saucepan. Add 1 teaspoon salt, margarine and 1/2 cup sugar; mix well. Dissolve yeast in 1/2 cup warm water in large warm bowl. Add lukewarm sour cream mixture, 2 eggs and flour; mix well. Chill, covered, overnight. Roll into four 8 x 12-inch rectangles on floured surface. Combine cream cheese, 3/4 cup sugar, 1 beaten egg, 1/8 teaspoon salt and 2 teaspoons vanilla in blender container. Process until smooth. Spread on rectangles to within 1/2-inch of edges. Roll as for jelly roll from long side, sealing edges. Place seam side down on foil-lined baking sheet. Cut diagonal slashes 3/4 inch apart to but not through bottom alternating sides to resemble braid. Let rise until doubled in bulk. Bake at 375 degrees for 12 to 15 minutes or until brown. Mix confectioners' sugar with milk and 2 teaspoons vanilla in bowl. Spread on hot coffee cakes. Yield: 4 loaves.

COCONUT PRALINE COFFEE CAKE

Evaporated milk
3/4 c. sugar
1/2 tsp. salt
2 eggs
Butter, softened
Flour
2 pkg. dry yeast
Brown sugar
2/3 c. flaked coconut
1 c. confectioners' sugar

Beat 2/3 cup evaporated milk and next 3 ingredients in mixer bowl. Add 1/2 cup butter and 2 cups flour; beat until smooth. Add yeast dissolved in 1/2 cup warm water and 1 cup flour. Beat at medium speed for 3 minutes. Stir in 2 cups flour. Let rise, covered, until doubled in bulk. Knead lightly on floured surface; roll to 10 x 15-inch rectangle. Mix 1/4 cup butter, 2 tablespoons flour, 2/3 cup packed brown sugar and coconut in small bowl. Spread over dough; roll as for jelly roll from long side. Place seam side down in greased tube pan. Let rise, covered, until doubled in bulk. Bake at 350 degrees for 45 minutes. Remove to wire rack. Blend 1/4 cup packed brown sugar, 2 tablespoons evaporated milk, 2 tablespoons butter and confectioners' sugar in bowl. Spread over warm coffee cake.

Photograph for this recipe on page 138.

CINNAMON-RAISIN BREAD

1 1/2 c. milk, scalded
Sugar
2 tsp. salt
3/4 c. butter
1 c. unseasoned mashed potatoes
2 pkg. dry yeast
7 1/2 c. flour
1 1/2 c. raisins
2 tsp. cinnamon

Combine milk, 1/4 cup sugar, salt and 1/2 cup butter in saucepan; stir until butter melts. Add mashed potatoes; mix well. Cool to lukewarm. Dissolve yeast in 1/2 cup warm water in large mixer bowl. Add milk mixture and 3 1/2 cups flour. Beat for 2 minutes. Stir in raisins. Mix in enough remaining flour to make stiff dough. Knead on floured surface for 10 minutes or until smooth and elastic. Place in greased bowl, turning to grease surface. Let rise, covered, until doubled in bulk. Roll into two 8 x 16-inch rectangles. Sprinkle with mixture of 1/2 cup sugar and cinnamon. Roll as for jelly roll; seal edges and ends. Place in greased loaf pans. Melt 1/4 cup butter. Brush each top with 1 tablespoon melted butter. Let rise until doubled in bulk. Brush with remaining butter. Bake at 375 degrees for 35 to 40 minutes or until bread tests done.

Breads

ITALIAN PEPPERONI BREAD

1 loaf frozen bread dough,
thawed
1/4 c. pizza sauce
1/2 lb. cheese, grated
1/2 lb. pepperoni, thinly sliced

Roll dough on floured surface into 1-inch thick rectangle. Spread with pizza sauce. Top with cheese and pepperoni. Roll as for jelly roll; place on baking sheet. Cut 4 or 5 slits on top. Bake at 350 degrees for 20 to 25 minutes or until brown. Yield: 10 servings.

EASY WHITE BREAD

6 1/2 to 7 c. flour
2 tbsp. sugar
1 tbsp. salt
2 pkg. yeast
1/2 c. softened margarine
Oil

Mix 2 cups flour, sugar, salt and yeast in large mixer bowl; add margarine and 2 cups hot water. Beat for 2 minutes at medium speed. Add 1 cup flour. Beat at high speed for 2 minutes. Stir in enough remaining flour to make soft dough. Knead on lightly floured board for 10 minutes or until smooth and elastic. Let rest, covered, for 20 minutes. Shape into 2 loaves. Place in greased loaf pans. Brush with oil. Cover pans loosely with plastic wrap. Refrigerate for 2 to 24 hours. Uncover dough carefully. Let stand at room temperature for 10 minutes. Puncture any bubbles. Bake at 400 degrees for 30 to 40 minutes. Remove from pans to cool on wire racks.

HIGH-PROTEIN DARK BREAD

2 pkg. yeast
1 tbsp. sugar
1 c. cottage cheese
1/4 c. butter
1 tbsp. salt
1 tbsp. honey
2 c. milk, scalded
3 c. whole wheat flour
1/2 c. rye flour
1/4 c. wheat germ
3 c. all-purpose flour

Dissolve yeast and sugar in 1/2 cup warm water in large bowl. Add cottage cheese, butter, salt and honey to milk. Stir until butter is melted. Cool to lukewarm. Stir whole wheat flour, rye flour, wheat germ and cottage cheese mixture into yeast; beat until smooth. Stir in enough all-purpose flour to make soft dough. Knead on lightly floured surface for 10 minutes or until smooth and elastic. Place in greased bowl, turning to grease surface. Let rise, covered, in warm place until doubled in bulk. Shape into 2 loaves. Place in greased loaf pans. Let rise, covered, until doubled in bulk. Place on low rack of preheated 375-degree oven so that tops are in center of oven. Bake for 1 hour. Brush warm loaves with additional butter.

CARAWAY PUFF ROLLS

1 pkg. dry yeast
2 1/2 c. sifted flour
1/4 tsp. soda
1 c. cream-style cottage cheese
2 tbsp. sugar
1 tbsp. butter
1 tsp. salt
1 egg, beaten
2 tsp. grated onion
2 tsp. caraway seed

Combine yeast, 1 1/2 cups flour and soda in large mixer bowl. Heat cottage cheese, 1/4 cup water, sugar, butter and salt in saucepan until butter melts. Add to dry ingredients with egg, onion and caraway seed. Beat at medium speed for 3 minutes. Stir in remaining flour. Place in greased bowl, turning to grease surface. Let rise, covered, in warm place until doubled in bulk. Divide into 12 portions; place in greased muffin cups. Let rise, covered, until doubled in bulk. Bake at 350 degrees for 12 to 15 minutes or until brown. Remove from pan immediately.

CLOVERLEAF DINNER ROLLS

1/2 c. shortening
1 pkg. yeast
1 egg
1/3 c. sugar
1 tsp. salt
3 c. (heaping) flour
Butter

Melt shortening in 1/2 cup boiling water in large bowl. Cool to lukewarm. Dissolve yeast in 3/4 cup lukewarm water; add to shortening mixture. Blend egg, sugar, salt and 1/2 cup water; add to yeast mixture. Mix in flour. Place in greased bowl, turning to grease surface. Refrigerate, covered, overnight. Shape into cloverleaf rolls in greased muffin cups. Let rise for 30 minutes. Dot with butter. Bake at 400 degrees for 10 minutes.

MARMALADE STICKY BUNS

1 c. milk, scalded
1/4 c. sugar
1 tsp. salt
Butter
2 pkg. dry yeast
2 eggs
5 to 5 1/2 c. flour
1 3/4 c. orange marmalade
1 c. finely chopped walnuts
3/4 tsp. cinnamon

Combine milk, sugar, salt and 1 cup butter. Cool to lukewarm. Dissolve yeast in 1/2 cup warm water in large bowl. Add milk mixture, eggs and 3 cups flour; beat until smooth. Stir in enough remaining flour to make stiff dough. Let stand, covered, for 20 minutes. Combine 1 cup marmalade with 3 tablespoons butter in saucepan. Heat over low heat until blended, stirring constantly. Spoon into greased muffin cups. Mix walnuts with cinnamon. Knead dough lightly on floured surface. Roll into 2 rectangles. Spread with remaining marmalade and sprinkle with walnut mixture. Roll as for jelly roll from long side; seal seam. Slice 1 inch thick; place in prepared muffin cups. Let rise until doubled in bulk. Bake at 375 degrees until golden brown. Invert on serving plate.

Breads

RICH CROISSANTS

7/8 c. milk, scalded
1 tbsp. lard
1 1/2 tbsp. sugar
3/4 tsp. salt
1 pkg dry yeast
2 1/2 c. sifted flour
1 c. butter, softened

Combine hot milk, lard, sugar and salt in bowl; mix well. Cool to lukewarm. Dissolve yeast in 1/3 cup warm water. Add to milk mixture; mix well. Stir in flour. Knead on floured surface until smooth and elastic. Place in greased bowl, turning to grease surface. Let rise, covered with damp cloth, for 1 1/2 hours or until doubled in bulk. Chill, covered, for 20 minutes or longer. Roll 1/4 inch thick. Spread 1/4 cup butter over 2/3 of the surface. Fold unbuttered dough to center; fold doubled dough over remaining buttered portion. Turn dough 1/4 turn. Roll, butter and fold 3 additional times. Chill, covered, for 2 hours or longer. Roll 1/4 inch thick; trim any hardened edges. Cut into 3-inch squares; cut squares in half into triangles. Roll up from wide end, stretching dough slightly. Shape into crescents on baking sheet. Chill for 1/2 hour. Do not let rise. Bake in preheated 400-degree oven for 10 minutes. Reduce temperature to 350 degrees. Bake for 10 to 15 minutes longer or until crisp and golden brown.

MINI CHIP SWIRL BUNS

1 pkg. dry yeast
2/3 c. buttermilk
1 egg
3 to 3 1/4 c. flour
Butter
1/4 c. sugar
1 tsp. baking powder
1 tsp. salt
1/2 c. packed brown sugar
3/4 c. chopped nuts
3/4 c. semisweet miniature
chocolate chips

Dissolve yeast in 1/4 cup warm water. Combine with buttermilk, egg, 1 1/4 cups flour, 1/4 cup softened butter, sugar, baking powder and salt in large mixer bowl. Blend on low speed. Beat at medium speed for 2 minutes. Stir in enough remaining flour until dough is easy to handle. Knead on floured surface for 5 minutes. Roll into 9 x 16-inch rectangle. Combine brown sugar, 3 tablespoons melted butter and nuts in bowl; mix well. Spread over dough. Sprinkle with chocolate chips. Roll as for jelly roll from long side; pinch edges to seal. Cut into 1/2-inch slices. Place in circle cut sides up on greased baking sheet. Let rise, covered, for 1 hour or until doubled in bulk. Bake at 350 degrees for 20 minutes. Cover outer edges with foil. Bake for 5 to 10 minutes longer. Glaze if desired. Serve warm. Yield: 11 servings.

Photograph for this recipe on page 70.

NO-KNEAD CINNAMON ROLLS

1 pkg. dry yeast
1/2 c. scalded milk
3 tbsp. shortening
3 tbsp. sugar
1 1/2 tsp. salt
1 egg
3 1/4 c. flour
1/2 c. packed brown sugar
1 tsp. cinnamon
2 tbsp. butter, softened
Confectioners' sugar glaze

Dissolve yeast in 1/4 cup warm water in large bowl. Combine milk with next 3 ingredients and 1/4 cup cold water. Stir milk mixture and egg into yeast. Add flour gradually; mix well. Let rise, covered, for 15 minutes. Mix brown sugar with cinnamon in bowl. Roll dough into 12 x 18-inch rectangle. Spread with butter. Sprinkle with brown sugar mixture. Roll as for jelly roll. Cut into 1-inch slices. Place in greased baking pan. Let rise for 1 hour or until doubled in bulk. Bake at 375 degrees for 20 to 25 minutes or until golden brown. Drizzle with confectioners' sugar glaze. Yield: 18 servings.

FROSTED ORANGE CRESCENT ROLLS

1 pkg. dry yeast
3/4 c. milk, scalded
1/4 c. shortening
1/4 c. sugar
1 tsp. salt
3 c. sifted flour
1 egg, beaten
1 tsp. grated orange rind
Confectioners' sugar
Orange juice

Soften yeast in 1/4 cup warm water. Combine milk, shortening, sugar and salt in large bowl. Cool to lukewarm. Add 1 cup flour; beat well. Beat in yeast mixture, egg and orange rind. Add remaining flour; mix well. Place dough in greased bowl, turning to grease surface. Chill, covered, for 2 hours or longer. Roll into two 9-inch circles. Cut each into 12 wedges. Roll each from wide end. Arrange rolls, points down, on greased baking sheet. Let rise for 1 1/4 hours. Bake at 350 degrees for 15 minutes. Blend confectioners' sugar with enough orange juice to make glaze. Drizzle over warm rolls.

OATMEAL YEAST ROLLS

1 pkg. dry yeast
3/4 c. milk, scalded
1/4 c. sugar
2 tsp. salt
1/3 c. butter
1 egg
4 1/2 to 5 c. sifted flour
1 c. cooked oatmeal, cooled
Melted shortening

Dissolve yeast in 1/4 cup warm water. Pour scalded milk over sugar, salt and butter in bowl; cool to lukewarm. Stir in egg and 1 cup flour. Add yeast and oatmeal. Stir in enough remaining flour to make soft dough. Knead on lightly floured surface until smooth and elastic. Place in greased bowl, turning to grease surface. Let rise, covered, in warm place until doubled in bulk. Punch dough down. Let rest, covered, for 10 minutes. Shape into rolls; place on greased baking sheets. Brush with melted shortening. Let rise, covered, in warm place until nearly doubled in bulk. Bake at 375 degrees for 15 to 18 minutes or until golden brown. Yield: 3 1/2 dozen.

Desserts

Crown your meal with a dessert masterpiece. There's no better way for the cook to draw raves from satisfied diners than to end a meal with a sweet delicacy from her own kitchen.

Choose your dessert to complement the meal that precedes it. Serve a light taste-tempter if your main course is substantial. Go to a rich concoction when your menu is not too heavy. Select just the right flavor, texture, and color to provide a perfect ending to that special meal.

The favorite dessert recipes that follow are among the most delectable ever assembled. Here you will find elegant cakes frosted to perfection and even an easy microwave cake. The collection of mouth-watering homemade pies brings you never-fail instructions for a sparkling array of pastries. There is a choice of fruit desserts, cream puffs, rich cheesecakes, or an elegant mousse. There are also recipes that will help you fill your cookie and candy jars to the top with homemade sweets.

You'll discover desserts that take hours to prepare, and others that take only minutes with the magic of microwave cooking.

Desserts offer adventure and excitement to every cook. Discover the satisfaction and pride of serving your family eye-appealing, taste-tempting confections.

CREAM PUFFS FILLED WITH CLASSIC CHOCOLATE CREAM PUDDING, Recipe on page 168.

Desserts

FRESH APPLE CAKE

2 to 2 1/2 c. chopped apples
2 c. sugar
3 eggs
1 c. oil
3 c. self-rising flour
2 tsp. soda
1 tsp. each cloves, cinnamon
and nutmeg
1 c. chopped pecans

Combine apples and sugar in bowl; mix well. Let stand for 10 minutes. Add eggs and oil; mix well. Mix in sifted dry ingredients and pecans. Pour into greased tube pan. Bake at 350 degrees for 1 hour.

HEAVENLY ANGEL FOOD CAKE

1 3/4 c. egg whites
1 1/4 c. sifted cake flour
1 3/4 c. sugar
1/2 tsp. salt
1 1/2 tsp. cream of tartar
1 tsp. vanilla extract
1/2 tsp. almond extract

Place egg whites in large mixer bowl. Let stand for 1 hour. Sift flour and 3/4 cup sugar together 5 times. Beat egg whites with salt and cream of tartar at high speed until soft peaks form. Add 1 cup sugar, 1/4 cup at a time, beating well after each addition; beat until stiff peaks form. Fold in vanilla and almond extracts. Sift 1/4 cup flour mixture at a time over egg whites; fold in gently after each addition. Spoon gently into 10-inch tube pan. Cut through batter twice with knife; spread evenly. Bake at 375 degrees for 35 to 40 minutes. Invert pan over neck of bottle to cool completely. Yield: 12-16 servings.

BUTTERSCOTCH-RUM RIPPLE CAKE

1 c. butter
2 c. sugar
1 c. sour cream
3 c. flour
1 tsp. each soda, salt
1 tsp. vanilla extract
1 tbsp. rum extract
6 eggs
1 sm. package butterscotch
instant pudding mix
3/4 c. butterscotch ice cream
topping

Combine first 8 ingredients and 5 eggs in mixer bowl. Beat for 3 minutes. Mix 2 cups prepared batter, pudding mix, topping and 1 egg in small mixer bowl. Beat for 1 minute. Spoon half the cake batter into greased and floured bundt pan. Add half the butterscotch batter. Cut with knife to marbleize. Repeat with remaining batters. Bake at 350 degrees for 1 1/4 hours or until cake tests done. Cool in pan for 10 to 15 minutes. Garnish with rum-flavored confectioners' sugar glaze. Yield: 12 servings.

CARROT-PINEAPPLE CAKE

1 c. oil
1 1/2 c. sugar
4 eggs, beaten
2 c. grated carrots
1 c. drained crushed pineapple
1 c. chopped walnuts
2 c. sifted flour
1 1/2 tsp. soda
2 tsp. baking powder
1 1/2 tsp. salt
1/2 lb. confectioners' sugar
1/2 c. butter, softened
1/2 tsp. vanilla extract
1 3-oz. package cream cheese,
softened

Combine oil and sugar in bowl. Add eggs; mix well. Stir in carrots, pineapple and walnuts. Sift in next 4 ingredients; mix well. Pour into greased and floured 9 x 13-inch baking pan. Bake at 350 degrees for 35 to 40 minutes. Cool. Combine confectioners' sugar, butter, vanilla and cream cheese in bowl; beat well. Spread on cooled cake.

ONE-STEP CHOCOLATE CAKE ROLL

1/4 c. butter
1 can sweetened condensed milk
1 tsp. vanilla extract
1/4 tsp. salt
1 1/3 c. flaked coconut
1/2 c. chopped pecans
4 eggs
2/3 c. sugar
2 1-oz. envelopes premelted
unsweetened chocolate
1/2 c. flour
1/2 c. (or more) confectioners'
sugar

Melt butter in foil-lined 10 x 15-inch jelly roll pan, spreading to coat surface. Mix condensed milk, 1/2 teaspoon vanilla and 1/8 teaspoon salt in small bowl. Pour over butter. Do not stir. Sprinkle coconut and pecans over top; set aside. Beat eggs in large mixer bowl at high speed until thick and lemon colored. Add sugar gradually, beating well after each addition. Blend in chocolate, 1/2 teaspoon vanilla, 1/8 teaspoon salt and 1/4 cup cold water. Stir in flour gradually. Spread over coconut mixture. Bake at 350 degrees for 18 to 20 minutes or until cake tests done. Sprinkle with confectioners' sugar; invert on towel. Roll in towel from 10-inch side as for jelly roll; cool. Unroll. Remove towel. Reroll. Cut into slices to serve. Yield: 8 servings.

PISTACHIO MARBLE CAKE

1 box white cake mix
1 pkg. pistachio pudding mix
4 eggs
1/2 c. oil
1 c. orange juice
3/4 c. chocolate syrup
Confectioners' sugar

Combine first 5 ingredients in bowl. Mix, using cake mix directions. Pour 2/3 of the batter into greased bundt pan. Blend syrup into remaining batter. Spoon over white batter; swirl to marbleize. Bake at 350 degrees for 50 to 60 minutes or until cake tests done; cool. Invert onto serving plate. Sprinkle with confectioners' sugar.

Desserts

CHOCOLATE FUDGE CAKE

3 1-oz. squares unsweetened
chocolate
Milk
3 eggs
1 2/3 c. sugar
1/2 c. shortening
1 tsp. vanilla extract
2 c. flour
1 tsp. soda
1/2 tsp. salt
1 recipe Fast Fudge Frosting

Combine chocolate, 1/2 cup milk, 1 egg and 2/3 cup sugar in saucepan. Bring to a boil, stirring constantly. Cream 1 cup sugar and shortening in bowl. Beat in vanilla and remaining 2 eggs. Add sifted dry ingredients alternately with 1 cup milk, beating well after each addition. Blend in chocolate mixture. Pour into 2 greased 9 x 12-inch pans. Bake at 350 degrees for 25 to 30 minutes. Frost with Fast Fudge Frosting.

Fast Fudge Frosting

1 lb. confectioners' sugar,
sifted
1/2 c. cocoa
1/4 tsp. salt
1/3 c. butter, softened
1 tsp. vanilla extract

Combine first 4 ingredients with 1/3 cup boiling water in bowl; blend well. Stir in vanilla. Beat until creamy.

MARBLE POUND CAKE

Butter
1 1/2 c. sugar
3 eggs
2 tsp. vanilla extract
1 1/2 c. flour
1/8 tsp. soda
1/2 c. sour cream
3 sq. unsweetened chocolate
Cinnamon
1/2 c. confectioners' sugar

Cream 3/4 cup softened butter in bowl. Beat in sugar until fluffy. Mix in eggs and 1 1/2 teaspoons vanilla. Mix flour and soda in bowl. Add half to the creamed mixture; mix well. Mix in half the sour cream. Repeat with remaining flour and sour cream. Blend 1 1/2 cups batter with 2 squares melted chocolate in bowl. Add 1/2 teaspoon cinnamon to remaining batter; mix well. Spoon half the cinnamon batter into greased and floured loaf pan. Spoon half the chocolate batter on top. Repeat with remaining batters. Swirl with knife to marbleize. Bake at 325 degrees for 1 1/2 hours or until cake tests done. Cool in pan for 10 minutes before turning onto wire rack to cool completely. Melt 1 square chocolate and 1 1/2 tablespoons butter in saucepan over low heat; remove from heat. Stir in confectioners' sugar, 1/8 teaspoon cinnamon and 1/2 teaspoon vanilla. Mix in 5 teaspoons hot water 1 teaspoon at a time to make thin glaze. Drizzle over cooled cake.

Photograph for this recipe on page 104.

BRANDIED POUND CAKE

2 sticks margarine, softened
3 c. sugar
6 egg yolks
1/2 tsp. rum extract
1 tsp. each orange, vanilla
extract
1/4 tsp. almond extract
1/2 tsp. lemon extract
1 tsp. butter flavoring
3 c. flour
1/4 tsp. soda
1/2 tsp. salt
1 c. sour cream
1/4 c. apricot Brandy

Cream margarine and sugar in large mixer bowl. Add egg yolks 1 at a time, beating well after each addition. Add flavorings. Sift dry ingredients together. Add to creamed mixture alternately with sour cream and Brandy. Pour into greased tube pan. Bake at 325 degrees for 1 hour and 10 minutes. Yield: 20-24 servings.

SOUR CREAM POUND CAKE

2 3/4 c. sugar
1 c. butter, softened
6 eggs
3 c. sifted flour
1/2 tsp. each salt, soda
1 c. sour cream
1/2 tsp. each lemon, orange
and vanilla extract
Confectioners' sugar

Cream sugar and butter in bowl. Add eggs 1 at a time, beating well after each addition. Sift dry ingredients together. Add to creamed mixture alternately with sour cream, beating well after each addition. Stir in flavorings. Pour into greased and floured 10-inch tube pan. Bake at 325 degrees for 1 1/2 hours. Cool in pan for 15 minutes. Sprinkle with confectioners' sugar.

MICROWAVE PUDDING CAKE

2 tbsp. melted butter
1 c. flour
1 tsp. baking powder
1 tsp. vanilla extract
1/2 c. milk
1/2 c. chopped pecans
1/2 c. flaked coconut
1 c. sugar
7 tbsp. cocoa
3/4 tsp. salt

Combine first 7 ingredients with 1/2 cup sugar, 3 tablespoons cocoa and 1/2 teaspoon salt in bowl; mix well. Microwave 1 2/3 cups water in 8 x 8-inch glass baking pan until boiling. Stir in remaining 1/2 cup sugar, 4 tablespoons cocoa and 1/4 teaspoon salt. Microwave to boiling point; mix well. Drop batter by spoonfuls into hot liquid. Microwave on Medium for 6 minutes; turn dish. Microwave on High for 6 minutes.

Desserts

FRESH PLUM CAKE

2 eggs
Sugar
1/2 c. milk
1 tbsp. butter
1 tsp. vanilla extract
1 c. flour
1 tsp. baking powder
1/2 tsp. salt
4 lg. plums, cut into eighths

Beat eggs in mixer bowl at high speed for 10 minutes or until very thick. Beat in 1 cup sugar gradually. Heat milk and butter in small saucepan. Stir into eggs and sugar gradually. Add vanilla. Blend in mixture of flour, baking powder and salt. Pour into greased 9-inch springform pan. Bake at 350 degrees for 30 minutes. Arrange plum slices skin side down on top of cake. Sprinkle with 2 tablespoons sugar. Bake for 10 to 12 minutes longer. Cool. Remove side of springform pan. Yield: 8 servings.

Photograph for this recipe on page 103.

SPICED PUMPKIN LAYER CAKE

1 16-oz. can pumpkin
1/2 c. packed light brown sugar
3 eggs
1 pkg. yellow cake mix
4 tsp. grated orange rind
2 tsp. pumpkin pie spice
1 c. chopped walnuts
1 3-oz. package cream cheese, softened
1/3 c. butter, softened
4 c. confectioners' sugar
1/2 tsp. nutmeg
1 tsp. vanilla extract

Combine pumpkin, brown sugar, 1/4 cup water and eggs in mixer bowl; mix well. Add cake mix, orange rind and pumpkin pie spice. Beat at low speed until blended. Beat at medium speed for 5 minutes. Stir in walnuts. Pour into 2 greased and floured 9-inch layer cake pans. Bake at 350 degrees for 30 to 35 minutes or until layers test done. Cool in pans for 10 minutes before turning onto wire rack to cool completely. Beat cream cheese and butter in bowl until blended. Add confectioners' sugar gradually, mixing well after each addition. Stir in nutmeg and vanilla. Beat in 1 1/2 to 2 tablespoons water gradually until of spreading consistency. Spread between layers and over top and side of cake. Garnish with additional walnuts.

Photograph for this recipe on page 104.

CHOCOLATE FINGERS

2 c. graham cracker crumbs
1 box confectioners' sugar
2 sticks margarine, melted
1 c. peanut butter
1 c. finely chopped pecans
1 12-oz. package semisweet chocolate chips
1 bar paraffin

Mix crumbs and confectioners' sugar in bowl. Add margarine, peanut butter and pecans; mix well. Shape into fingers. Melt chocolate chips and paraffin in double boiler. Cool slightly. Dip candy into mixture to coat. Cool on waxed paper.

MICROWAVE FUDGE

1 1-lb. package confectioners'
sugar
1/4 tsp. salt
1/2 c. cocoa
1/4 c. evaporated milk
1 stick margarine, sliced
1 tbsp. vanilla extract
1/2 c. chopped pecans

Sift first 3 ingredients together into 3-quart glass casserole. Add milk; mix until partially blended. Place margarine over top. Microwave for 2 minutes. Add vanilla; beat until smooth. Add pecans; mix well. Pour into 8 x 8-inch buttered dish. Chill in refrigerator for 1 hour or in freezer for 20 minutes. Cut into squares.

HONEY-WALNUT BALLS

1/2 c. peanut butter
1/4 c. honey
1/2 c. (or more) nonfat dry
milk powder
1 tbsp. sunflower seed
1 tbsp. chopped walnuts
1 tbsp. chopped raisins
3 tbsp. sesame seed

Combine peanut butter and honey in bowl; mix well. Add milk powder gradually; mix well. Stir in next 3 ingredients. Shape into small balls. Roll in sesame seed. Chill in refrigerator. Yield: 1 1/2 dozen.

MAPLE WALNUT BRITTLE

2 c. packed light brown sugar
1/2 c. maple syrup
1/4 c. butter
1/2 tsp. maple flavoring
1 1/2 c. chopped walnuts
1/4 tsp. soda

Combine brown sugar, maple syrup and 1/2 cup water in large saucepan. Cook to 300 degrees on candy thermometer, stirring constantly. Add butter, flavoring and walnuts; mix well. Stir in soda. Spread in thin layer on buttered baking sheet. Break into pieces when cool. Yield: 1 1/2 pounds.

MUDDY BOTTOM DIVINITY

2 8-oz. bars milk chocolate
2 1/2 c. sugar
1/2 c. light corn syrup
1/4 tsp. salt
2 egg whites, stiffly beaten
1 tsp. vanilla extract
1/2 c. pecans

Line 9 x 9-inch pan with large piece of foil. Place chocolate bars in bottom. Combine sugar, corn syrup, salt and 1/2 cup water in saucepan. Cook over medium-high heat until sugar dissolves, stirring constantly. Cook to hardball stage or to 250 degrees on candy thermometer. Do not stir. Beat hot syrup gradually into egg whites at high speed. Add vanilla. Beat for 4 to 5 minutes or until candy holds its shape. Stir in pecans. Spread evenly over chocolate bars; cool. Lift foil to remove from pan. Cut into 1-inch squares. Store in tightly covered container. Yield: 3 dozen.

Desserts

PECAN PRALINES

1 6 1/2-oz. can evaporated milk
2 c. light corn syrup
3/4 c. sugar
1 can sweetened condensed milk
1/2 stick margarine
1 tsp. salt
3 c. broken pecans

Combine first 3 ingredients in saucepan; mix well. Cook over medium heat to 248 degrees on candy thermometer, stirring constantly. Mixture will curdle. Add condensed milk and margarine. Cook to 238 degrees on candy thermometer, stirring constantly. Remove from heat; stir in salt and pecans. Drop by tablespoonfuls onto foil-lined surface. Wrap individually in plastic wrap when cool.

ALMOND FUDGE BARS

2 c. packed brown sugar
Butter, softened
2 eggs
4 tsp. vanilla extract
2 1/2 c. baking mix
3 c. quick-cooking oats
1 12-oz. package semisweet chocolate chips
1 c. sweetened condensed milk
1/2 tsp. salt
1 1/2 c. chopped almonds

Combine brown sugar, 3/4 cup butter, eggs and 2 teaspoons vanilla in large bowl; mix well. Add baking mix and oats; mix well. Heat chocolate chips, condensed milk, 2 tablespoons butter and salt in 2-quart saucepan over low heat until chocolate melts, stirring constantly. Stir in 1/2 cup almonds and 2 teaspoons vanilla. Press 2/3 of the oatmeal mixture into greased 10 x 15-inch baking pan. Drizzle chocolate mixture over top. Sprinkle with 1 cup almonds; press lightly into mixture. Sprinkle remaining oats mixture over top. Bake at 350 degrees for 30 minutes or until lightly browned. Cut into bars when cool. Yield: 6 dozen.

LUSCIOUS APRICOT BARS

2/3 c. dried apricots
1/2 c. butter
1/4 c. sugar
1 1/3 c. sifted flour
1 c. packed brown sugar
2 eggs, well beaten
1/2 tsp. baking powder
1/4 tsp. salt
1/2 tsp. vanilla extract
1/2 c. chopped pecans
Confectioners' sugar

Combine apricots with enough water to cover in saucepan. Boil for 10 minutes; cool. Drain and chop. Mix butter, sugar and 1 cup flour in bowl until crumbly. Press into greased 8 x 8-inch baking pan. Bake at 350 degrees for 25 minutes. Beat brown sugar gradually into eggs. Sift in 1/3 cup flour, baking powder and salt. Add vanilla, pecans and apricots; mix well. Spread over baked layer. Bake for 30 minutes longer. Cool. Cut into bars. Roll in confectioners' sugar. Yield: 2 1/2 dozen.

CHOCOLATE-CREAM CHEESE BARS

1 box chocolate cake mix
3 eggs
1 tsp. vanilla extract
1 stick butter
1 box confectioners' sugar
1 8-oz. package cream cheese,
softened

Combine cake mix, 1 egg, 1/2 teaspoon vanilla and butter in bowl; mix well. Pat into greased 9 x 13-inch baking pan. Mix remaining ingredients, 2 eggs and 1/2 teaspoon vanilla in bowl. Pour over crust. Bake at 350 degrees for 30 minutes. Cut into bars when cool.

PEPPERMINT BROWNIES

3 sq. chocolate
Margarine
2 eggs
1 c. sugar
1 tsp. vanilla extract
1/2 c. flour
1/2 c. pecans
1 c. confectioners' sugar
1 tbsp. milk
3/4 tsp. peppermint flavoring
Green food coloring

Melt 2 squares chocolate and 1/2 cup margarine in saucepan. Combine with next 5 ingredients in bowl; mix well. Pour into greased 8 x 8-inch baking pan. Bake at 300 degrees for 25 minutes; cool. Mix confectioners' sugar, milk, flavoring and food coloring in bowl until smooth. Spread over baked layer. Melt 1 square chocolate and 1 tablespoon margarine together in saucepan. Drizzle over peppermint layer. Cut into 1-inch squares when cool.

LEMON SQUARES

2 sticks margarine
1/2 c. confectioners' sugar
1/2 tsp. salt
Flour
4 eggs
1/2 tsp. vanilla extract
2 c. sugar
2 tbsp. lemon juice

Combine first 3 ingredients with 2 cups flour in bowl; mix until crumbly. Pat into buttered 8 x 8-inch baking dish. Bake at 350 degrees for 25 minutes. Combine eggs, 6 tablespoons flour and remaining ingredients. Beat for 1 minute. Pour over crust. Bake for 30 minutes longer. Cut into squares. Sprinkle with additional confectioners' sugar.

TOFFEE COOKIES

40 saltine crackers
1 c. melted butter
1 c. packed brown sugar
2 c. chocolate chips
1 c. chopped pecans

Line large cookie sheet with foil; coat with oil. Arrange crackers in single layer on foil. Combine butter and brown sugar in saucepan. Boil for 2 1/2 minutes. Pour over crackers. Bake at 300 degrees for 5 minutes. Sprinkle chocolate chips over crackers. Spread to cover when melted. Sprinkle pecans over top; press in lightly. Cut while warm.

Desserts

CHESS SQUARES

2 sticks margarine
1 16-oz. package light brown
sugar
1/2 c. sugar
4 eggs
2 c. flour
1 tsp. baking powder
Pinch of salt
1 tsp. vanilla extract
1 c. chopped pecans
1 c. confectioners' sugar (opt.)

Combine margarine and brown sugar in saucepan. Cook over low heat until blended, stirring constantly. Pour into mixer bowl. Add sugar then eggs 1 at a time, beating well after each addition. Add flour sifted with baking powder and salt; stir in vanilla and pecans. Pour into greased and floured 9 x 13-inch baking pan. Bake at 300 degrees for 40 to 50 minutes or until set. Cut into squares while warm; roll in confectioners' sugar. Yield: 2 dozen.

PEANUT BUTTER SURPRISE COOKIES

1 c. margarine, softened
1 c. crunchy peanut butter
1 c. packed brown sugar
1 1/2 c. sugar
2 eggs
1/4 c. milk
2 tsp. vanilla extract
1 c. chocolate chips
1 1/2 c. flour
2 c. whole wheat flour
2 tsp. soda
1 tsp. salt

Cream margarine, peanut butter, brown sugar and 1 cup sugar in bowl. Add eggs, milk and vanilla 1 at a time, beating well after each addition. Stir in chocolate chips. Sift in next 4 dry ingredients; mix well. Shape into 1-inch balls. Roll in remaining 1/2 cup sugar. Place on cookie sheet. Bake at 375 degrees for 8 to 10 minutes or until golden brown. Yield: 8 dozen.

CINNAMON TEA CAKES

1 c. butter, softened
2 1/2 c. confectioners' sugar
2 1/4 c. sifted flour
1 1/2 tsp. cinnamon
1/4 tsp. salt
1 tsp. vanilla extract

Cream butter and 1/2 cup confectioners' sugar in large bowl. Stir in flour, 1/2 teaspoon cinnamon, salt and vanilla. Chill for several hours. Shape into 1-inch balls. Place on buttered baking sheet. Bake at 400 degrees for 14 to 17 minutes or until golden brown. Roll in mixture of 2 cups confectioners' sugar and 1 teaspoon cinnamon while hot; cool. Roll in remaining cinnamon mixture. Yield: 4 dozen.

Desserts

APPLE PIE WITH CINNAMON CREME SAUCE

1 c. sugar
1 tsp. cinnamon
1/4 c. flour
6 c. thinly sliced peeled tart apples
1 recipe 2-crust pie pastry
2 tbsp. butter
Evaporated milk
Cinnamon Creme Sauce

Combine sugar, cinnamon and flour in small bowl. Mix with apples in large bowl. Turn into pastry-lined pie plate. Dot with butter. Top with remaining pastry; seal edge and cut vents. Brush evaporated milk lightly over top. Bake at 425 degrees for 45 to 50 minutes or until apples are tender and crust is golden brown. Serve warm or cold with vanilla ice cream and Cinnamon Creme Sauce.

Cinnamon Creme Sauce

2/3 c. light corn syrup
1 1/2 c. sugar
1 1/2 tsp. cinnamon
2/3 c. evaporated milk

Combine corn syrup, sugar, 1/3 cup water and cinnamon in saucepan. Bring to a boil over medium heat, stirring constantly. Cook for 4 minutes. Cool for 10 minutes. Stir in evaporated milk. Yield: 2 cups.

Photograph for this recipe above.

165

Desserts

APRICREAM PIE

1 tbsp. unflavored gelatin
3 eggs, separated
1 c. packed brown sugar
1/2 tsp. salt
1 1/2 c. apricot puree
1 tbsp. lemon juice
2 tbsp. sugar
1/2 c. whipping cream, whipped
1 baked 9-in. pie shell

Soften gelatin in 1/4 cup cold water. Combine beaten egg yolks, brown sugar, salt, apricot puree and lemon juice in saucepan. Cook over low heat until thick, stirring constantly. Add gelatin; stir until dissolved. Chill until partially set. Beat sugar gradually into beaten egg whites until stiff. Fold egg whites and whipped cream into apricot mixture. Spoon into pie shell. Chill until firm. Garnish with additional whipped cream.

BLACKBERRY-SOUR CREAM PIE

4 c. fresh blackberries
1 unbaked 9-in. pie shell
Sugar
1 c. sifted flour
1/4 tsp. salt
1 c. sour cream

Place blackberries in pie shell. Sift 1 1/4 cups sugar, flour and salt into sour cream in bowl; mix well. Pour over blackberries. Sprinkle 2 tablespoons sugar over top. Bake at 450 degrees for 10 minutes. Reduce temperature to 350 degrees. Bake for 30 minutes longer. Cool on wire rack.

CHOCOLATE FUDGE PIE

1/2 c. melted butter
1/3 c. cocoa
4 eggs
1/4 tsp. salt
1 tsp. vanilla extract
1 c. sugar
1 unbaked 9-in. pie shell

Combine first 6 ingredients in bowl; mix well. Pour into pie shell. Bake at 350 degrees for 1/2 hour or until set. Do not overbake. Yield: 6 servings.

BROWNIE PIE

1 can sweetened condensed milk
1/4 tsp. salt
1 6-oz. package semisweet
chocolate chips
1 tsp. vanilla extract
2 tbsp. flour
2 eggs, separated
1/2 c. coarsely chopped pecans
2 tbsp. sugar
1 unbaked 9-in. pie shell

Combine condensed milk and salt in saucepan. Bring to a boil; remove from heat. Beat in chocolate, vanilla and flour. Add egg yolks, 1 at a time, beating well after each addition. Stir in pecans. Add sugar gradually to stiffly beaten egg whites, beating until very stiff. Fold into chocolate mixture. Pour into pie shell. Bake at 350 degrees for 40 minutes or until firm. Serve with ice cream.

Desserts

CANTALOUPE-ORANGE PIE

4 eggs, separated
1 c. sugar
1/2 tsp. salt
1 tbsp. lemon juice
1 tbsp. grated lemon rind
1 pkg. orange gelatin
1/2 c. orange juice
1/4 tsp. cream of tartar
1 1/2 c. chopped cantaloupe
1 baked 10-in. pie shell
1 c. whipping cream, whipped

Beat egg yolks lightly in double boiler. Add 1/2 cup sugar, salt, lemon juice and rind. Cook until mixture coats spoon, stirring frequently; remove from heat. Dissolve gelatin in boiling orange juice. Stir into egg yolk mixture; cool. Beat egg whites and cream of tartar until stiff. Beat in remaining 1/2 cup sugar gradually. Fold in gelatin mixture; add cantaloupe. Spoon into pie shell. Chill for 4 hours or longer. Top with whipped cream.

CHERRY MELBA MERINGUE PIE

1 8-oz. jar maraschino cherries
1 tbsp. cornstarch
1/2 c. currant jelly
4 tsp. lemon juice
1/4 tsp. grated lemon rind
4 egg whites
1/2 tsp. vanilla extract
1/4 tsp. salt
1/4 tsp. cream of tartar
1 1/3 c. sugar
8 fresh peach halves, chilled
1 qt. vanilla ice cream

Puree cherries in blender. Blend cornstarch with 1 tablespoon cold water in saucepan. Add cherries, jelly, lemon juice and rind. Cook over medium heat until thick and clear, stirring constantly. Chill in refrigerator. Combine egg whites, vanilla, salt and cream of tartar in large mixer bowl. Beat at high speed until soft peaks form. Add sugar very gradually, beating until stiff. Spread 1/4 inch thick in pie plate, building up side. Bake at 250 degrees for 45 minutes. Turn oven off. Let stand in closed oven for 30 minutes longer. Arrange peach halves in meringue shell. Top with ice cream. Spoon cherry melba sauce over top.

TWO-CRUST LEMON PIE

1 1/4 c. sugar
2 tbsp. flour
1/8 tsp. salt
1/4 c. butter, softened
3 eggs
1 tsp. grated lemon rind
1 med. lemon, peeled, thinly sliced
1 recipe 2-crust pie pastry

Combine first 3 ingredients in bowl. Blend in butter. Reserve 1 teaspoon egg white. Beat remaining eggs together. Add to flour mixture with lemon rind and 1/2 cup water; mix well. Stir in lemon. Pour into pastry-lined 8-inch pie plate. Top with remaining pastry; seal edge and cut vents. Brush top with reserved egg white. Bake at 400 degrees for 30 to 35 minutes or until golden brown.

Desserts

POPPY SEED CHEESECAKE

1/2 c. graham cracker crumbs
1 tsp. cinnamon
1 1/4 c. sugar
3 tbsp. flour
3 tbsp. poppy seed
2 8-oz. packages cream cheese, softened
1 c. sour cream
1 1/2 tsp. vanilla extract
6 eggs, separated
1/8 tsp. salt
1/2 tsp. cream of tartar

Mix graham cracker crumbs with cinnamon. Coat sides and bottom of buttered 9-inch springform pan with crumbs. Combine 3/4 cup sugar, flour and poppy seed in mixer bowl. Add cream cheese, sour cream and vanilla. Beat until smooth. Blend in beaten egg yolks. Beat egg whites and salt until foamy. Add cream of tartar. Beat until soft peaks form. Beat in remaining 1/2 cup sugar gradually until stiff. Fold into cheese mixture. Pour into prepared pan. Bake at 275 degrees for 1 1/2 hours. Turn off oven. Open oven door about 6 inches. Let cake stand for about 2 hours. Garnish with whipped cream.

Photograph for this recipe on page 104.

CREAM PUFFS FILLED WITH CLASSIC CHOCOLATE CREAM PUDDING

1/2 c. butter
1/4 tsp. salt
1 c. flour
4 eggs
Classic Chocolate Cream Pudding

Bring 1 cup water, butter and salt to a rolling boil in saucepan; reduce heat. Add flour all at once. Cook for 1 minute or until mixture forms ball, stirring constantly. Remove from heat; cool slightly. Beat in eggs 1 at a time. Drop by scant 1/4 cupfuls 2 inches apart onto baking sheet. Bake at 400 degrees for 35 to 40 minutes or until puffed and golden brown. Slice off and reserve tops. Scoop out soft centers. Fill with Classic Chocolate Cream Pudding. Replace tops. Chill. Garnish with sprinkle of confectioners' sugar.

Classic Chocolate Cream Pudding

1 c. sugar
1/4 c. cocoa
1/3 c. cornstarch
1/4 tsp. salt
3 c. milk
3 egg yolks, slightly beaten
2 tbsp. butter
1 1/2 tsp. vanilla extract
1/2 c. whipping cream, whipped (opt.)

Combine sugar, cocoa, cornstarch and salt in heavy saucepan; stir in milk and egg yolks. Bring to a boil over medium heat, stirring constantly. Cook for 1 minute, stirring constantly; remove from heat. Blend in butter and vanilla. Chill, covered with plastic wrap. Fold in whipped cream.

Chocolate-Berry Parfaits

Fold 3/4 cup pureed strawberries into 2 cups sweetened whipped cream. Layer chocolate pudding and strawberry mixture alternately in parfait glasses.

Photograph for this recipe on page 154.

Desserts

CAFE AU LAIT PUFFS

1 c. sugar
3 c. whipping cream
6 tbsp. instant coffee powder
8 doz. Miniature Cream Puffs
3 c. confectioners' sugar

Blend sugar into whipping cream gradually, beating until stiff. Dissolve coffee in 6 tablespoons boiling water. Fold half the coffee into whipped cream. Spoon into puffs. Blend remaining coffee with confectioners' sugar. Spread over puffs.

Miniature Cream Puffs

1/2 c. butter
1/4 tsp. salt
1 c. sifted flour
4 eggs

Combine 1 cup water, butter and salt in saucepan. Bring to a full rolling boil; reduce heat. Stir in flour quickly, mixing vigorously with wooden spoon until mixture forms ball. Remove from heat. Beat in eggs 1 at a time. Drop by heaping measuring teaspoonfuls onto greased baking sheet. Bake at 400 degrees for 20 minutes. Yield: 8 dozen.

ICE CREAM KOLACHES

4 c. flour
1 lb. butter, softened
1 pt. vanilla ice cream, softened
Apricot jam
Strawberry preserves
Confectioners' sugar

Combine first 3 ingredients in bowl; blend well. Roll 1/8 inch thick on floured surface. Cut into small circles. Place on baking sheet. Spoon 1/2 teaspoon jam or preserves on each circle. Bake at 350 degrees for 20 minutes or until golden. Sprinkle with confectioners' sugar.

MERINGUE-TOPPED APPLES SARONNO

4 lg. apples, peeled, cored, sliced
Juice of 1 lemon
1 1/2 c. sugar
Amaretto di Saronno
Grated rind and juice of 1 orange
3 egg whites

Sprinkle apple slices with lemon juice. Combine 1 cup sugar, 1 cup Amaretto di Saronno, orange rind and juice in saucepan. Bring to a boil. Add apple slices. Simmer until apples are just tender. Spoon into individual casseroles. Beat 1/2 cup sugar and 1 teaspoon Amaretto di Saronno gradually into stiffly beaten egg whites. Spoon meringue into pastry bag with large star tip. Pipe meringue over apples. Bake at 350 degrees for 15 to 20 minutes or until lightly browned. Serve warm or cold. Yield: 6 servings.

Photograph for this recipe on page 2.

Desserts

STEAMED APPLE PUDDING

1 1/2 c. fine dry bread crumbs
1/2 c. flour
1 tsp. baking powder
1/2 tsp. each soda, salt
1 tsp. cinnamon
1/2 c. sugar
2 eggs
1/2 c. molasses
2 tbsp. butter, melted
2 c. chopped tart cooking apples
1 c. whole fresh cranberries

Combine dry ingredients in bowl. Stir in mixture of eggs, molasses and butter. Fold in apples and cranberries. Pour into greased and sugared pudding mold. Cover tightly with greased foil; secure with string. Place mold on rack in deep saucepan. Add enough simmering water to cover half the mold. Cover saucepan. Steam for 2 to 2 1/2 hours or until pudding tests done. Cool in mold for 10 minutes. Unmold on serving plate. Serve with whipped cream or ice cream. Yield: 8-12 servings.

Photograph for this recipe on page 1.

BLUEBERRY BUCKLE

1/2 c. butter, softened
1 c. sugar
1 egg
1/2 tsp. grated fresh lemon rind
4 tsp. fresh lemon juice
1/4 tsp. mace
1 1/3 c. unsifted all-purpose flour
1 tsp. baking powder
1/4 tsp. salt
1/4 c. milk
2 c. fresh blueberries

Cream 1/4 cup butter and 1/2 cup sugar in bowl. Beat in egg, 1/4 teaspoon lemon rind, lemon juice and 1/8 teaspoon mace. Mix 1 cup flour, baking powder and salt. Blend into creamed mixture alternately with milk. Turn into greased 9 x 9-inch baking pan. Sprinkle blueberries over batter. Mix 1/2 cup sugar, 1/3 cup flour, 1/4 teaspoon lemon rind and 1/8 teaspoon mace in bowl. Cut in 1/4 cup butter until crumbly. Sprinkle over blueberries. Bake at 375 degrees for 60 to 65 minutes or until cake tests done. Serve warm with whipped cream or lemon sauce. Yield: 8 servings.

Photograph for this recipe on page 103.

FRESH BLUEBERRY COBBLER

1/2 c. sugar
1 tbsp. cornstarch
4 c. fresh blueberries
1 tsp. lemon juice
1 c. flour
1 tbsp. sugar
1 1/2 tsp. baking powder
1/2 tsp. salt
3 tbsp. shortening
1/3 c. milk

Combine first 4 ingredients in saucepan; mix well. Simmer for 1 minute or until mixture thickens, stirring constantly. Pour into 2-quart casserole; keep warm. Combine flour and next 3 ingredients in bowl. Cut in shortening until crumbly. Stir in milk. Drop by spoonfuls onto hot fruit. Bake at 400 degrees for 25 to 30 minutes or until brown. Serve warm with cream.

BLUEBERRY-PEACH SHORTCAKE

2 c. sifted flour
1 tbsp. baking powder
1/2 tsp. salt
1 1/3 c. sugar
1/2 c. butter
1/3 c. milk
1 egg, slightly beaten
1/4 tsp. grated fresh lemon rind
2 c. fresh blueberries
6 c. sliced fresh peaches
1 c. whipping cream, whipped
1 tsp. vanilla extract

Sift flour, baking powder, salt and 1/3 cup sugar into large bowl. Cut in butter until crumbly. Add milk, egg and lemon rind. Mix lightly with fork. Stir in 1 cup blueberries. Shape into 2 balls. Press into 2 greased 8-inch layer cake pans. Bake at 450 degrees for 12 to 15 minutes or until golden brown. Remove from pans. Cool for 10 minutes. Sprinkle peaches with 1 cup sugar. Add 1 cup blueberries. Let stand at room temperature. Whip cream with vanilla. Chill in refrigerator. Place 1 short-cake layer on plate. Spread with 1/3 of the whipped cream. Top with 2/3 of the fruit. Pour sugared fruit syrup over top. Spread half the remaining whipped cream over fruit. Layer remaining shortcake, whipped cream and fruit over top. Yield: 8 servings.

Photograph for this recipe on page 103.

BROWNIE BAKED ALASKA

1 pkg. brownie mix
1 c. each strawberry ice cream, vanilla ice cream, softened
1 c. each lime sherbet, rainbow sherbet, softened
5 egg whites
1 c. sugar

Prepare and bake brownie mix according to package directions using 9-inch round baking pan. Layer ice cream and sherbets in foil-lined 1-quart bowl. Freeze until firm. Beat egg whites until soft peaks form. Add sugar gradually, beating until stiff. Unmold ice cream on brownie layer on baking sheet. Frost with meringue, sealing to baking sheet. Bake at 500 degrees for 2 to 3 minutes or until golden brown. Serve immediately. Yield: 10 servings.

EASY CHOCOLATE MOUSSE

1 1/2 c. miniature marshmallows
1/3 c. milk
1 6-oz. package chocolate chips
1 tsp. vanilla extract
1 c. whipping cream, whipped

Combine marshmallows and milk in saucepan. Cook over very low heat until melted, stirring constantly; remove from heat. Add chips and vanilla. Stir until melted; cool completely. Fold in whipped cream. Spoon into dessert dishes. Garnish with fresh strawberries. Yield: 4-6 servings.

Desserts

FRESH FRUIT BETTY

1 1/3 c. graham cracker crumbs
1/4 c. melted butter
1/4 c. sugar
1 tsp. grated fresh lemon rind
1/2 tsp. cinnamon
1/4 tsp. nutmeg
1 lg. apple, peeled, thinly sliced
1 lg. pear, peeled, thinly sliced
1 banana, sliced
2/3 c. coarsely chopped nuts
1 1/4 c. fresh orange juice
2 tbsp. fresh lemon juice

Combine graham cracker crumbs, butter, sugar, lemon rind, cinnamon and nutmeg in bowl; mix well. Combine apple, pear, banana and nuts in bowl. Spoon half the fruit mixture into buttered 1 1/2-quart casserole. Sprinkle with half the crumb mixture. Repeat layers. Combine orange and lemon juice; pour over casserole. Bake at 350 degrees for 1 hour. Serve warm with cream or ice cream. Yield: 8 servings.

Photograph for this recipe on page 36.

LIME SUMMER FRUIT COMPOTE

1 1/2 c. sugar
1/8 tsp. salt
1/4 tsp. grated fresh lime rind
1/4 c. fresh lime juice
4 peaches, peeled, sliced
1 c. fresh green grapes
1 c. fresh blueberries
3 plums, halved

Mix sugar, 2 cups water and salt in saucepan. Cook over low heat until sugar dissolves, stirring constantly. Simmer for 5 minutes; remove from heat. Stir in lime rind and juice. Cool. Combine peaches, grapes, blueberries, plums and lime syrup in bowl. Chill, covered, for several hours. Yield: 8 servings.

Photograph for this recipe on page 103.

PINEAPPLE-BUTTERMILK SHERBET

1/2 c. sugar
1/2 c. orange juice
1 4-lb. ripe pineapple
1 c. buttermilk

Combine sugar and orange juice in saucepan. Cook until sugar dissolves. Cut pineapple in half lengthwise through crown; scoop out pulp, reserving shells. Drain pineapple chunks, reserving 1/2 cup juice. Puree 2 cups pineapple with reserved juice in blender. Add orange juice and buttermilk. Process until just blended. Pour into 8-inch square pan. Freeze, covered, for 3 hours. Stir until smooth. Freeze for several hours longer. Spoon into reserved pineapple shells. Freeze until firm. Let stand at room temperature for 10 minutes before serving. Garnish with mint and orange rind.

Desserts

PEACHES IN SPICED WINE

1/4 c. dry Sauterne
2 tbsp. sugar
1 tbsp. lemon juice
Dash each of cinnamon, cloves
2 c. sliced peeled peaches

Combine Sauterne, sugar and lemon juice in small saucepan. Cook until sugar is dissolved. Do not boil. Stir in cinnamon and cloves. Pour hot wine mixture over peaches in deep bowl. Chill in refrigerator. Yield: 4 servings.

BURGUNDY PLUMS AND NECTARINES

2 c. sugar
1 c. Burgundy
3 whole cloves
2 cinnamon sticks
2 whole allspice
3 strips orange rind
3 strips lemon rind
1 tbsp. fresh lemon juice
4 lg. plums, cut into halves
4 nectarines, sliced

Combine sugar, Burgundy and 1 cup water in saucepan. Cook over low heat until sugar dissolves, stirring constantly. Add cloves, cinnamon sticks, allspice, orange rind, lemon rind and lemon juice. Simmer for 5 minutes; remove from heat. Strain into large bowl. Add plums and nectarines. Chill, covered, for several hours. Yield: 6-8 servings.

Photograph for this recipe on page 103.

YOGURT AMBROSIA

2 bananas, sliced
1 red Delicious apple, chopped
1 pear, peeled, chopped
Lemon juice
2 navel oranges, peeled, sectioned
1 1/3 c. flaked coconut
1 c. pineapple yogurt

Dip bananas, apple and pear in lemon juice; drain. Combine with orange sections in glass bowl. Chill for 1 hour. Fold in coconut and yogurt.

WATERMELON FREEZE

1/2 lg. watermelon
Juice of 4 oranges
Juice of 2 lemons
1 c. sugar
1 egg white, stiffly beaten

Scoop pulp from watermelon; reserve rind. Place pulp in cloth bag. Squeeze juice into bowl. Add citrus juices and sugar; mix well. Pour into 1-gallon freezer container. Freeze until partially set. Fold in egg white. Freeze until firm. Serve in watermelon rind. Garnish with melon balls. Yield: 24 servings.

Cake Tips

WHAT WENT WRONG . . .	AND WHY?
Holes in cake	Too little mixing; too little liquid or shortening; or too cool an oven.
Cake humped or cracked in center	Too hot an oven; too much flour; or a combination of the two.
Dry cake	Too little shortening or sugar; too much baking powder; or overbaked.
Sticky	Too much sugar or shortening; or underbaked.
Cake too brown	Baked too long; oven too hot; or too much sugar.
Not brown enough	Too big a pan; too little baking powder or inactive baking powder; not baked enough; or too little sugar.
Cake falls	Underbaked; or substituting self-rising flour and not reducing leavening.
Crumbly texture	Too little mixing; or too much shortening or sugar.

CAKE LAYER SIZE . . .	AMOUNT OF FROSTING NEEDED
1 9-inch round layer	3/4 cup
2 9-inch round layers	1 1/2 cups
3 9-inch round layers	2 1/4 cups
9 1/2 x 5 1/2 x 3-inch loaf pan	1 to 1 1/2 cups
16 x 5 x 4-inch loaf pan	2 to 2 1/2 cups
16 large or 24 small cupcakes	1 to 1 1/4 cups
10 x 15-inch sheet cake	1 1/3 cups
10 x 15-inch roll	2 cups

Pie and Pastry Tips

- *For perfectly round pie crusts,* form a ball with the dough and flatten it by pressing the side of your hand into it three times in a top-to-bottom direction and three times in a side-to-side direction. Then roll as usual.

- *To put the top crust onto your pie easily,* roll it out until it is ready to be put on the pie. Cut the slits you want for air vents, then pick up one edge of the crust on your rolling pin and roll to wrap the entire crust loosely around the pin. "Roll" the top crust over your pie.

- *To fit a crumb crust into a 9-inch plate,* place the crumb dough into the plate and press down with an 8-inch plate. The crust will shape itself between the two plates.

- *For a non-stick crumb crust,* when you're ready to serve your pie, wrap a hot, wet towel around the outside of the pie plate. Hold it there for two or three minutes. Every slice you cut will come out of the pan easily.

- *To save yourself the trouble of thickening juices* for fruit pies, substitute tapioca for the flour. Combine the tapioca with the sugar and seasoning you use then add liquid and fruit according to your recipe, turn the mixture into a pie crust and bake. The tapioca thickens the juices during baking.

- *To prevent a soggy bottom crust if your pie has a juicy filling,* brush the crust with an egg white or melted butter before adding the filling. And do be sure that the filling is very hot.

- *When pie juices spill into your oven,* sprinkle the spill with salt to prevent smoke and smell.

- *To avoid spills* when you're preparing to bake custard pie, place the shell on your oven rack and pour the filling into it. This trick bypasses the precarious balancing of a full custard pie as you carry it to the oven.

- *To prevent ragged edges on your pie meringue* when it is cut, dip the knife you use in warm water. Repeat as often as necessary while you're cutting your slices.

- *To freeze pies and crusts,* remember: fruit, mince, and chiffon pies freeze well, but custard and meringue ones don't; freeze a filled pie without wrapping it until it is almost solid — then wrap it, using moisture-and vapor-proof freezer paper. These pies can be frozen for two to three months.

- *When thawing a frozen pie baked before freezing,* heat at 350 degrees just until warm. The exception to this rule is chiffon pie which must never be heated. Thaw a chiffon pie in the refrigerator for three hours or at room temperature for 45 minutes.

- *When cooking a frozen, unbaked pie,* bake at the temperature specified in your recipe for the given time plus 15 to 20 minutes.

Quantity

Eating together, like working together, has long been a part of the American way of life. Large groups of people gathering for fun, fellowship and food were as much a common sight in pioneer days as they are now. While rural America has changed considerably, its people seem to have changed very little. Still quite popular today are Sunday picnics and Fourth of July barbecues when hearty dishes of all kinds completely cover the table. But preparing meals in large quantities that taste as delicious as they are inviting, doesn't have to be difficult.

In this excellent selection of recipes there are quantity dishes that are just right for large gatherings . . . transport well . . . are liked by people of all ages . . . and don't require an excessive amount of preparation. Many can be made ahead of time, frozen or refrigerated and then reheated. None require exotic, expensive ingredients, so they'll certainly suite a food committee's budget. And some are flexible enough to be stretched if a larger crowd than expected arrives for dinner!

You'll discover a variety of recipes for main dishes, vegetables, salads, breads, desserts and even a pancake treat for a crowd on the following pages. Simply add good friends, and you're certain to have all the ingredients for success!

← BORSCHT, Recipe on page 178. PIROSHKIS, Recipe on page 180.

Quantity

BORSCHT

2 lb. boneless beef chuck,
cubed
1 lb. marrow soup bones (opt.)
2 6-oz. cans tomato paste
2 tbsp. salt
1/2 tsp. pepper
4 c. grated peeled beets
4 c. finely shredded cabbage
2 c. shredded carrots
1/2 c. instant minced onions
2 tbsp. dillseed
1/4 tsp. instant minced garlic
2 to 4 tbsp. lemon juice

Combine 6 quarts water, beef and soup bones in soup kettle. Bring to a boil; skim foam. Stir in tomato paste, salt and pepper. Simmer, covered, for 1 1/2 hours. Add beets, cabbage, carrots, minced onions, dillseed and garlic. Simmer, uncovered, for 45 minutes or until vegetables are tender. Stir in lemon juice. Serve with sour cream and Piroshkis on page 180. Yield: 6 quarts.

Photograph for this recipe on page 180.

BRUNCH EGG AND SAUSAGE BAKE

9 lb. sausage
3 loaves bread, cubed
2 1/2 lb. Cheddar cheese,
shredded
3 1/2 doz. eggs
3 qt. milk
1 tbsp. salt
1 tsp. pepper
1 1/2 tbsp. dry mustard

Brown sausage in skillet, stirring until crumbly; drain. Layer bread cubes, sausage and cheese in two 12 x 20-inch baking pans. Combine remaining ingredients in large bowl; mix well. Pour over cheese. Chill, covered, for 12 hours. Bake, uncovered, at 350 degrees for 1 hour or until set. Cut into squares. Yield: 50 servings.

BRUNSWICK STEW

1 3 1/2-lb. chicken, cooked,
boned, chopped
2 lg. cans tomatoes
3 onions, chopped
6 carrots, sliced
1/2 bunch celery, sliced
1 can tomato sauce
3 lb. frozen baby lima beans
1 lg. potato, chopped
4 lb. frozen niblet corn
2 lb. cooked beef, chopped
2 lb. cooked pork, chopped
2 hot peppers, chopped
Tabasco sauce, salt and pepper
to taste

Combine all ingredients in stock pot. Simmer for 12 hours, stirring occasionally. Stew should be thick enough to eat with fork. Yield: 30-35 servings.

OLD-FASHIONED CHICKEN SALAD

6 c. chopped cooked chicken
2 c. chopped celery
12 hard-boiled eggs, chopped
3 c. chopped red Delicious
apples
1 c. chopped sweet pickle
1 1/2 c. chicken broth
1/2 c. sweet pickle juice
3 c. mayonnaise
2 tbsp. sugar
Salt and pepper to taste

Combine first 5 ingredients in large bowl. Blend broth and remaining ingredients in bowl. Add to chicken mixture; mix well. Serve on lettuce-lined plates. Yield: 24 servings.

CROWD-PLEASER SPAGHETTI SAUCE

9 c. finely chopped onions
2 1/2 c. finely chopped celery
3 tbsp. instant garlic
3/4 c. shortening
15 lb. ground beef
12 3/4 lb. canned tomatoes
1 1/2 qt. catsup
7 6-oz. cans tomato paste
4 8-oz. cans sliced mushrooms
3 bay leaves, crumbled
1 tsp. soda
1 tbsp. cayenne pepper
1 tsp. chili powder
7 tbsp. salt
1 tbsp. monosodium glutamate

Saute onions, celery and garlic in hot shortening in large saucepan until lightly browned. Add ground beef. Cook until brown and crumbly, stirring frequently. Add tomatoes, catsup, tomato paste, mushrooms with liquid, bay leaves, soda and 4 cups water. Cook over low heat for 2 1/2 hours, adding additional water if necessary and stirring occasionally. Add seasonings. Cook for 1/2 hour longer. Skim. Serve over cooked spaghetti with Parmesan cheese. Yield: 80 servings.

PARTY MEAT LOAVES

.5 lb. each ground beef, ham
and pork
2 c. cracker crumbs
1/2 tsp. pepper
9 eggs
4 1/2 cans tomato soup
1/2 c. mustard
1/2 c. vinegar
1/2 c. sugar
1/2 c. melted butter

Combine beef, ham, pork, crumbs and pepper in large bowl; mix well. Add 6 eggs and 4 cans tomato soup; mix well. Shape into 2 x 4-inch loaves. Place in large baking pans. Bake at 350 degrees for 1 hour. Mix mustard, vinegar, sugar and butter with 1/2 can tomato soup and remaining 3 eggs. Cook over low heat until thickened, stirring constantly. Serve over meat loaves. Yield: 50 servings.

Quantity

PIROSHKIS

3 tbsp. instant minced onion
3 tbsp. butter
1/2 lb. lean ground beef
2 hard-boiled eggs, chopped
1 tbsp. dillweed
1 tsp. parsley flakes
3/4 tsp. salt
1/2 tsp. paprika
1/8 tsp. pepper
2 tbsp. sour cream
1 tsp. lemon juice
2 pkg. frozen patty shells, thawed

Rehydrate minced onion in 3 tablespoons water for 10 minutes. Saute onion in butter in skillet for 2 minutes. Add ground beef. Cook until brown, stirring frequently; remove from heat. Stir in eggs, dillweed, parsley flakes, salt, paprika and pepper. Add sour cream and lemon juice; mix well. Press patty shells together on lightly floured surface; roll 1/8-inch thick. Cut into 2-inch circles. Place 1 teaspoon ground beef mixture on each circle; moisten edges lightly with water. Fold over to enclose filling; seal edge. Place on baking sheets. Bake at 400 degrees for 12 minutes or until golden. Yield: 6 dozen.

Photograph for this recipe on page 176.

PARTY TUNA BAKE

3/4 c. chopped green pepper
3 c. sliced celery
2 onions, chopped
1/4 c. butter
3 cans cream of mushroom soup
1 1/2 c. milk
3 c. cubed Cheddar cheese
1 1/2 c. mayonnaise
24 oz. medium noodles, cooked, drained
3   9 1/4-oz. cans tuna
3/4 c. chopped pimento
1 c. slivered almonds

Saute first 3 ingredients in butter in skillet for 5 minutes. Combine soup, milk and cheese in large saucepan; mix well. Cook until cheese is melted, stirring frequently; remove from heat. Mix in mayonnaise. Combine noodles, sauteed vegetables, tuna and pimento in large bowl; mix well. Stir in soup mixture. Pour into large greased baking pan. Sprinkle with almonds. Bake at 400 degrees for 30 to 35 minutes or until bubbly. Yield: 24-30 servings.

SUGAR AND SPICE YAM CASSEROLE

2   6 1/2-lb. cans yams, drained
Butter, melted
2 c. light cream
2 c. sugar
2 tsp. cornstarch
2 tsp. nutmeg
2 tsp. cinnamon
8 eggs, beaten

Combine yams with 1 cup butter, cream, sugar, cornstarch and spices in large mixer bowl. Add eggs; beat until smooth. Pour into large baking pan generously coated with butter. Bake at 350 degrees for 45 minutes. Yield: 30 servings.

RICE DOLLAR PANCAKES

3 c. sifted flour
1 tbsp. baking powder
1 1/2 tsp. soda
3/4 tsp. salt
1 tbsp. sugar
6 eggs, separated
3 c. buttermilk
9 tbsp. melted butter
1 1/2 c. cooked rice

Sift dry ingredients together. Beat egg yolks in bowl until light. Add buttermilk and butter; mix well. Stir in dry ingredients; beat until just blended. Fold in rice and stiffly beaten egg whites. Pour batter by tablespoonfuls onto hot lightly greased griddle. Bake until brown on both sides. Yield: 9 dozen.

Photograph for this recipe above.

Quantity

MAKE-AHEAD REFRIGERATOR ROLLS

Sugar
2 pkg. dry yeast
1 c. oil
1 tbsp. salt
15 c. flour

Mix 2 tablespoons sugar with 1/2 cup warm water in large bowl. Add yeast. Let stand for 10 minutes. Add 1 1/2 cups sugar, 4 cups lukewarm water, oil, salt and flour; mix well. Let rise, covered, in warm place for 3 hours. Punch dough down. Let rise for 1 1/2 hours. Shape into rolls; place on greased baking sheets. Chill, covered, for several hours to overnight. Bake at 350 degrees for 20 minutes or until brown. Yield: 5 dozen.

STRAWBERRY AMBROSIA

1 qt. strawberries, sliced
4 bananas, sliced
4 apples, sliced
1 16-oz. can pineapple chunks, drained
2 12-oz. cans mandarin oranges, drained
2 16-oz. cans fruit cocktail, drained
1 16-oz. package chopped walnuts
1 16-oz. package slivered almonds
4 pkg. whipped topping mix, prepared

Combine fruits and half the nuts in large bowl; mix well. Mix in half the whipped topping. Spread remaining whipped topping over top. Sprinkle with remaining nuts. Yield: 30-40 servings.

BLUEBERRY PARFAITS

1 c. unflavored gelatin
10 1/2 qt. grapefruit juice
2 1/2 lb. sugar
6 qt. fresh blueberries
4 qt. stemmed green grapes

Soften gelatin in 2 quarts grapefruit juice in saucepan. Cook over low heat until gelatin is dissolved, stirring constantly. Stir in remaining grapefruit juice and sugar until sugar is dissolved. Pour into shallow 3-gallon pan. Chill until firm. Cut gelatin into 1/2-inch cubes. Layer half the blueberries, half the gelatin cubes, grapes, remaining gelatin and remaining blueberries in serving dishes. Chill until serving time. Yield: 48 servings.

PEANUT BUTTER BROWNIES

10 c. flour
12 c. sugar
3 c. dried egg powder
2 1/4 c. butter, softened
4 1/2 tbsp. vanilla extract
1 3/4 lb. peanut butter

Combine first 3 ingredients in large mixer bowl. Add butter, vanilla, peanut butter and 3 cups warm water. Beat for 3 minutes or longer. Spread in 4 large greased baking pans. Bake at 350 degrees until brown. Cut into squares. Yield: 8 dozen.

CREAM-FILLED CUPCAKES

4 8-oz. packages cream cheese, softened
1 1/3 c. sugar
4 eggs
1/2 tsp. salt
2 12-oz. packages chocolate chips
4 pkg. cake mix

Combine first 4 ingredients in bowl; blend well. Stir in chocolate chips. Prepare cake mixes, using package directions. Fill paper-lined muffin cups 2/3 full. Drop 1 rounded teaspoonful cheese mixture into each cupcake. Bake at 350 degrees for 20 to 25 minutes or until golden brown. Yield: 8 dozen.

OLD-FASHIONED STRAWBERRY SHORTCAKE

4 c. flour
1/3 c. baking powder
2 1/2 tsp. salt
1 1/2 c. sugar
1 lb. butter
1 pt. heavy cream
7 to 8 qt. strawberries, sliced, sweetened

Mix dry ingredients in bowl. Cut in butter until crumbly. Mix cream and 1 cup water. Stir into flour mixture. Drop by large spoonfuls 2 inches apart onto baking sheets. Bake at 450 degrees for 15 minutes. Split in half. Fill shortcakes with strawberries. Spoon remaining strawberries over tops. Serve with whipped cream. Yield: 50 servings.

RICH PASTRY FOR EIGHT PIE SHELLS

5 c. sifted flour
1 tsp. baking powder
1 1/2 tsp. salt
3 tbsp. packed brown sugar
2 1/2 c. shortening
1 egg, beaten
2 tbsp. vinegar

Sift flour, baking powder, salt and brown sugar into large bowl. Cut in shortening until crumbly. Add enough water to egg to measure 3/4 cup; stir in vinegar. Pour over flour mixture; toss until moistened. Divide into 8 portions. Wrap in foil. Store in freezer. Thaw overnight in refrigerator.

Microwave Tips

- Always choose the minimum cooking time. Remember, food continues to cook after it is removed from the microwave.

- Keep your microwave clean. Built-up grease or spatters can slow cooking times.

- When poaching or frying an egg in a browning dish, always prick the center of the yolk with a fork to keep the egg from exploding.

- Do not try to hard-cook eggs in the shell in a microwave. They will build up pressure and burst.

- To prevent soggy rolls, elevate rolls on roasting rack or place on paper towels while heating.

- Do not use metal dishes or aluminum foil except as specifically recommended by the manufacturer of your microwave.

- Never use a foil tray over 3/4-inch deep in your microwave.

- When heating TV-style dinners, remove the foil cover, then place tray back in carton. Food will heat only from the top.

- Be sure to prick potatoes before baking to allow steam to escape.

- Cut a small slit in pouch-packed frozen foods before heating to allow steam to escape.

- When placing more than one food item in microwave, arrange foods in a circle near edges of oven.

- Cover foods that need to be steamed or tenderized.

- Do not try to pop popcorn unless you have a microwave-approved corn popper.

DID YOU KNOW YOU CAN . . .?
(Use High setting for the following unless otherwise indicated.)

- Use your microwave oven to melt chocolate, soften cream cheese and butter.

- Roast shelled nuts for 6 to 10 minutes, stirring frequently.

- Peel fruit or tomatoes. Place in 1 cup hot water. Microwave for 30 to 45 seconds; remove skins easily.

- Plump dried fruit by placing in a dish with 1 to 2 teaspoons water. Cover tightly with plastic wrap. Heat for 1/2 to 1 1/2 minutes.

- Precook barbecued ribs or chicken until almost done then place on the grill to sear and add a charcoal flavor.

- Soften brown sugar by placing in a dish with a slice of bread or apple. Heat for 30 to 45 seconds, stirring once.

- Dry bread for crumbs or croutons. Place cubed or crumbled bread on paper towels. Heat for 6 to 7 minutes, stirring occasionally.

- Warm baby food or bottles by removing metal lid and heating for 10 to 20 seconds.

- Freshen chips and crackers by heating for 15 to 30 seconds. Let stand for 2 to 3 minutes.

- Dry herbs by placing on paper towels and heating for 2 to 3 minutes or until dry.

- Ripen an avocado by heating on Low for 2 to 4 minutes.

Cooking With Wine

When used in cooking, wine provides a special goodness to the food by accenting the natural flavor of the food ... at the same time adding its own inviting fragrance and flavor. The only secret in cooking successfully with wine is to use a quality wine, as the alcohol evaporates during the cooking, leaving only the actual flavor of the wine. A fine wine with rich body and aroma will insure a distinct, delicate flavor.

	FOOD	AMOUNT OF WINE	TYPE OF WINE
Soups	Cream soups	1 T. per cup	Sauterne or Sherry
	Meat and Vegetable Soups	1 T. per cup	Burgundy or Sherry
Sauces	Brown	1 T. per cup	Sherry or Burgundy
	Cheese	1 T. per cup	Sherry or Sauterne
	Cream	1 T. per cup	Sherry or Sauterne
	Dessert	1 T. per cup	Port or Muscatel
	Tomato	1 T. per cup	Sherry or Burgundy
Meats	Ham, baked	2 c. for basting	Port or Muscatel
	Liver, braised	¼ c. per pound	Burgundy or Sauterne
	Pot Roast	¼ c. per pound	Burgundy
	Gravy for Roasts	2 T. per cup	Burgundy or Sherry
	Stew, Beef	¼ c. per pound	Burgundy
	Stew, Lamb or Veal	¼ c. per pound	Sauterne
	Tongue, boiled	½ c. per pound	Burgundy
Fish	Baked, Broiled or Poached	½ c. per pound	Sauterne
Poultry and Game	Chicken or Turkey	¼ c. per pound	Sauterne or Burgundy
	Gravy	2 T. per cup	Sauterne, Burgundy or Sherry
	Duck, roasted	¼ c. per pound	Burgundy
	Pheasant	¼ c. per pound	Sauterne, Burgundy or Sherry
	Venison	¼ c. per pound	Burgundy
Fruits (Fresh, Canned, Frozen)	In syrup or juice (Fruit cups, compotes, etc.)	2 T. per cup over fruit or in syrup or juice	Port, Muscatel, Sherry, Rose, Sauterne, Burgundy
	Drained fruits	At the table, pour undiluted over fruits	Champagne or other Sparkling Wine

Size of Bottle	Ounces	Appetizer & Dessert Wines	Dinner Wines & Champagne
Split (2/5 pt.)	6.4	2 servings	2 servings
Tenth (4/5 pt.)	12.8	4 servings	4- 6 servings
Pint	16.0	5 servings	5- 7 servings
Fifth	25.6	8 servings	8-12 servings
Quart (4/5 qt.)	32.0	10 servings	10-14 servings
Magnum	52.0	16 servings	16-20 servings
½ Gallon	64.0	20 servings	20-30 servings
Gallon	128.0	40 servings	40-60 servings

Charts

Count-Your-Calories Chart

Almonds, shelled, 1/4 cup 213
Apples: 1 med 70
   chopped, 1/2 cup 30
Apple juice, 1 cup .117
Applesauce: sweetened, 1/2 cup 115
   unsweetened, 1/2 cup 50
Apricots: fresh, 3 55
   canned, 1/2 cup 110
   dried, 10 halves 100
Apricot nectar, 1 cup 140
Asparagus: fresh, 6 spears 19
   canned, 1/2 cup 18
Avocado, 1 med. 265
Bacon, 2 sl. crisp-cooked, drained 90
Banana, 1 med. 100
Beans: baked, 1/2 cup 160
   dry, 1/2 cup 350
   green, 1/2 cup 20
   lima, 1/2 cup 95
   soy, 1/2 cup 95
Bean sprouts, 1/2 cup 18
Beef, cooked, 3 oz. serving:
   roast, rib 375
   roast, heel of round 165
   steak, sirloin 330
Beer, 12 oz. 150
Beets, cooked, 1/2 cup 40
Biscuit, from mix, 1 90
Bologna, all meat, 3 oz. 235
Bread: roll, 1 85
   white, 1 slice 65
   whole wheat, 1 slice 65
Bread crumbs, dry, 1 cup 390
Broccoli, cooked, 1/2 cup 20
Butter: 1/2 cup 800
   1 tbsp. 100
Buttermilk, 1 cup 90
Cabbage: cooked, 1/2 cup 15
   fresh, shredded, 1/2 cup 10
Cake: angel food, 1/12 pkg. prepared 140
   devil's food, 1/12 pkg. prepared 195
   yellow, 1/12 pkg. prepared 200
Candy: caramel, 1 oz. 115
   chocolate, sweet, 1 oz. 145
   hard candy, 1 oz. 110
   marshmallows, 1 oz. 90
Cantaloupe, 1/2 med. 60

Carrots, cooked, 1/2 cup 23
   fresh, 1 med. 20
Catsup, 1 tbsp. 18
Cauliflower: cooked, 1/2 cup 13
   fresh, 1/2 lb. 60
Celery, chopped, 1/2 cup 8
Cereals: bran flakes, 1/2 cup 53
   corn flakes, 1/2 cup 50
   oatmeal, cooked, 1/2 cup 65
Cheese: American, 1 oz. 105
   Cheddar: 1 oz. .113
     shredded, 1 cup 452
   cottage: creamed, 1/2 cup 130
     uncreamed, 1/2 cup 85
   cream: 1 oz. 107
   mozzarella, 1 oz. 80
     shredded, 1 cup 320
   Parmesan, 1 oz. .110
   Velveeta, 1 oz. 84
Cherries: canned, sour in water, 1/2 cup 53
   fresh, sweet, 1/2 cup 40
Chicken, meat only, 4 oz. serving:
   boned, chopped, 1/2 cup 170
   broiled 155
   canned, boned .230
   roast, dark meat 210
   roast, light meat 207
Chili peppers: green, fresh, 1/2 lb. 62
   red, fresh, 1/2 lb. 108
Chili powder with seasoning, 1 tbsp. 51
Chocolate, baking, 1 oz. 143
Cocoa mix, 1-oz. package 115
Cocoa powder, baking, 1/3 cup 120
Coconut, dried, shredded, 1/4 cup 166
Coffee 0
Corn: canned, cream-style, 1/2 cup 100
   canned, whole kernel, 1/2 cup 85
Corn bread, mix, prepared, 1 x 4-in. piece 125
Corn chips, 1 oz. 130
Cornmeal, 1/2 cup .264
Cornstarch, 1 tbsp. 29
Crab, fresh, meat only, 3 oz. 80
   canned, 3 oz. 85
Cracker crumbs, 1/2 cup 281
Crackers: graham, 2 1/2-in. square 28
   Ritz, each 17
   saltine, 2-in. square 13

Charts

Cranberries: fresh, 1/2 lb. 100
 juice, cocktail, 1 cup 163
 sauce, 1/2 cup 190
Cream: half-and-half, 1 tbsp. 20
 heavy, 1 tbsp 55
 light, 1 tbsp. 30
Creamer, imitation powdered, 1 tsp. 10
Cucumber, 1 med. 30
Dates, dried, chopped, 1/2 cup 244
Eggs: 1 whole, large 80
 1 white 17
 1 yolk 59
Eggplant, cooked, 1/2 cup 19
Fish sticks, 5 200
Flour: rye, 1 cup .286
 white: 1 cup 420
 1 tbsp. 28
 whole wheat, 1 cup 400
Fruit cocktail, canned, 1/2 cup 98
Garlic, 1 clove 2
Gelatin, unflavored, 1 env. 25
Grapes: fresh, 1/2 cup 35-50
 juice, 1 cup 170
Grapefruit: fresh, 1/2 med. 60
 juice, unsweetened, 1 cup 100
Ground beef, patty, lean 185
 regular 245
Haddock, fried, 3 oz. 140
Ham, 3 oz. servings:
 boiled 200
 country-style 335
 cured, lean 160
 fresh, roast 320
Honey, 1 tbsp. 65
Ice cream, 1/2 cup 135
Ice milk, 1/2 cup 96
Jams and preserves, 1 tbsp. 54
Jellies, 1 tbsp. 55
Jell-O, 1/2 cup 80
Lamb:
 3 oz. serving, leg roast 185
 1 1/2 oz., rib chop 175
Lemon juice, 1 tbsp. 4
Lemonade, sweetened, 1 cup 110
Lentils, cooked, 1/2 cup 168
Lettuce, 1 head 40
Liver, 2 oz. serving:
 beef, fried 130
 chicken, simmered 88
Lobster, 2 oz. 55
Macaroni, cooked, 1/2 cup 90
Mango, 1 fresh 134
Margarine: 1/2 cup 800
 1 tbsp. 100
Mayonnaise: 1 tbsp. 100

Milk: whole, 1 cup 160
 condensed, 1 cup 982
 evaporated, 1 cup 345
 dry nonfat, 1 cup 251
 skim, 1 cup 89
Muffin, plain 120
Mushrooms: canned, 1/2 cup 20
 fresh, 1 lb. 123
Mustard: prepared, brown, 1 tbsp. 13
 prepared, yellow, 1 tbsp. 10
Nectarine, 1 fresh 30
Noodles: egg, cooked, 1/2 cup 100
 fried, chow mein, 2 oz. 275
Oil, cooking, salad, 1 tbsp. 120
Okra, cooked, 8 pods 25
Olives: green, 3 lg. 15
 ripe, 2 lg. 15
Onion: chopped, 1/2 cup 32
 dehydrated flakes, 1 tbsp. 17
 green, 6 20
 whole, 1 40
Orange: 1 whole 65
 juice, 1 cup 115
Oysters, meat only, 1/2 cup 80
Pancakes, 4-in. diameter, 1 60
Peaches: fresh, 1 med. 35
 canned, 1/2 cup .100
 dried, 1/2 cup 210
Peanut butter, 1 tbsp. 100
Peanuts, shelled, roasted, 1 cup 420
Pears: fresh, 1 med. 100
 canned, 1/2 cup 97
 dried, 1/2 cup 214
Peas: black-eyed, 1/2 cup 70
 green, canned, 1/2 cup 83
 green, frozen, 1/2 cup 69
Pecans, chopped, 1/2 cup 400
Peppers: sweet green, 1 med. 14
 sweet red, 1 med. 19
Perch, white, 4 oz. 50
Pickles: dill, 1 lg. 15
 sweet, 1 average 30
Pie crust, mix, 1 crust 626
Pie, 8-in. frozen, 1/6 serving
 apple 234
 cherry 300
 peach 280
Pimento, canned, 1 avg. 10
Pineapple: fresh, diced, 1/2 cup 36
 canned, 1/2 cup 90
 juice, 1 cup 135
Plums: fresh, 1 med. 30
 canned, 3 101
Popcorn, plain, popped, 1 cup 54
Pork, cooked, lean:

Charts

Boston butt, roasted, 4 oz. 280
chop, broiled, 3.5 oz. 260
loin, roasted, 4 oz. 290
Potato chips, 1 oz. 322
Potatoes, white:
baked, 1 sm. with skin 93
boiled, 1 sm. 70
French-fried, 10 pieces 155
hashed brown, 1/2 cup 225
mashed, with milk and butter, 1/2 cup 90
Potatoes, sweet:
baked, 1 avg. 155
candied, 1 avg. .295
canned, 1/2 cup 110
Prune: 1 lg. 19
dried, cooked, 1/2 cup 137
juice, 1 cup 197
Puddings and pie fillings, prepared:
banana, 1/2 cup 165
butterscotch, 1/2 cup 190
chocolate, 1/2 cup 190
lemon, 1/2 cup .125
Puddings, instant, prepared:
banana, 1/2 cup 175
butterscotch, 1/2 cup 175
chocolate, 1/2 cup 200
lemon, 1/2 cup .180
Pumpkin, canned, 1/2 cup 38
Raisins, dried, 1/2 cup 231
Rice: cooked, white, 1/2 cup 90
cooked, brown, 1/2 cup 100
precooked, 1/2 cup 105
Salad dressings, commercial:
blue cheese, 1 tbsp. 75
French, 1 tbsp. 70
Italian, 1 tbsp. 83
mayonnaise, 1 tbsp. 100
mayonnaise-type, 1 tbsp. 65
Russian, 1 tbsp. 75
Thousand Island, 1 tbsp. 80
Salami, cooked, 2 oz. 180
Salmon: canned, 4 oz. 180
steak, 4 oz. 220
Sardines, canned, 3 oz. 175
Sauces: barbecue, 1 tbsp. 17
hot pepper, 1 tbsp. 3
soy, 1 tbsp. 9
white, med., 1/2 cup 215
Worcestershire, 1 tbsp. 15
Sauerkraut, 1/2 cup 21
Sausage, cooked, 2 oz. 260
Sherbet, 1/2 cup 130
Shrimp: cooked, 3 oz. 50
canned, 4 oz. 130
Soft drinks, 1 cup 100

Soup, 1 can, condensed:
chicken with rice 116
cream of celery 215
cream of chicken 235
cream of mushroom 331
tomato 220
vegetable-beef .198
Sour cream, 1/2 cup 240
Spaghetti, cooked, 1/2 cup 80
Spinach: fresh, 1/2 lb. 60
cooked, 1/2 cup 20
Squash: summer, cooked, 1/2 cup 15
winter, cooked, 1/2 cup 65
Strawberries, fresh, 1/2 cup 23
Sugar: brown, packed, 1/2 cup 410
confectioners', sifted, 1/2 cup 240
granulated: 1/2 cup 385
1 tbsp. 48
Syrups: chocolate, 1 tbsp. 50
corn, 1 tbsp. 58
maple, 1 tbsp. 50
Taco shell, 1 shell 50
Tea, 1 cup 0
Tomatoes: fresh, 1 med. 40
canned, 1/2 cup 25
juice, 1 cup 45
paste, 6 oz. can 150
sauce, 8-oz. can 34
Toppings: caramel, 1 tbsp. 70
chocolate fudge, 1 tbsp. 65
Cool Whip, 1 tbsp. 14
Dream Whip, prepared, 1 tbsp. 8
strawberry, 1 tbsp. 60
Tortilla, corn, 1 65
Tuna: canned in oil, drained, 4 oz. 230
canned in water, 4 oz. 144
Turkey: dark meat, roasted, 4 oz. 230
light meat, roasted, 4 oz. 200
Veal: cutlet, broiled, 3 oz. 185
roast, 3 oz. 230
Vegetable juice cocktail, 1 cup 43
Vinegar, 1 tbsp. 2
Waffles, 1 130
Walnuts, chopped, 1/2 cup 410
Water chestnuts, sliced, 1/2 cup 25
Watermelon, fresh, cubed, 1/2 cup 26
Wheat germ, 1 tbsp. 29
Wine: dessert, 1/2 cup 140
table, 1/2 cup 85
Yeast: compressed, 1 oz. 24
dry, 1 oz. 80
Yogurt: plain, w/whole milk, 1 cup 153
plain, w/skim milk, 1 cup 123
with fruit, 1 cup 260

Nutrition Labeling Chart

The Food and Nutrition Board of the National Research Council, National Academy of Sciences, periodically reviews the scientific literature to determine the daily human needs, from birth to old age, for the various nutrients needed for health. This information then appears as the Recommended Dietary Allowances (RDA). These allowances are updated about every five years.

The Food and Drug Administration (FDA) used the 1974 RDAs as the basis for setting the United States Recommended Daily Allowances (U.S. RDA). The U. S. RDAs are the standards for nutrition labeling — the basis for measuring and comparing nutritive value of foods — to help consumers make informed choices.

UNITED STATES RECOMMENDED DAILY ALLOWANCE CHART

Protein	.45-65 Grams
Carbohydrates	125 Grams
Vitamin A	5,000 International Units
Thiamine (Vitamin B_1)	.1.5 Milligrams
Riboflavin (Vitamin B_2)	.1.7 Milligrams
Vitamin B_6	2 Milligrams
Vitamin B_{12}	6 Micrograms
Folic Acid (B Vitamin)	.0.4 Milligrams
Pantothenic Acid (B Vitamin)	10 Milligrams
Vitamin C (Ascorbic Acid)	.55-60 Milligrams
Vitamin D	400 International Units
Vitamin E	30 International Units
Iron	18 Milligrams
Calcium	1 Gram
Niacin (Nicotinic Acid)	.13-20 Milligrams
Magnesium	400 Milligrams
Zinc	15 Milligrams
Copper	2 Milligrams
Phosphorus	1 Gram
Iodine	150 Micrograms
Biotin (Vitamin H)	.0.3 Milligrams

IMPORTANT NUTRIENTS YOUR DIET REQUIRES

PROTEIN

Why?   Absolutely essential in building, repairing and renewing of all body tissue. Helps body resist infection. Builds enzymes and hormones, helps form and maintain body fluids.

Where? Milk, eggs, lean meats, poultry, fish, soybeans, peanuts, dried peas and beans, grains and cereals.

Charts

CARBOHYDRATES
Why?   Provide needed energy for bodily functions, provide warmth, as well as fuel for brain and nerve tissues. Lack of carbohydrates will cause body to use protein for energy rather than for repair and building.

Where?   Sugars: sugar, table syrups, jellies, jams, etc., as well as dried and fresh fruits. Starches: cereals, pasta, rice, corn, dried beans and peas, potatoes, stem and leafy vegetables, and milk.

FATS
Why?   Essential in the use of fat soluble vitamins (A, D, E, K), and fatty acids. Have more than twice the concentrated energy than equal amount of carbohydrate for body energy and warmth.

Where?   Margarine, butter, cooking oil, mayonnaise, lard, bacon, vegetable shortening, whole milk, cream, ice cream, cheese, meat, fish, eggs, poultry, chocolate, coconut, nuts.

VITAMIN A
Why?   Needed for healthy skin and hair, as well as for healthy, infection-resistant mucous membranes.

Where?   Dark green, leafy and yellow vegetables, liver. Deep yellow fruits, such as apricots and cantaloupe. Milk, cheese, eggs, as well as butter and fortified margarine.

THIAMINE (VITAMIN B_1)
Why?   Aids in the release of energy of foods, as well as in normal appetite and digestion. Promotes healthy nervous system.

Where?   Pork, liver, kidney. Dried peas and beans. Whole grain and enriched breads and cereals.

RIBOFLAVIN (VITAMIN B_2)
Why?   Helps to oxidize foods. Promotes healthy eyes and skin, especially around mouth and eyes. Prevents pellagra.

Where?   Meats, especially liver and kidney, as well as milk, cheese, eggs. Dark green leafy vegetables. Enriched bread and cereal products. Almonds, dried peas and beans.

VITAMIN B_6
Why?   Helps protein in building body tissues. Needed for healthy nerves, skin and digestion. Also helps body to use fats and carbohydrates for energy.

Where?   Milk, wheat germ, whole grain and fortified cereals. Liver, kidney, pork and beef.

VITAMIN B_{12}
Why?   Aids body in formation of red blood cells, as well as in regular work of all body cells.

Where?   Lean meats, milk, eggs, fish, cheese, as well as liver and kidney.

FOLIC ACID
Why?   Aids in healthy blood system, as well as intestinal tract. Helps to prevent anemia.

Where?   Green leaves of vegetables and herbs, as well as liver and milk. Wheat germ and soybeans.

PANTOTHENIC ACID
Why?   Aids in proper function of digestive system.

Where?   Liver, kidney and eggs. Peanuts and molasses. Broccoli and other vegetables.

VITAMIN C (ASCORBIC ACID)
Why?   Promotes proper bone and tooth formation. Helps body utilize iron and resist infection. Strengthens blood vessels. Lack of it causes bones to heal slowly, failure of wounds to heal and fragile vessels to bleed easily.

Where?   Citrus fruits, cantaloupe and strawberries. Broccoli, kale, green peppers, raw cabbage, sweet potatoes, cauliflower, tomatoes.

VITAMIN D
Why?   Builds strong bones and teeth by aiding utilization of calcium and phosphorus.
Where? Fortified milk, fish liver oils, as well as salmon, tuna and sardines. Also eggs.

VITAMIN E
Why?   Needed in maintaining red blood cells.
Where? Whole grain cereals, wheat germ, beans and peas, lettuce and eggs.

IRON
Why?   Used with protein for hemoglobin production. Forms nucleus of each cell, and helps them to use oxygen.
Where? Kidney and liver, as well as shellfish, lean meats, and eggs. Deep yellow and dark green leafy vegetables. Dried peas, beans and fruits. Potatoes, whole grain cereals and bread. Enriched flour and bread. Dark molasses.

CALCIUM
Why?   Builds and renews bones, teeth and other tissues, as well as aids in the proper function of muscles, nerves and heart. Controls normal blood clotting. With protein, aids in oxidation of foods.
Where? Milk and milk products, excluding butter. Dark green vegetables, oysters, clams and sardines.

NIACIN
Why?   Helps body to oxidize food. Aids in digestion, and helps to keep nervous system and skin healthy.
Where? Peanuts, liver, tuna, as well as fish, poultry and lean meats. Enriched breads, cereals and peas.

MAGNESIUM
Why?   Aids nervous system and sleep.
Where? Almonds, peanuts, raisins and prunes. Vegetables, fruits, milk, fish and meats.

ZINC
Why?   Needed for cell formation.
Where? Nuts and leafy green vegetables. Shellfish and meats.

COPPER
Why?   Helps body to utilize iron.
Where? Vegetables and meats.

PHOSPHORUS
Why?   Maintains normal blood clotting function, as well as builds bones, teeth and nerve tissue. Aids in utilization of sugar and fats.
Where? Oatmeal and whole wheat products. Eggs, milk and cheese, dried beans and peas. Nuts, lean meats, and fish and poultry.

IODINE
Why?   Enables thyroid gland to maintain proper body metabolism.
Where? Iodized salt. Saltwater fish and seafood. Milk and vegetables grown in iodine-rich soil.

BIOTIN (VITAMIN H)
Why?   Helps to maintain body cells.
Where? Eggs and liver. Any foods rich in Vitamin B.

Charts

Equivalent Chart

	WHEN RECIPE CALLS FOR:	YOU NEED:
BREAD & CEREAL	1 c. soft bread crumbs	2 slices
	1 c. fine dry bread crumbs	4-5 slices
	1 c. small bread cubes	2 slices
	1 c. fine cracker crumbs	24 saltines
	1 c. fine graham cracker crumbs	14 crackers
	1 c. vanilla wafer crumbs	22 wafers
	1 c. crushed cornflakes	3 c. uncrushed
	4 c. cooked macaroni	1 8-oz. package
	3 1/2 c. cooked rice	1 c. uncooked
DAIRY	1 c. freshly grated cheese	1/4 lb.
	1 c. cottage cheese or sour cream	1 8-oz. carton
	2/3 c. evaporated milk	1 sm. can
	1 2/3 c. evaporated milk	1 tall can
	1 c. whipped cream	1/2 c. heavy cream
SWEET	1 c. semisweet chocolate pieces	1 6-oz. package
	2 c. granulated sugar	1 lb.
	4 c. sifted confectioners' sugar	1 lb.
	2 1/4 c. packed brown sugar	1 lb.
MEAT	3 c. diced cooked meat	1 lb., cooked
	2 c. ground cooked meat	1 lb., cooked
	4 c. diced cooked chicken	1 5-lb. chicken
NUTS	1 c. chopped nuts	4 oz. shelled
		1 lb. unshelled
VEGETABLES	4 c. sliced or diced raw potatoes	4 medium
	2 c. cooked green beans	1/2 lb. fresh or 1 16-oz. can
	1 c. chopped onion	1 large
	4 c. shredded cabbage	1 lb.
	2 c. canned tomatoes	1 16-oz. can
	1 c. grated carrot	1 large
	2 1/2 c. lima beans or red beans	1 c. dried, cooked
	1 4-oz. can mushrooms	1/2 lb. fresh
FRUIT	4 c. sliced or chopped apples	4 medium
	2 c. pitted cherries	4 c. unpitted
	3 to 4 tbsp. lemon juice plus 1 tsp. grated rind	1 lemon
	1/3 c. orange juice plus 2 tsp. grated rind	1 orange
	1 c. mashed banana	3 medium
	4 c. cranberries	1 lb.
	3 c. shredded coconut	1/2 lb.
	4 c. sliced peaches	8 medium
	1 c. pitted dates or candied fruit	1 8-oz. package
	2 c. pitted prunes	1 12-oz. package
	3 c. raisins	1 15-oz. package

COMMON EQUIVALENTS

1 tbsp. = 3 tsp.	4 qt. = 1 gal.
2 tbsp. = 1 oz.	6 1/2 to 8 oz. can = 1 c.
4 tbsp. = 1/4 c.	10 1/2 to 12-oz. can = 1 1/4 c.
5 tbsp. + 1 tsp. = 1/3 c.	14 to 16-oz. can (No. 300) = 1 3/4 c.
8 tbsp. = 1/2 c.	16 to 17-oz. can (No. 303) = 2 c.
12 tbsp. = 3/4 c.	1-lb. 4-oz. can or 1-pt. 2-oz. can (No. 2) = 2 1/2 c.
16 tbsp. = 1 c.	1-lb. 13-oz. can (No. 2 1/2) = 3 1/2 c.
1 c. = 8 oz. or 1/2 pt.	3-lb. 3-oz. can or 46-oz. can or 1-qt. 14-oz. can = 5 3/4 c.
4 c. = 1 qt.	6 1/2-lb. or 7-lb. 5-oz. can (No. 10) = 12 to 13 c.

Substitution Chart

	INSTEAD OF:	USE:
BAKING	1 tsp. baking powder	1/4 tsp. soda plus 1/2 tsp. cream of tartar
	1 c. sifted all-purpose flour	1 c. plus 2 tbsp. sifted cake flour
	1 c. sifted cake flour	1 c. minus 2 tbsp. sifted all-purpose flour
	1 tbsp. cornstarch (for thickening)	2 tbsp. flour or 1 tbsp. tapioca
SWEET	1 1-oz. square chocolate	3 to 4 tbsp. cocoa plus 1 tsp. shortening
	1 2/3 oz. semisweet chocolate	1 oz. unsweetened chocolate plus 4 tsp. sugar
	1 c. granulated sugar	1 c. packed brown sugar or 1 c. corn syrup, molasses, honey minus 1/4 c. liquid
	1 c. honey	1 to 1 1/4 c. sugar plus 1/4 c. liquid or 1 c. molasses or corn syrup
DAIRY	1 c. sweet milk	1 c. sour milk or buttermilk plus 1/2 tsp. soda
	1 c. sour milk	1 c. sweet milk plus 1 tbsp. vinegar or lemon juice or 1 c. buttermilk
	1 c. buttermilk	1 c. sour milk or 1 c. yogurt
	1 c. light cream	7/8 c. skim milk plus 3 tbsp. butter
	1 c. heavy cream	3/4 c. skim milk plus 1/3 c. butter
	1 c. sour cream	7/8 c. sour milk plus 3 tbsp. butter
	1 c. bread crumbs	3/4 c. cracker crumbs
SEASONINGS	1 c. catsup	1 c. tomato sauce plus 1/2 c. sugar plus 2 tbsp. vinegar
	1 tbsp. prepared mustard	1 tsp. dry mustard
	1 tsp. Italian spice	1/4 tsp. each oregano, basil, thyme, rosemary plus dash of cayenne
	1 tsp. allspice	1/2 tsp. cinnamon plus 1/8 tsp. cloves
	1 medium onion	1 tbsp. dried minced onion or 1 tsp. onion powder
	1 clove of garlic	1/8 tsp. garlic powder or 1/8 tsp. instant minced garlic or 3/4 tsp. garlic salt or 5 drops of liquid garlic
	1 tsp. lemon juice	1/2 tsp. vinegar

Index

Index

Index

Index

197

Index

PHOTOGRAPHY CREDITS

Cover: Artist, Jonathan Wilde; United Fresh Fruit and Vegetable Association; Amaretto di Saronno; Florida Fruit and Vegetable Association; American Lamb Council; Hershey Foods Corporation; American Spice Trade Association; Campbell Soup Company; National Dairy Council; Pineapple Growers Association; San Giorgio-Skinner Foods; The McIlhenny Company-Tabasco; Spanish Green Olive Commission; Pickle Packers International; National Pasta Institute; Florida Citrus Commission; Stove Top Stuffing Mix — General Foods Consumer Center; American Dry Milk Institute; National Macaroni Institute; The Borden Company; Evaporated Milk Association; Rice Council.

To Order Copies of

NATIONAL WILDLIFE FEDERATION COOKBOOK

Write to: National Wildlife Federation
1412 16th Street, N.W.
Washington, D.C. 20036

When ordering, please use code number 67850DG to help expedite your request. Thank you.

For your convenience MasterCard and Visa are accepted for all orders.

122 Hash brown casserole   93 Lemon chicken
120 Crunchy Broccoli "
120 Carrot Souffle
119 Swt + Sour gr beans (Bocolli
126 Orange Glazed Swt Pot
126 Zucchini Au Grater